6/99

WITHDRAWN

D1249235

 St. Louis Community College

Forest Park
Florissant Valley
Meramec

Instructional Resources
St. Louis, Missouri

ALSO BY LENORE TERR, M.D.

Too Scared to Cry: Psychic Trauma in Childhood
Unchained Memories: True Stories of Traumatic Memories, Lost and Found

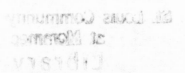

Beyond Love and Work

WHY ADULTS NEED TO PLAY

Lenore Terr, M.D.

SCRIBNER

SCRIBNER
1230 Avenue of the Americas
New York, NY 10020

SCRIBNER and design are trademarks of Simon & Schuster Inc.

Designed by Brooke Zimmer
Set in Spectrum
Manufactured in the United States of America

1   3   5   7   9   10   8   7   6   4   2

Library of Congress Cataloging-in-Publication Data
Terr, Lenore, 1936–
Beyond love and work : why adults need to play / Lenore Terr.
p.   cm.
Includes bibliographical references and index.
1. Play—Psychological aspects. 2. Adulthood—
Psychological aspects. I. Title.
BF717.T47   1999
155.6—dc21   98-37138
CIP

ISBN 0-684-82239-3

To Ab
husband, lover, friend, playmate

Contents

The communal life of human beings had, therefore, a two-fold foundation: the compulsion to work . . . and the power of love.

—Sigmund Freud, *Civilization and Its Discontents*

Preface

I am two, perhaps three, years old and somebody—a neighbor, I think—has just had a backyard wedding. And today, I'm outside scavenging, looking for bottle caps. Blue ones, red ones, orange and black ones, gleaming silvers and golds. I cannot read, so I don't know if they are soda-pop or beer-bottle caps—whether they're drinks I might like or drinks I would hate. It doesn't matter—what I do is collect the caps and then spread them out on the grass by type—all of the reds together, the blues, the oranges. Like jewels, they are so beautiful. I love them. But look there. Some of the reds have big letters and some reds have small letters. They're different. And some of the blues are of slightly different shades—oh my, these are different bottle tops, too. So I sort all of this out and finally get it right—a huge panoply of bottle caps all arranged, all grouped, all categorized. This is the most perfect kind of play. A great afternoon in solitude doing exactly what I like.

That day—a sunny June day in Cleveland, I would guess—remains in my mind. It is never lost. An epiphany, perhaps. A great day of play. And as an adult, I have played that way at my best, too. I've sorted out children's behaviors, and sorted out their miseries and traumas, and sorted out their symptoms and the possible ways to treat them. Sometimes when it's complicated, I've put everything on a great big chart—about as big, the way I remember it now, as that assortment of post-wedding-day bottle caps. Sometimes I've had to put it all into a computer because the whole business is too huge and ungainly to set up in any kind of backyard. But that grand day is still there in what I do. Because whenever I go out to do some research—or set out to treat a human being—I am struck with people's sortings. I feel intrigued with their samenesses and differences. I guess I must admit it now—I go to work in order to play.

So when somebody tries to tell me that I *work* at psychiatry, I laugh a little inside. Psychiatry is my form of play. A hidden pleasure. And if somebody says that adults are too deep to play, I giggle silently, too. I love the surfaces of nature and I play at them all the time—hopefully in the way that Johannes Vermeer played at the exquisite surfaces he created on canvas, but even more hopefully, in my own individual fashion.

In his 1930 *Civilization and Its Discontents,* Sigmund Freud wrote that love and work *(Lieben und Arbeiten)* were the two occupations that principally enable us to endure the pressures common to all civilizations. But where, I often wonder, is play in all of this? According to Freud, a metaphoric marriage has been made between Eros (love) and Ananke (necessity, the reason that we work), and this marriage helps most of us to control our rage while adhering to society's prohibition against it. But cannot play be considered a child of Freud's metaphoric marriage? If mankind loved and worked well, Freud said, some wars might be averted. But playing, too, helps avert the outward manifestations of anger, and dangerous sexual instincts can be masked or redirected by play as well.

I imagine that Freud disregarded play because he himself was not noticeably playful. In his writings, he did not observe play in a serious or systematic way (although in *Beyond the Pleasure Principle* he produced a finely detailed account of the play of his eighteen-month-old grandson). Even though he wrote extensively about the psychology of art, for example, Freud seemed uninterested in the playfulness of the people who produced this art. And since Freud drew his primary inspiration from what he perceived in his own psychology, he may have failed to recognize play as the powerful force it is.

Of the psychoanalytic generation after Freud, it was most notably the gifted writer and clinician Erik Erikson who emphasized play as crucial to a child's development. But Erikson did not consider play a necessary part of adult life. He chose not to expand upon Freud's two requirements for normal adulthood. ("We cannot improve on the professor's formula," he wrote in *Childhood and Society* [1950].) In fact, in 1972, Erikson remarked that grown-up play looks phony and forced: "The adult who is playing in a sphere set aside for 'play' is not comparable to a playing child; wherefore he often seems to be playing at playing."

Erikson believed that active play disappears as a person gets older. The lasting legacy of child's play is, rather, an adult attitude achieved by too few—the mature quality of playfulness. In one of the later lectures of his life, given at the Harvard School of Government, Erikson recalled that Freud had expressed regret that adults generally lack what Freud called *"die strahlende Intelligenz des Kindes"* (the radiant intelligence of children). Erikson urged people to cultivate this radiant intelligence by being playful. From Erikson's point of view, playfulness was as essential to the institutional boardroom, the political cloakroom, the halls of government, as it was to the playground. But he did not show much interest in what adult play might consist of—what he felt adult lives lacked was the quality, not the activity.

In my readings on play, I have not yet come across the explicit suggestion that play ought to be added to Freud's two-pronged equation or any other. But I have become convinced that play is crucial to successful, healthy adult living.

With this book, I attempt to bring play into our contemporary thinking about adult mental health. For those many people who hardly play at all, they might consider this writing a giant "how-to" book. For those readers who consistently play, I hope they will enjoy some insight into what they are already doing.

Whatever you are, dear reader—and I'd guess you fall somewhere in the middle—I hope you find some fun in looking into a subject almost as mysterious and beautiful as a soda-pop bottle cap is to a preschooler. Adult play is a subject not ordinarily encountered in psychology or in one's everyday reading. Yet it is a necessity to us all.

Procedures and Acknowledgments

The true names, and at times, the vocations, locations, marital status, even a gender or two, of the people about whom I write are altered to protect their identities. The inherent qualities of their psychologies, however, are laid out as directly and as fully as I am able. Most of the stories have been garnered from my psychiatric practice, although I have also included some situations that I know from my life. My children's names are undisguised. All other names, except where indicated in the text, are changed.

I have tried to enable the reader to get through this book smoothly without any pauses for further explanation or references. For those readers who wish to use the book as an entryway into the professional and general literature in and around play, I have included end notes, an index to both text and notes, and a bibliography. It was not my goal in this writing, however, to review the entire world of play and its psychology. Rather, I wished to hit a number of the high spots, especially those that would apply to my particular interest in the play of healthy adults. Therefore, the sophisticated reader may be aware of several important researchers in the play field who were virtually or completely left out—not because their work is minor or insignificant, but because their work did not directly fit in with my theme.

I wish to acknowledge a number of professionals in my own field—and in other fields having to do with play—who have helped me with their ideas, reading suggestions, and encouragement. I know that I will miss naming a few, and for this I sincerely apologize. Over the last few years, many of my colleagues have responded with enthusiasm to my ongoing talk about play. Let me particularly thank Robert Michels, M.D., professor of psychiatry at Cornell, for reading the entire first draft—a yeoman's job far beyond the call of friendship. And my thanks to Stuart Brown, M.D., Irving Berkowitz, M.D., Richard Sarles, M.D., Gilbert Levin, Ph.D., Larry Hartmann, M.D., Robert Dorman, M.D., Bessel van der Kolk, M.D., Joan and Bob McGrath, Linda Donely Reed, Ph.D., Martin Drell, M.D., Walter Menninger, M.D., Jeff Dolgan, Ph.D., Russell Gardner Jr., M.D., Justice Kay Werdegar, and my examination "team" from psychiatry boards, who threw ideas and materials at me, often faster than I could process them. Special thanks to four great current researchers on play, Brian Sutton-Smith, Ph.D., Barrie Thorne, Ph.D., Helen Schwartzman, Ph.D., and Robert Fagen, Ph.D., who helped me with references and reprints, and who originally promised to join me in presenting a symposium on play to our professional colleagues in child and adolescent psychiatry—until it turned out that not one of the pharmaceutical companies or toy manufacturers we applied to would extend to us the relatively small amount of financial aid we needed for the project. There and then, I learned how difficult it is to get backing for research and education about play.

My office staff, Joanna Musgrove, Scott Lindstrom, Darney Martin, and Marsha Bessey, continue to make it possible for me to practice medicine and to write. Thanks to them all. To Marsha Bessey, I extend special thanks—not only do you type like a study in perpetual motion, Marsha, but you edit, correct, and suggest as you go along. You are one of the outstanding examples of humankind out-performing—and hopefully outplaying—the machines.

For the writing in this book, I wish to acknowledge the tremendous help afforded me by the publishing team who assisted and encouraged me at Scribner—my editors, Jane Rosenman and Nan Graham, and the company publisher, Susan Moldow. I also sought and received advice from an editor and friend, Sara Lippincott, my son-in-law and writer of fiction, Vince Colvin (published as Vince Montague), my close friend who composes college textbooks on writing, Rosemary Patton, and my book attorney, Debbie Orenstein. Each of you reviewed the manuscript and helped me invaluably. Finally to my agent, Joy Harris, I offer kudos galore. Not only were you an efficient business manager for the project, but you fulfilled my needs at various times for a literary critic and a pal.

Last, thanks to my husband, Ab. You fully earned this book's dedication.

1

Why Play? And How Do We Know We're Playing?

Some people know how to play. I can tell as I spot them from my garden. And some people don't; I can tell that, too. Directly across the street from my house, folks of any age from five to seventy-five hop the Presidio Wall, the stonework boundary of San Francisco's newest addition to the National Park System. Right at that place, the height of the jump is manageable. With a running start, a young person might leap it in one fluid motion the way a horse leaps a hedge. That looks lively and frolicking—like play. Or a less athletic person might back up to it, sit, sling both legs onto the top, and then turn around and slide backward down the other side, all the while appearing totally unconcerned and unself-conscious. That look, too, conveys a sense of play.

Sometimes I see couples sitting on the wall, swinging their legs, gazing at some point on the horizon, listening to music on a small portable radio, or just chatting idly. They are playing, though it might not be easy to define their sport. Their faces and their bearing show it, though—they're relaxed, carefree, enjoying the moment itself.

A young man vaults the wall in the company of his dog. He carries a chewed-up tennis ball and talks in a lilting cadence to the animal, who is already well beyond my sight. This boy, too, has that semblance—not ecstatic but at peace, yesterday's drop in the stock market forgotten, tomorrow's tasks tucked well away in the future, where they belong.

A moment or two later, a smartly dressed, tall, trim man hurls himself at the Presidio, just behind two perfectly groomed and matched hounds, all of them bullets on unstoppable trajectories. He carries a switch, and every couple of seconds he barks "Heel!" or "Sit!" and again, "Sit!" On their way back, he pauses at my ironwork fence, which barely manages to contain the forty or fifty varieties of flowers that border my house. "I see you're having as much trouble controlling your plants as I have with my dogs," the man says. Yes, maybe, I smile. But my own goals have nothing at all to do with control—I want to experience the pleasure of watching new shoots and blossoms develop, of seeing various combinations of color come and go, of observing life cycles far more accelerated than my own. I go outside to my garden in order to play. Do this man and his dogs ever go somewhere for that sort of thing? Where, I wonder, is the happiness in all of this "Sit!" "Heel!" and "Sit!"?

I think about play. I have been playing with children all of the years that I have been a psychiatrist. I loved watching the play of my own two children, David and Julia, as they grew up. In the last ten years or so, I have encouraged my adult patients to bring me the products of their play—their poems, journals, paintings, stories, photos. Sometimes we rehash a golf game, a hike, a dance lesson, an afternoon at the beach. And we laugh, too. We joke. We make metaphors. Sometimes we toss one-liners back and forth across an imaginary net. And it helps. Play makes people scintillate. It creates a kind of mental click that frees you to begin sorting things out. The lack of play dulls a person—and it may well be that an overall lack of play dulls a society.

I define play as "activity aimed at having fun." In his classic 1938 book on adult play, *Homo Ludens* ("Man the Player"), the Dutch historian Johan Huizinga wrote that he believed the English word *fun* was essential to any definition of play. (He could find no equivalent word in either German or Dutch.) But though Huizinga said that play is "nonserious" at heart, to an outside observer it often looks deadly serious. It carries a tension of its own that must be resolved. It is suspenseful. And it often requires intense concentration. Mihaly Csikszentmihalyi, a University of Chicago psychologist who has conducted fascinating experiments on pleasurably intense human concentration, defines play as "grounded in the concept of possibility." When we play, we sense no limitations. In fact, when we are playing, we are usually unaware of ourselves. Self-observation goes out the window. We forget all those past lessons of life, forget our potential foolishness, forget ourselves. We immerse ourselves in the act of play. And we become free.

PLAY HAS repeatedly appeared in my research as a behavior of great importance and interest—not only as a clue to a child's mental state or as therapy for a troubled child, but as an activity that generates excitement and ideas within the scientific project itself. Early in my studies of what happens to traumatized people, for instance, I spotted a kind of play that no one had characterized or explained before—a behavior that I eventually named "post-traumatic play." I discovered that the play of traumatized people spreads into our culture as jump-rope rhymes, horror novels, art, film, poetry— some of it, strong and cleansing; some of it, the impetus for a nightmare or two. Post-traumatic play has a ripple effect with an extremely broad reach. And I recognized that when a child is inspired to play because of a terrible event, that play tends to be frightening to the child, yet at the same time irresistible. This temptation to play out a traumatic episode lasts—often until or past the time the child is entirely grown up. I came to realize that a person's play is an opening to that person's being.

The psychotherapeutic situation can itself be seen as a game of sorts, requiring considerable humor and a sense of sport, both on the part of the patient and of the therapist. A generation ago, the English psychoanalyst D. W. Winnicott wrote that a lack of playfulness made a person a poor candidate for psychotherapy; a nonplaying patient might have to be taught how to play before psychotherapy could begin. Today, many psychotherapists, including myself, find that without some enjoyment in playing with situations, roles, analogues, solutions, a patient's chances of psychotherapeutic success are diminished.

Take the time-hallowed tea party, for example. It's easy to scoff at tea parties as useless relics of a mannered era that is gone forever . . . but a tea party exemplifies the benefits that play offers both to the individual and to society. (Though teas are a particularly feminine style of play, I have noticed a number of men over the years playing at tea in some of the grand, formal hotels.) Tea play generates moments of perfect manners, perfect peace in communal settings. Teas, in fact, bridge the gap between play and ritual. There are several pleasures in tea parties: the dressing up, the good manners, the delicious and dainty food, the chance to sit down to good conversation.

I learned how helpful teas could be from a three-year-old girl named Janie, a veteran sufferer of parental sexual and physical abuse. Medical examinations had revealed human bite marks all over her body, and when she was four, surgeons would find old scars in her urinary and genital regions. When she was just a year old, Janie had been a horrified witness to her two-week-old sister Sandra's murder. Sandra was shaken and bitten to death by one and possibly two adults. Janie's father was eventually arrested and convicted of murder in the second degree, and the authorities placed Janie in excellent foster care. She came to see me a couple of years later—after her biological mother (who at the very least had looked the other way while these horrors were going on) had gone to court to try to get Janie back. After a period of evaluation, I wrote to the court explaining why Janie could not return to her mother and emotionally survive. The court went along with my recommendation, and on her first therapy visit, the little girl suggested that we get out my nested tables and make tea.

After that, Janie and I took our imaginary tea once a month for a little over a year. What was most important to Janie in playing "tea" was whom to invite. The rabbit and the raccoon puppets? Yes, they were nice. The lion? Janie wasn't so sure. He could bite. The Madam Alexander dolls? Of course. The baby doll? Janie didn't know. How could we be sure that this baby would be okay? Might it die? Would we need somebody to protect it? We eventually figured all of this out, and the lion and the baby received their long-overdue invitations. We deliberated and deliberated over the Russian nutcracker (who, of course, bites and is of human form) and the painted Zuni snake (who, to this child, resembled a penis). Finally, Janie decided that she could handle both the nutcracker and the snake. We'd know what to do if one of them acted up. These two play objects stood for Janie's two most horrible experiences; yet with no conscious, verbal memories of her past ordeals, she was sharing with me through her tea parties these dark and formative secrets.

Janie gained considerable personal control by dint of her teas. Through play, what had previously been disastrous for her could come under her own powers. In play, Janie was the one to decide. She could set up the procedures for a ritual, a civilized form of play, a "tea."

When Janie was four and a half years old, her foster mother was at last allowed to adopt her. How did Janie want to celebrate? "A tea party!" she chirped without a moment's hesitation. And so the next time she came, we had a real one—real tea, real cookies, my real office staff, and Janie's very real mom. As a matter of fact, that party turned out to be the last of our teas. Janie was off and running with new and more flexible kinds of play: "Little Red Riding Hood," "Chase the Army," "Get the Dinosaur"—although, as I write this, the five little dinosaurs who live in my desk drawer have still not learned to behave in the way that a Janie-tamed animal should.

One of my adult patients—I'll call her Marie—has for years given an elaborate annual tea party at Christmastime. Mothers and daughters, aunts and nieces, grandmothers and grandchildren, are invited to come. Marie doesn't provide any particular entertainment or develop any particular customs for these teas. Her form of play relies on the pleasure of reunion—of knowing that she will see her old friends this way, again and again. Marie derives some of her joy from adding a few new people each year; occasionally, a child she considers interesting is invited. It gives Marie almost as much pleasure in July to plan a new decoration scheme, invent a new kind of tea sandwich, dream up an idea for an invitation, as it gives her in December. Marie assesses herself from one year to the next in terms of her annual tea. How has she related with her friends? And how has she progressed with her personal goals?

Marie's tea parties originated years ago, when she first went away to college. Her mother, an elegant and loving lady who enjoyed teas herself, was killed in an automobile accident just before the Christmas of Marie's freshman year. Marie's father had been driving the family car and plowed it into a tree, emerging uninjured himself. Shocking as the accident was to Marie, her father added immeasurably to her horror by remarrying within only a few months. Marie had lost her mother to death and her father to deceit. She stopped going home for Christmas. She started giving Christmas teas. And in her own way, Marie began to create a surrogate family through her play—play that could carry her through the holiday season, play that could surround her with a large and happy clan. Marie never consciously connected her annual tea party to her tragic and traumatic late-adolescent loss. But the connection was clear all the same.

When I analyzed the frightened little girl's teas and the mature and sophisticated woman's teas, I found many of the same powerful play functions at work. Through play, Janie and Marie had reorganized their lives, both of which had been disrupted by violent death. Janie and Marie both relied on a ritual form of play—a form hallowed by tradition. In tea parties, they were provided with clearly defined "playgrounds"—places to play—and with clearly defined timing and rules. Through their play, Janie and Marie could regain control of their lives. Through the tiny, tidy metaphor of tea, they created pleasure, the sense of belonging, the sense of "family." Both learned from their play: Janie learned how to judge a person's vulnerability or dangerousness; Marie learned how to judge whom she could depend on. Both Marie and Janie used their teas for problem solving. Through the special language of human play, each one revealed her secrets.

HERE IT becomes necessary to ask, "How do we know when we are playing?" Many of us may suppose that, in our waking hours, when we are not at work, we are in one way or another at play. But leisure (the "freedom or spare time provided by the cessation of activities," according to *Webster's Third New International Dictionary*) is not at all the same thing as play. Play is active; leisure is by definition passive. And leisure appears to be something that people look forward to in the future: we wait for retirement, so that we will have the leisure time to "play," when what we need to do instead is to make the time for play now.

Unfortunately, people today devalue their play. We tend to play less and less, the older we become. And this is sometimes due to our circumstances: in too many middle-class American households today, two adults have to work to support themselves and their family, and leisure time is a luxury. We are spending more money and ending up with less spare time. (We even sleep less, according to the Harvard economist Juliet Schor, who has defined our new lifestyle in her 1993 book, *The Overworked American.*) People are overtired, overstressed. We are forgetting how to play. And we are failing to realize how important play really is. When we jog through the park or work out on our muscle-toning, bodybuilding machinery, we may be fooling ourselves into thinking we are at play, but we're not.

Even our dictionaries, those mirrors of our assumptions and our ways of looking at things, almost uniformly omit adulthood when it comes to defining *play*. *Webster's Third* says that play is "the spontaneous or organized recreational activity of children," and the *New*

Shorter Oxford English Dictionary defines play as "exercise or action by way of recreation or amusement, note especially as a spontaneous activity of children or young animals."

The practice of relegating play exclusively to children appears to hark back to the ancient Greeks. Their words for "play" and for "education" both derive from the word for "child" (*pais* [pie ees']). In the Greek language, play (*paitheia* [pie dee āh']) and education (*paitheia* [pie dee' ah]) are distinguished aurally only by the accented syllable. The common origin of the words implies that play and education are supposed to stop when childhood ends. The Greeks had a second word, *agon* (the root of our *agonist* and *agonize*), meaning "contest," and they used this word to designate various competitive aspects of their society, including the Olympic games. You could "play" if you were a child, but if you were grown up you "competed."

Our dictionaries go even further, in setting play in opposition to work. There is an implied value judgment in these definitions: work is necessary; play is frivolous, unnecessary, the province of children.

But I wondered—did work always have to be drudgery? Boring? Don't many jobs inspire great pleasure? Did Mozart, for instance, taking out a new sheet of composition paper, necessarily think, "It's time now to get to work"? Mozart wrote on commission, but he also wrote just for the pleasure of it. His "Musical Joke" must have been done purely for fun, as were the string quartets, composed so that he could play chamber music with his amiable peer Joseph Haydn; and so were the four-hand duets, written to amuse himself while—who knows?—driving his piano students crazy on their side of the keyboard. The dictionaries, however, consistently take a non-Mozartian tack. *Webster's Third:* "Play in its most general sense suggests an opposition to work; it implies activity, often strenuous, but emphasizes the absence of any aim other than amusement, diversion, or enjoyment." *Webster's* also points to a less important, British definition of *play*—"to be out of work or idle, take a holiday." How does Mozart fit into this sort of definition? More important, how do we all fit in?

This black-and-white opposition of work and play crops up in all segments of our society—even in kindergarten, where one might least expect to find it. In his syndicated "Families Today" newspaper column, T. Berry Brazelton, M.D., reprinted a letter from the mother of a five-year-old preschooler. She said she was wondering about her "smart little boy's" readiness for school. Should this child, who could "spell his name and occasionally sit and practice writing," go to kindergarten when "his primary interest [was] playing"? The boy had shown "so little interest in schoolwork," she said, that despite his father's objections, she wanted to hold him back for a year.

The eminent pediatrician implicitly concurred with the woman's point of view. If the boy was not yet interested in work, he was not yet ready for school. Although Brazelton's main point was that parents shouldn't feel too bad about holding their kindergarten-age children back from school, he also appeared to be reasoning as the dictionaries do: work counted more than play. But why, I wondered, should play diminish a child's capacity for work? Play, if it truly characterized this particular boy's state of mind, might well have made his schoolwork that much more creative, that much more enjoyable. When my son, David, was two or so, his favorite "toys" were numbers—magnetic numbers on refrigerators, brass numbers on the fronts of houses, embossed numbers on license plates. Today he is hard at work on a dissertation on number theory. But is this really work for him? I think not.

Obviously, any person, even a kindergarten child, must occasionally settle down to an activity that is sheer drudgery. But a playful state of mind applied to work allows for clever solutions to work-related problems and a sense of well-being. Work and play need not be mutually exclusive; many of us discovered this for ourselves long ago. We recognize that the best players—basketball stars, for instance, or chess champions or barbershop-quartet contestants—work diligently at their play. And we recognize, too, that the best workers—Nobel Prize winners, computer scientists, philosophers—seem to play as hard as they work. The Swiss psychologist C. G. Jung saw play and work as inseparable; in 1923 he wrote, "Without playing with fantasy, no creative work has ever yet come to birth." And Robert Frost, in "Two Tramps in Mud-Time," made the ideal explicit:

> My object in living is to unite
> My avocation and my vocation
> As my two eyes make one in sight.

Clearly, we need simpler, broader definitions of *work* and *play*. I have already defined play as "activity directed primarily at having fun." I would define work as "activity directed primarily at personal and family sustenance, the achievement of power, the making of societal contributions"; but work often carries with it a secondary goal—"having fun"—and a great deal of our work is also play for us.

So how do we know that we are playing? We know partly because we deliberately decide to go in this direction. We invariably make a decision—albeit most often a split-second one—to play. As an activity directed primarily at having fun, play usually carries with it a certain span of time, certain boundaries, a certain format. Huizinga called the necessary space drawn up in advance for play "a play-ground." The psychologist Gregory Bateson referred to play as "always a framed event," in which "players must consistently know that they are playing. . . . When involving more than one player, there must be an agreement to play. This agreement is often entirely nonverbal, but it must clearly be communicated."

We know we are playing when we are suddenly removed from all cares and worries. We know because afterward we feel cleansed and refreshed, despite our tired bodies, our aching muscles, our sleepiness. The interlude has been a healthy one. It takes place entirely outside, or at the very edge of, our drive for personal success or survival. Play is disinterested, removed.

The play I've watched my patients indulge in over the years has often been extraordinarily elastic, allowing any number of directions for its expression and action. Much music and art is play.

Huizinga thought that human rituals and rites were play. Erikson saw evidence of playfulness in the behind-the-scenes machinations of leadership and government. Sitting around the family room watching television with the kids, talking back to the TV set, talking with one another about the show, is a kind of play. And having your own fun all alone—daydreaming, wishing, toying with ideas—is play. In fact, any activity done with the primary aim of having fun is play.

A game is a special form of play, in which there are fixed rules. But not all games are play; some games are not play because they are too frightening, too murderously competitive, too likely to result in injury. The gladiators in the amphitheaters of ancient Rome were not playing. Steffi Graf agonized and contested but did not play at Madison Square Garden in November 1995, when, "crippled with blisters" and with "her home ripped apart by tax investigators and her father . . . in jail," she won the Women's Tennis Association championship. ("The closer she came to winning," wrote Robin Finn, of the *New York Times*, "the more painful the process became.") When pushed to excess, some play becomes the entire meaning to a person's life. Some people become fixated on their computer games, squash courts, exercise classes, calorie consumption, athletic shoes. But healthy play has nothing to do with perfect equipment or perfect bodies.

Moreover, healthy play seldom takes place at anyone else's expense. Gossip, cruel teasing, life-and-death struggle, scapegoating, demeaning or baiting one's competitors—none of these are play. They are instead direct expressions of aggression. David Mamet's film *House of Games* offers an extreme example of adult play gone awry. The young protagonist destroys his psychologist's life while coming to her for counseling—all in the name of a so-called game. Toying with other people's lives is something that people with disordered characters do. These pathological forms of play will be considered, too, as we move further along in this book.

For an activity to be play, it must be lighthearted. When people are playing, there is a sense of good-humored, spirited, even sparkling, pleasure. There is an infectiousness to play. It beckons us to join in. The playwright S. N. Behrman, in writing about his friend George Gershwin, said that as Gershwin sat down at the piano to play for friends, you "felt on the instant the newness, the humor, above all the great heady surf of vitality. The room became freshly oxygenated; everybody felt it, everybody breathed it." My own office reoxygenates itself every time someone plays there. I sense an instantaneousness, a freshness, good humor, vitality. My garden renews itself whenever my little next-door neighbors, five-year-old Frankie and one-year-old Robin, stop by to toss a few coreopsis petals in the air or talk into a snapdragon's mouth.

Play permits us emotional discharge without huge risk. Our cares, worries, sadness, secrets, are released. Our tensions are built into our play, but unlike the direct discharges produced in the sexual act or in battle, the release of play is more prolonged, more subtle, less the sought-after, ultimate goal. Laughing, hitting a ball, pinching back spent flowers, moving our bodies around, moving our ideas around, gently teasing, playing a role—these diversions create a series of shallow, slow releases that relax us and leave us satisfied, set for another day.

THE EXAMPLES afforded by people who do not play at all—who have never played—have something to tell us here. Consider Charles Whitman, the young man who on August 1, 1966, shot a large number of people at random from Austin's University of Texas Tower. After the tower was stormed and Whitman was gunned down, a psychiatrist, Stuart Brown, conducted a psychological "autopsy" of the mass killer. What did Dr. Brown find? He learned that Charles Whitman had not played as a child; he had spent much of his childhood earning Boy Scout medals, serving as an altar boy, trying to duck his father's brutal physical attacks. His teachers recalled a frightened little kid who slumped against a schoolyard wall and watched his peers at play. Others recalled that Charles's father had controlled his after-school time so closely that the boy had virtually no time for play, even by himself.

Play is necessary to a normal childhood. Much of our current knowledge about the importance of play comes from the observation of animals. Among higher species, play does not stop with the assumption of adulthood. Play is biologically important to adult animals as well as to their young. In this regard, the everyday behavior of our own pets is interesting. Dogs don't stop their chasing and burrowing games just because they've grown up. I know one seven-year-old Gordon setter from Vermont around whom you can't use the word *Frisbee* without having to go outside, whether it's freezing or not, and toss her twenty, thirty, shots. Dierdre just stands there, almost on top of you, panting until you capitulate—there is no other choice. I know a San Francisco mutt named Pearl who is impelled to dive into the ocean every time you take her for a walk on the beach. She will doubtless have to be given a much-hated bath afterward, but Pearl takes her chances. And she is well beyond puppyhood.

In adult animals, the need to play is so important that sometimes it takes precedence over the need to eat. In its December 1994 issue, *National Geographic* ran a photo story about animal play that featured a polar bear in the Canadian Arctic. Because the ice had not yet fully formed over Hudson Bay, the adult bear had probably not eaten his dietary staple, seal meat, for around four months. As the hungry bear lumbered toward the magazine's team of huskies, the journalists became concerned that their sled dogs would be eaten. But surprisingly, one of the huskies approached the fluffy white monster and, with a slight smile on his face, bowed. This was an instinctive canine invitation to play. *Click!*—the *National Geographic* photographer went into action. The polar bear "got it." Rather than attack the dog, he proceeded to cavort with him. *Click! Click!* Wrestling, wrapping the dog within his furry embrace, romping along the ice, this bear chose play over food. He eventually became so tired that he lay down on his back, paws up in the air, another great photo opportunity; in fact, that was the shot they chose for a centerfold.

According to Prof. Robert Fagen, a wildlife biologist at the University of Alaska, play teaches animals how to get along in groups, how to traverse their terrain, how to master their own bodies, how to anticipate the patterns that will end in successful mating, dominance, hunting. Dr. Fagen points out that as animals grow to full adulthood, they no longer need to learn as much from their play, but their play keeps them behaviorally flexible. Through play, adult animals can deal better with challenges and change. Through play, they can better relate to their young and their mates. We have all seen photos, at least, of adult mammals and birds at play—shots of fully grown mountain sheep and goats frolicking with such wild abandon that it's easy to see how they earned their family zoological name of Caprinae (caperers). I've seen pictures of adult crows, even hippopotamuses, letting their bodies be jostled and carried by currents of the wind or water. Animals look particularly beautiful at these times. I'd bet that if animals were able to set up species-specific roller-coaster rides, quite a few of them might try it.

We fully grown human animals should be playing, too, yet we refuse to learn the lessons available to us from our pets and from the animal behaviors recorded in the wild. When we play as young children, we are working toward understanding things. How do our bodies work? What feels good? What doesn't? And we are grappling with the future. What will happen when we're big? What will happen tomorrow? Achieving an understanding of these things should motivate us to play all through our lives.

We can trace the movement of human play up its developmental ladder, beginning with two primitive forms, instinctive play and mimicry. Instinctive play is something adults help babies do. We toss our infants up gently or whirl them around, and they show quick, involuntary, startled reflexes and then laugh, often signaling us for more. Playful mimicry also begins within weeks to a couple of months after birth. Much of it, at first, centers on faces: we smile at our babies, they smile at us. Plays on separation and reunion (peekaboo) begin within the next few months. Peekaboo, in fact, is the first type of play to be based on fantasy—about the loss and return of somebody crucial. When our children are around six months old, they start handling rudimentary objects—spoons, rattles, teething rings; within the next few months, they begin playing on word sounds—"Ba ba, ma ma, ga ga"—linguistic play that appears to be uniquely human.

In the toddler years, the rough-and-tumble and cavorting play behaviors of nonhuman animals become possible for children as well. The tot also begins to "pretend," and this playful expression of fantasy dominates youngsters' preschool and early school years. Child psychiatrists love it, and a good round of pretend is one of the particular enjoyments I get from my work. During this same period of development, children also begin to learn how to play games, and their games become more complex and difficult as their childhoods progress. As children reach age seven or so, they develop two other strictly human forms of play, practice and hobbies. (I define a hobby as a play activity that involves collecting things and/or information.) School-age children also develop the ability to play alone, entirely within their minds.

With adolescence, young people achieve the ability to dare, and a predilection for playing while hanging out (something that Winnie the Pooh apparently knew how to do but the average nonhuman mammal does not). And with adolescence, I have found, a turning point appears in our children's play. Will they go on to play in their adult lives? The lucky ones do.

I find that the kind of play that adults prefer often harks back to the kinds they most enjoyed during their childhood. We step back down the developmental ladder, revisiting old rungs. Even if we are driven in adulthood by inner demons, we may be impelled to play in the old ways. Consider the case of Theodore Kaczinski. Kaczinski was picked up by the FBI in early April 1996, in his rural Montana cabin, on suspicion of being the Unabomber, who had eluded the authorities for eighteen years. On the evening of Kaczinski's arrest, I wondered aloud to my husband and a couple of friends whether this man, who was known to be a mathematical and scientific whiz, had amused himself as a teenager by building bombs.

The second day after Kaczinski's arrest, a Dartmouth anthropology professor, Dale E. Eickelman, came forward and confirmed my hunch. Ted and Dale, as adolescent boys near Chicago, had constructed bombs with supplies from their chemistry sets. Once, the two boys exploded a metal garbage can in a vacant lot in Evergreen Park. For Kaczinski, a childhood mode of play allegedly became the trademark behavior of his maturity. But of course every child "bomber" does not grow up to become a Unabomber—as evidenced by Theodore Kaczinski's old friend Professor Eickelman.

Although many people find entirely new modes of play in their adult lives, a number of us recapitulate old modes or old themes that were our favorites in childhood. A healthier example than Kaczinski is in order here.

Tom Kennedy, a Portland, Oregon, gardener, began planting a little plot of land that his father had given him when Tom was five. Planting quickly established itself as Tom's favorite pastime. And it remains his favorite pastime today. There was a good reason for five-year-old Tom's choice of gardening. His life-threatening asthma forced him to stay away from sports. And a second factor was that gardens were his father's favorite playground. Old Jake Kennedy spent more time in his garden than anywhere else. Tom loved his father. So the garden was the place where Tom was sure to find his dad.

"My father was very much into gardening," Tom told me. "Each one of us, me and my sisters, was given the same-size garden plot. I remember liking to raise unusual plants, like godetia and salpiglossis, so that my plot could be unusual and interesting. I took pride in growing big cukes and humongous squashes. I competed. And I always beat my sisters. Not that it was very hard—they weren't the least bit interested in gardening.

"There's another part from my childhood about raising plants," Tom went on. "As a little kid, I always wanted to please my father, especially about his gardening interests. He liked the different varieties of roses and the upkeep of a beautiful lawn. As a child, I never felt I was doing the lawn quite well enough for him. I'd see my dad edging it after I'd finished, and that would devastate me. I wonder now if I've made up for those old feelings of inadequacy. My dad died from cancer when I was ten years old. And I went on to become more and more interested in gardening, maybe as part of my lasting connection to him."

Tom spent much of his early adulthood concentrating on three types of plants—magnolias, rhododendrons, and true firs. Lucky enough to live in the Pacific Northwest, one of the greenest parts of the world, Tom put into his garden as many varieties of his three favorite plants as he could. Almost every February, Tom came south to Golden Gate Park to check out the varieties of magnolias blooming there. Sometimes we went over to the park together; I was repeatedly amazed at Tom's mastery of botanical details. He was a gardening Whiz Kid. Tom tracked species rhododendrons—the parent plants of the hybrids—all around the world. He often brought back unusual specimens for his garden. Some of these plants were iffy, to say the least, in Portland. But Tom particularly enjoyed working with plants that were having a hard time. "I have this fantasy," he told me once, "that they're all going to get better."

Tom is a doctor. He has never married, has no children, and lives alone. Specializing in child and adolescent psychiatry, Tom has done such notable work with the saddest, the most undergrown children of Oregon that I have often heard him called "the Saint of Portland" (never to his face; he wouldn't stand for it). And look at his play! Tom preferred tending to the species plants, the ones that weren't really at home in his garden. Although, as the most devoted sort of hobbyist, he knew the Latin names, the places of origin, Tom's play had earlier roots: it was a piece of four- and five-year-old pretend. Tom liked to maintain his plants in families, putting the species specimens close to their hybrids. His attempts to arrange family groupings may well have partly fulfilled his wish to have a family of his own. In the world of fantasy, Tom had grown, yet remained entirely true to himself. His garden play revolved around establishing and keeping family ties. A childhood fantasy of pleasing his father had been replaced by an adult fantasy of preserving families and continuing relationships, even past death.

Over the past few years, ever since he moved into a ground-floor condo on the Willamette, Tom has developed techniques for indoor and patio gardening that would bring envy to the heart of many a pro. For Tom, the potted plant became the same kind of challenge that his old species magnolias used to be—or, for that matter, what Oregon's neediest children still are today. "I take care of basket-case plants these days," he told me. "A rare orange begonia recently tried to commit suicide by jumping off my shelf. My cleaning lady disliked another plant and almost drowned it. I had to go into action on both plants quickly. I guess I've always tended to the things that other people don't care about. Some of them make it. And some of them don't. I guess I just have to live with that."

WE EMBELLISH our play with meanings unique to ourselves. And these meanings continue to develop as our lives become more complex. Underlying meanings make each person's play special and individual, almost as if our play carried a personal trademark or logo. Long before I became a gardener myself, my gardening friends fascinated me. When I saw adults play so differently in their gardens, I realized that each of us had individual psychological ways to play in our own backyards.

Kim Armstrong, for instance, painted, with a rural Vermont flower garden as her paint box. Her goal, she told me, was to create beautiful colors and textures and place them in arrays that gave one the feeling of living inside a watercolor. As a child, Kim loved to draw. She sketched more horses and flowers than the ordinary child does, because for years she could not read. She suffers from dyslexia. Her family was wealthy but not well-adjusted: her father, an alcoholic, beat the boys into bettering themselves while expecting nothing from the girls. On the grounds of their house in Connecticut was a formal garden that was off-limits to the children. Nobody expected Kim to do well in school. If she became a sportswoman, that was just fine with her family. And so they bought Kim a horse of her own and didn't help her much with her struggles to read.

When she reached fifth grade, Kim finally began to read. She was intensely motivated. Her schoolwork now became a manage-able challenge. She studied more diligently the older she became. She checked and double-checked her work to catch any inadver-tent mistakes. Eventually, Kim became a professional in the new field of adult dyslexia—but despite her advanced training, no read-ing, naming, or decoding skill ever came easy. As an escape, she played in the same ways that had always been successful for her as a child. Her playgrounds became the small corral she kept for her daughter's horse and a garden plot of her own. With her flowers, Kim did not have to be as mentally disciplined as she felt she needed to be in her working life. "In my garden," she told me, "it doesn't matter if I call something the wrong name. My dysnomia and dyslexia can be entirely forgotten."

Kim's play is a hobby. It began, as do many hobbies, during the skill-building phase of her middle childhood. In her adult garden, Kim plays with hues of one color, arranging things so that one new color wave will emerge every three weeks or so, while the other occasional colors are "just a little splash." She purposely constructs no overall scheme for her garden: "I want things to be free-flowing. I don't want things structural or formal"—as her parents' garden was. "It's a very impressionistic thing for me. I really love it messy, with little seedlings that don't belong"—Kim herself?—"coming up in the pebble path." She chooses soft colors—blue, pink, violet, salmon, pale yellow, white. In her garden, Kim plays a kind of inte-rior game with considerable room for fantasy. Although she is beautiful, she likes to remain consistently understated. In her school days, being noticed brought along with it too many humili-ating remarks about her dumbness, her failures. As an adult, Kim plays so subtly that you can recognize the beauty of her flowers without paying much attention to her. Her garden is famous enough to have inspired color spreads in a couple of national mag-azines, but at her request it was listed as belonging to an "anony-mous" gardener.

One June, I ran into Andy, Kim's husband, and asked him how the garden grew. "All blues right now," he said. "A couple of weeks ago it was almost all violet. Can you come up and see what's happening? It's incredible!" Andy also wanted me to know that one of Kim's attitudes had recently changed. "She's decided to let us show it in the gardening magazines under our own name," he told me. I wondered whether the act of play itself was beginning to bring Kim out of the shadows.

In contrast to Kim Armstrong, Kelly McNamara was highly socialized before she ever became a gardener. A transplanted Midwesterner who had moved to Hawaii when her husband was hired as a professor by the university there, Kelly joined the Oahu Garden Club, not as a way to meet "the right people" but to make friends and learn about the flowers that inhabited her new environment. Her first project at home, in fact, was to create a bed of native plants. They flourished and in doing so made Kelly feel more comfortable on her adopted turf. Not a purist about what she would or would not set into a garden, she created an exciting mélange of bright orange birds-of-paradise juxtaposed with deep purple orchids and cream-colored hibiscus flowers. In Kim's terms, Kelly's garden may have been a little on the loud side—but it had a certain panache.

Then Kelly's husband was invited to spend five weeks in the spring as a Rockefeller scholar-in-residence at the Villa Serbelloni, the Rockefeller Foundation's study retreat high on a hill above Lake Como. For months before arriving in Italy, Kelly fretted that she might not fit in. "All those women professors and stuffy faculty wives," she recalled. "I was sure I wouldn't be accepted." She decided to do a wildflower survey of the villa's lands; the survey might keep her busy enough not to feel bad about all those snubs she expected. She borrowed a few botanical books from her club, selected some drawing supplies, bought a camera of her own. Now she felt ready. If nobody would talk to her, then she would do what came the hardest to her—play all by herself.

That spring, while her husband worked on a scholarly monograph, Kelly named, identified, sketched, and photographed every wildflower she could find. She immediately "belonged" in the Lake

Como region. People, Americans and Italians alike, wanted to follow Kelly around—meet her, learn from her, watch her. Like Kim, Kelly had developed an adult hobby. But the interior meaning of her hobby was quite different from Kim's—it hinged on socialization. Kelly found herself surrounded by unsnobbish women professors and not-at-all-stuffy spouses. Upon returning home, she submitted a handmade book to the Rockefeller scholars-of-the-future so that they could walk the trails of this magnificent estate, one that Pliny the Elder is said to have owned, and be able to identify any April wildflower they spotted. Kelly's gift to the foundation was her play. What made it play was her most important aim—to have fun. But Kelly also gained what she has always gained from gardening—the sense of belonging.

Mature play doesn't originate out of a vacuum. It develops from childhood avoidances, losses, wishes, preferences, even rebellions. When Kelly was very young, her sister Lucy, two years her junior, was her primary playmate. Although Kelly enjoyed the other children who lived in her neighborhood, she never felt compelled to seek them out. Lucy was always there. Then, in the middle of one night, Lucy, who had been coughing, was taken to the hospital. The next morning, Kelly's parents were nowhere to be found; a short time later, they came home without Lucy. Kelly's little sister was dead; she had contracted "runaway" pneumonia. It was too much, too fast. The surviving six-year-old was shocked and, later, grievously sad.

Kelly still played. But she played rougher and dirtier. "After six, I was always in the mud," she remembered. "And I always had somebody there with me. I didn't enjoy being alone. I can't remember what my parents did about redoing my room—I had roomed with Lucy up to then, so they must have done something about it. But after Lucy died, I'd always have to be with kids. Somebody. I'd climb up onto the roof of the playhouse and make noises that would frighten the boys inside. Or I'd lock them into the playhouse, and then we girls would run away. We were always flying around, chasing, tricking. And I was always deep inside a group."

Obviously, Kelly's gardening did not spring, as Venus from the sea, from her responses to Lucy's death. But her groupiness did. From the devastating loneliness of a child suddenly robbed of her constant playmate came the need for a circle of friends, a circle that could easily be found through a mutual interest in flowers.

PLAY IS essential to maturity. It gives us pleasure, a sense of accomplishment, of belonging. It is an opportunity for learning. It reduces our stresses. It even inspires an occasional book (Izaak Walton's masterpiece *The Compleat Angler,* for one). Play is important to our relationships. And it gives us flexibility. As Robert Fagen has put it, "In a world continuously presenting unique challenges and ambiguity, play prepares [us] for an evolving planet."

People must pause to examine their lives. And these pauses must come at relatively frequent intervals. As adults, most of us have given up on playing. We're too busy, we believe—or we can't bring ourselves to behave in what we might consider frivolous ways. Most of us don't even think about playing anymore. Few people die, however, feeling that they did not work hard enough. When it is too late, the loss of play is what we too often regret. If we are already accustomed to playing, we must continue to upgrade our play, continue to find the time for it. If we don't play at all, then we must begin. In today's world, play is a lost key. It unlocks the door to our selves.

2

Revisiting the Lowest Rungs of the Play Ladder

My baby daughter used to wake up at two every morning. Somehow, it was special between us at that hour. No eager toddler named David was getting into our faces so early in the morning. In fact, there was not a single sound at two except for the ones that she and I made. When she reached her first birthday, Julia still awoke at the same time night after night. No sleeping the whole night through, the way babies a third of her age could do. At that time in Julia's life, I worked as a resident in psychiatry at the hospital. A nice baby-sitter named Jennie took good care of Julia every day Monday through Friday. And Ab and I took good care of her in the evenings. She ate enough dinner to last her until breakfast. She played. She explored. She walked all around the house and tired herself out.

So why did she wake up at two every morning? She wasn't hungry, it was clear. But she also refused to lie back down in less than half an hour. I talked to her. I lifted her up and held her high above my head. Sometimes I tossed her slightly and caught her. "Up in the air, with the greatest of ease-a, she's a superbaby! She's a superbaby!" Julia laughed. We settled down and she said a couple of words to me and mimicked my inflections. She smiled. We did it again. "Try patty-cake!" she signed by slapping her hands together. We clapped through a couple of rounds. She cuddled into my body and I held her. Then we tried the motions of "This little piggy" and "There was a little girl who had a little curl" a few times. I sang to her about our Ann Arbor address, "Twenty-three, twenty-four, York-*shy*-er." And then one round of "My Favorite Things," except that instead of using Oscar Hammerstein's words "Raindrops on roses and whiskers on kittens," I sang, "Mommy and Daddy and David and Julie; Mommy and Daddy and David and Julie; we all belong to the Terr family; we all belong to the Terr family." She tried to sing it, too. Finally, she looked a little sleepy and let me know it was time to go back to bed.

What were we doing? And why didn't I resent this invasion of my sleep? Because we both were having fun, I realized then and appreciate even more today. For around a year and a half, little Julia Beth Terr and I woke up every single night at two in order to play.

Up until fairly recent history, children were thought of as miniature adults. Even today, we hang on to a few old expressions that indicate this traditional view of children—"little man" or "young lady," for instance, when we address them formally or with ice in our voices. The twentieth century, however, brought a breakthrough in the way that the world thinks about children—the idea that young people develop in stages. This idea was inspired by the concept of evolution. However, it was not the product of one person or one field, but of many.

Staging means that as children physically grow, their thinking and emotions grow, too. They start low down on a developmental ladder, and then their maturation moves them upward through a predictable pattern. Once the idea of staging caught on in the early twentieth century, a boy of thirteen or fourteen with an adult's body, for instance, could no longer be considered an adult. He'd be considered, instead, an "adolescent." His thinking and his emotions would be seen as special to his teenage years. By reading about one youth or a group of young people, we might easily pick out qualities that applied to our own teenagers as well.

This new concept of developmental phases brought with it exciting new fields of study and of practice, such as juvenile justice, pediatrics, child psychiatry, child psychology, early childhood education, and child's rights. Without staging, the twentieth century would not have even begun to live up to the name it was given at its onset—"The Century of the Child." And without staging, we would not have been able to group our thoughts and observations about the phenomena inherent in child's play.

We must briefly pause to explore a few of these developmental theories before going further along our journey into play. Since a great deal of our adult play comes from deep in our own childhoods, it is interesting to note how the early developmental psychologists would have traced our recreational preferences. I will take you quickly through three of these schemes—those of G. Stanley Hall, Sigmund Freud, and Jean Piaget—as an outline of how we might look at the lifetime development of play.

As we move into the phases, however, one cautionary point. A number of contemporary experts on childhood, including myself, find these early theories overly rigid. And they were originally based, we recognize now, on just a few cases. One of the themes in child development theory is that once a new position on the developmental ladder is attained, it is not normal to stand still in that position (to "fixate," in Freud's terminology) or to dip backward (to "regress," according to Freud). This is not my view. I see each of the childhood stages as potentially extending directly into normal, healthy adulthood.

But we cannot overlook Freud and the other early classifiers of child development just because we disagree a little—their work is far too important. And it directly applies to play, enabling us to begin to understand where in our own backgrounds our play comes from. The important concept of developmental staging was first introduced by the American psychologist G. Stanley Hall in his 1904 book, *Adolescence*. In it, Hall suggested that when children of advancing phases play, they are gradually recapitulating the history of humankind from the earliest primitive cultures to the most complex, modern civilizations. Hall's attempt to fit the world's historical movements into a child's maturing play was a giant leap. And it wasn't provable. When we watch children at play, for instance, we cannot find consistent situations in which young tots behave like tribal warriors while teenagers play with the highest civility. Consider today's adolescents at a rock concert, for example. Would they be universally seen as the epitome of our progress through history?

So instead of taking G. Stanley Hall up on his historical recapitulation idea, the turn-of-the-twentieth-century psychoanalysts and psychologists, especially Sigmund Freud, took him up on his general approach to developmental staging. By categorizing the phases of youth according to the progress of the sexual and aggressive drives, Freud and his analytic circle proposed a ladder of development that is still actively argued back and forth today. Almost a hundred years after its introduction, this theory remains fresh and interesting.

Let's briefly think about how the early analysts fit play into their newly conceived childhood phases. Sigmund Freud divided childhood into the oral, anal, phallic (infantile genital) and oedipal (family triangle), latency, and adolescent (mature genital) periods. Before reaching adulthood, a person would pass through each of these phases and forgo the previous one. The psychoanalytic stages of development are based on where the center of sexual and aggressive drives, or pleasures, can supposedly be found at each age. So an oral-phase child would lick, suck, and manually toy with body parts or objects to express sexuality; bite and claw to express aggression. The child's play would include stroking, sucking, and teething. Adults who liked oral modes of playing—modes emphasizing skin sensations, as in spa vacations and tanning at the beach, or sexual foreplay that depended largely on oral and manual activities—would be considered to be somewhat regressed. An analyst might deem this kind of psychological rollback to be healthy, but only if the adult in question wasn't entirely centered on this sort of activity.

According to psychoanalysis, anal play, or the play of toddlers, is dedicated to exploration, mastery, and autonomy. Although the anus is not directly involved, the corresponding child's play involves tasks having to do with toilet training—messing, controlling, organizing, handling mistakes, taking responsibility. Anal-stage children pull playthings around, build with blocks, slop water and paints onto paper, organize their toys, stack items up, tear them down; and adults who play anally might collect coins or stamps, go around to quilting bees or antique shows, throw pots, paint with palette knives or spray cans, or adore organizing the things that they play with. Again, psychoanalysis would generally consider such types of adult play as potentially abnormal instances of freezing in place or of sliding backward.

I could go on to examples of child and adult pretend and competition (hallmarks of the phallic and oedipal phase) and games (representative of the latency [a relatively nonsexual] period), but I will cite a number of these as we move along. The main point I'd make here, however, has to do with what the psychoanalysts have seen as an important goal in growing up—giving up on what they named "the pleasure principle." Pleasure has to retreat before real life, "the reality principle," in order for a person to grow up healthy. Play is destined, according to the analysts, to bow entirely to work.

What Freudian psychology has said about the pleasure-reality trade-off certainly carries a good amount of truth to it. We adults do have to live in reality much of the time, forsaking numbers of immediate pleasures in order to make money, raise children, keep our houses habitable, eat. But Freud and his followers, in stressing the realities of adolescent and adult life so emphatically, gave mature play short shrift. They treated play as if it were some sort of vestige of childhood, much the way that the thymus gland is a residual of our growing years.

The best example of what eventually happened to this theoretical victory of work over play was Sigmund Freud's daughter Anna's late-life contribution to developmental staging theory. In the mid-1960s she thought up a way of looking at the phases of childhood that she called the "developmental lines"; and she organized one of her specific lines, "from play to work." Some of this progression would be evident, Miss Freud said, before a small child ever started school; but as children reached adolescence, most of the transition would already be complete. Otherwise, teenagers could not handle the pressures of academic or vocational training. Anna Freud was a keen enough observer to write that healthy adults continue to treasure their play. But she left the idea dangling. Her either-or theoretical strictness forced her into overvaluing work at the expense of play.

A very different approach to childhood staging, one developed in Geneva, Switzerland, from the 1920s into the late 1960s, has been extremely important to the fields of child psychology and psychiatry, especially to those professionals with an interest in how early thinking evolves. Jean Piaget painstakingly studied his own three children as they developed from infancy. He took meticulous notes on the statements and behaviors of his young Lucienne, Laurent, and Jacqueline. What fascinated Piaget was how his kids put their ideas together and how they eventually figured things out. But he also took notes on how they played. As opposed to the childhood-sexuality-driven observations of the psychoanalysts, Piaget's observations were cognition-driven. He was looking at an entirely different aspect of how children come of age.

Piaget concluded that youngsters, as infants and toddlers, first pass through a sensory-motor phase in which they practice their motor and thinking skills as they play. Preschool boys and girls then enter a stage in which they almost exclusively use pretend. Children who play imaginatively appear to bend reality to suit their inner desires—an important, but immature, thinking mechanism that the Swiss psychologist called "assimilation." Next, school-age youngsters come into a new and more realistic phase of cognition, in which they are able to join into games with rules. With their organized, but concrete, early-elementary-school thinking, these children appear able to make "accommodations" of thought, the opposite process from assimilation. Now inner realities are reshaped by the child to conform to external facts. In the Piagetian frame of reference, accommodation is a definite improvement over the earlier thinking styles. With accommodation, reality strikes young people as the most important factor in framing their ideas and explanations. Finally, at around age twelve or so, youngsters enter a phase in which their play begins to resemble reality itself. Adolescents are able to think abstractly, using formal logic and organization. In fact, according to Piaget, the teenager no longer has to play at all. After all, why *play* reality when one is already fully able to *live* reality?

We can see that Jean Piaget's carefully constructed staging theory leads inexorably from illogic (primitive thinking) to logic (mature thinking). Similar in this respect to Freud and his followers, Piaget leaves little to no room in his outline for adult play. After watching Lucienne, Laurent, and Jacqueline grow up, Piaget stopped making notes on their play and thought. So he never systematically learned what happened to their adult pleasures. (I can't help but wonder whether the great Swiss psychologist felt just a wee bit playful himself as he made all those minute observations of his kids. Once in a while, his examples make me chuckle.)

When I consider the Piagetian and the Freudian stagings of childhood play, I would say that the two theories work best when taken together. Even when merged, however, there are huge gaps and exceptions, especially in regard to the play of adults. Partly because of this incompleteness, other, more contemporary observers of children (and occasionally, of adults) would step in to enlighten us about play development. And we will become better acquainted with some of them—Brian Sutton-Smith, Robert Fagen, Barrie Thorne, Helen Schwartzman, for instance—as we move along.

Over the years, I have learned that our brains develop new and increasing capacities as we grow up and that our emotions allow for ever more complicated meanings and expressions. The old thoughts and feelings, however, are never entirely abandoned. And some of these old vestiges from our own developmental ladders continue to pose favorite themes for us—favorite ways of thinking, of reacting, of being. Our play begins during our infancies—with involuntary reflexive play, mimicry, object play, and word play. These primitive stages of play, despite what the early developmental psychologists and psychoanalysts might have said, extend into *normal* adult lives. We do not have to regress to play. We simply have to stay in control of ourselves, while remaining in close touch with our own beginnings.

BORN WITH flaccid little bodies that fail at first to completely support the weight of their own heads, full-term human infants cannot play right away. But within days of their births most of them are watching us, following us with their eyes, even making a facial gesture or two that indicate they are developing the ability to copy us. It seems to me that from the very first, human infants are trying to understand their worlds and to gain some control. They handle their parents' bodies to grasp and know them, almost the same way that a blind person reads braille. They handle their own bodies, too, sometimes scratching their skin or somebody else's skin with sharp little nails. Their worlds are narrow—their cribs, their bodies, a few faces, sounds, somebody's lap, a bottle or a breast. Yet within this narrow scope, infants begin to develop play. And they do this because play is so essential to their ongoing maturation.

Playing on infantile instincts is the earliest of all human forms of play. It originates in our first few months on earth. When a parent gently tosses a three- or four-month-old baby into the air, the baby, virtually helpless with no useful arm or leg responses except for its innate instincts, feels a sudden rush of danger and in a sudden, involuntary bodily response flexes and then extends the legs and fully extends the arms. Within another second or so, the infant feels a sudden sense of security back in its parent's grasp. The baby laughs with the reestablishment of safety. Then its parent intones something like "Allez-oop!" And again the rush of danger, the surprised look, instinctive full-body response, and that same sure catch. The baby giggles upon landing and signals for more. It's amazing how we lightly swoop our infants up, drop them a bit, whirl them around—and it's amazing how much jostling our babies can take and come to like.

Whenever they slip in space, or whenever they hear a sudden, loud noise, babies experience a full-body response. We physicians check infants for these reflexes because they indicate to us that a baby is properly wired. Most likely, these instincts represent ways that young babies, who for thousands of prehistoric years lived in the insecurity of trees or caves, occasionally saved themselves from falls or from animal attacks. These sudden flingings of arms and legs come only as responses to things that signify danger. Yet when a parent plays with a three- or four-month-old infant on these very same instincts, this danger is juxtaposed with a keen sense of safety. The fun revolves around trying to control the uncontrollable. The enjoyment sits at the meeting point of peril and security. This universal game is pleasurable for all—even for the accidental onlooker.

Instinctive play originates way, way down the developmental ladder, just a few months after birth. (As far as fetal life is concerned, who knows if the almost-term fetus plays? Mothers-to-be have reported to me the sense that at times their baby was "all elbows and knees," or that their fetus was "playing around" on a certain day.) As parents, we get a kick out of propping our infants up on locked little legs—this, like the startle reflex, is a primitive instinct. Or we tickle the bottoms of our babies' feet until they splay their minuscule toes in avoidance—the Babinski reflex. The sensation of playing on instincts is the sensation of finding a cusp between chaos and control. It is an edge between laughing and crying, pleasure and pain. And we adults recapture it—at the height of battle, of sexual experience, of surprise, of intense gratification.

Infants lose almost all of their primitive instincts within the last half of the first year of life. We can tell this because a fall eventually comes to be endured with arms and legs held close to the body. A loud noise comes to be experienced with a slight start, but with no spasmodic jerks of the extremities. Toes turn down once little feet are tickled; and an older infant comes to stand normally, locked knees or no. Once our infantile reflexes are quashed—because they are inhibited by our maturing frontal lobes—they do not ordinarily break through again, unless we suffer extreme damage to the foreparts of our brains. Immature reflexes remain permanently out of sight, but they are still there. And the memories are still there, too, although they cannot be verbalized.

As adults, we continue to flirt with these same, heavily masked, but innate responses. And what better way to flirt with something than to play with it? Instinctive play stimulates the same sense of helplessness that we repeatedly experienced during our infancies. But this time we have the means to master our helplessness. We have skateboards, race cars, parachutes, sails. We have rafts, kayaks, horses, bikes.

Instinctive play originates so low down in development that fantasy, wishes, understanding, barely figure in. We grown-ups indulge vicariously in instinctive play by savoring films, such as *Downhill Racer, Wind, Deliverance, River Wild,* the two *Endless Summer*s, and *Cliffhanger.* Closer at hand, we might opt to drive down to the beach to watch some sail surfers, or over to the hills to view somebody flying a glider. In doing so, we hark back to our almost forgotten infancies—our days in (and half out of) our parents' arms.

Some of us go to amusement parks to conjure up those old feelings. People on roller-coaster rides frequently throw out their arms atop the first dip. That's so close to the look of the infantile startle reflex, we must remind ourselves that this form of mature behavior is quite purposeful. Those flung-out arms at the tops of hills on bikes, or at the crests of city blocks on skateboards, demonstrate how close we older humans come to recapturing our ancient infantile sensations when we play. "Look, Ma! No hands!" Hardly any fantasy goes along with this. Here, the sensation is what counts.

Ironically enough, one of the most dedicated instinctive players

I have ever known is a young man with cerebral palsy. Rick Ruiz is an unmarried, thirty-year-old astrophysicist. He was working on his doctorate at Stanford when I first met him. Due to birth-related damage to the motor centers of his brain, Rick's muscles lock into tense, spastic bundles whenever he tries to use them.

As clumsy and ungainly as his crisscross gait makes him, Rick demonstrates a consistently strong urge to play. He is a physical player, and the sports he particularly likes are those that a person can do alone. Rick enjoys competing with Mother Nature. That, beyond doubt, is his favorite game.

During college, Rick's "playground" was the water. At the University of Pennsylvania, where he worked on his undergraduate degree in physics, he sculled on the Schuylkill River. Though gliding over the surface of a river looks easy and sometimes feels effortless, Rick had to do arm and chest exercises two or three hours a day in order to row competitively. There was a good dose of work to Rick's river play; but although he had to exert himself to exhaustion, each outing in his boat felt pleasurable. Although he never won a race at Penn, he eventually won something far more important: a sense of competence. He found himself able to challenge nature—the course of a river, its currents, its breezes—and he could challenge the nature of himself, too, locked muscles and all.

While studying astrophysics in graduate school at Stanford, however, Rick found himself unable to do the three hours or so of daily exercise that he needed in order to scull. There simply wasn't the time. Rick gradually became depressed—who was he if he could not master the elements? He spent a number of days in a psychiatric hospital and then sought outpatient treatment with me. We decided to use both antidepressant medications and psychotherapy.

After a few months of treatment, Rick got lucky. Some of his friends were going up to Lake Tahoe to ski. Did he want to come along? Rick agreed; but as he anticipated, his skiing buddies took off for the advanced slopes as soon as they arrived. Alone, Rick made his way over to a place labeled "Handicapped Skiing," and there, within minutes, he met a man with one leg.

The man was excited to spot Rick. He could tell without asking what Rick's condition was. "What I'm working on right now is boots, poles, and skis for people with CP! Do you want to come over to my cabin and experiment with some of my stuff? You'll be a kind of model."

Rick hoisted himself into the man's van, and off they went down the road to try on the man's equipment. The man himself skied and, as Rick soon observed, could get down a slope quickly and with style. But this man wanted to go further with his equipment. He had already developed successful designs for people with amputations. Now he wanted to tackle cerebral palsy. "Anyone who wants to ski should be able to!" he said.

Rick used the man's ski equipment that day; and the man served as his first instructor. "What you've got to get comfortable with," the man told his new student, "is having to admit to yourself that you will be using special equipment. In rowing, your boat wouldn't be distinguishable from anyone's. But with skiing, once you're on a hill, you won't think twice about the gadgets you're using. You'll just feel yourself fly!"

That year, Rick made amazing progress with both his skiing and his depression. Instead of having to exercise his upper body every single day, Rick needed only to go up to the mountains on winter and spring weekends. During the week, he stayed up late at night analyzing the data that his lab received from the Hubble space telescope. This way he could free his Saturdays and Sundays for the hills. His special equipment kept his weak ankles firm to the ground and provided him the steadying force of poles with small skis fastened to their ends. The man never charged Rick a cent for any of this. Rick was his "perfect" example of CP. All that Rick had to do was to keep coming up to the mountains for a little experimentation and fine-tuning.

After three years, Rick was appointed a member of the Handicapped Ski Patrol at Squaw Valley. After four years, he was named an instructor. In about the same period, he finished his doctoral thesis and graduated from Stanford with a fine future ahead of him. And where did he want to go? To Seattle, of course, to work in an astrophysics laboratory at the University of Washington—and to ski, ski, ski.

Before he left California, Rick summarized what he gets from his play: "I've always needed to feel in control. Ever since I was very young. Control hasn't come easy to me. It's not natural for me to walk. Not natural to take the stairs or—worse yet—to keep pace with a fast-moving crowd. But on a mountain, I can turn and face downhill all by myself. Every time I do that, I realize that the mountain is a huge force, bigger, much bigger, than me. When I ski, it's just us two alone. Me and the mountain. And I like it that way."

Perhaps Rick, because of his physical problems, gravitated almost exclusively to instinctive play because it harkened back to a time when his physical limitations weren't as obvious. Rick's parents, not recognizing the movement problems that would be in store for their little boy, would have tossed him around a little and he would have beckoned for more, with no fantasies, no goals, save the pleasure of a short, excitingly safe trip and the possibility of another.

An important difference between Rick and those among us without disabilities is that Rick's play dictated almost everything else in his life. It stood far ahead—in first place, ahead of black holes and exploding stars, ahead of friends and food. Rick became depressed when it was no longer possible for him to play against nature. And he became comfortable again when he found his own solution. Of course, Rick benefited from antidepressant medication and psychotherapy. But he and I agree that his discovery of skiing has helped more than anything else.

ALL OF US have noticed at some time or the other that babies are excellent mimics. Beginning as early as a couple of weeks after birth, infants study their parents' and siblings' facial expressions; and then they try to duplicate them with expressions of their own.

When babies get it right, and especially after they are able to smile, they show gleeful responses to their own successful mimicries. They begin to use copying as play. Like so many other forms of play, playful imitation carries considerable learning potential. And it carries more than a little fun. It is a strong stimulant to a child's development.

Miming remains a strong impetus to our adult play. It is a key to our proficiency at sports, for instance. "Do not as I say, but as I do" is the key operational phrase here. For years, we watched and admired Chris Evert's two-handed tennis backhand, and then everybody tried it. Before Kareem Abdul-Jabbar showed us his basketball "skyhook," nobody seemed to have considered it. Afterward, the hook became almost generic. Perhaps Kareem should have patented it. Millions of children emulate such sports figures as Wayne Gretzky, Brett Favre, Tara Lipinski, Michelle Kwan, Cal Ripken, Charles Barkley, Roberto Alomar, and Picabo Street. Not only do kids consider athletic legends to be role models, but they closely observe and copy their techniques. With videotaping, imitation becomes far easier. A spectacular player can be studied in slow motion. And our own play can then be considered in tandem. When we amateur players see exactly what we have been doing, we can often mimic a professional and correct our mistakes. If we play better, we enjoy it more.

Mimicry is frequently used in infantile play. And it lasts to some extent into our maturity. Michael Lewis, a psychologist who does fascinating infant research at the Institute for the Study of Child Development, Robert Wood Johnson Medical School, New Brunswick, New Jersey, has demonstrated that from just a few weeks after birth, babies communicate elaborately with their caretakers with a combination of nonverbal signals and mimicry. Imitation helps babies to get what they want, and it helps them as well to play. Mirroring is often characterized by the same lighthearted smiles and infectiousness that we associate with play.

Our adult play also includes bits of mimicry. If we adults didn't like to ape, why would we laugh so much at the "roast" of a colleague or roar so hard at a takeoff on our own behaviors? Why would we spend so many evenings at the movies or in front of the TV set with Robin Williams or Dana Carvey? Why would congressional representatives, politicians, even presidents, laugh out loud while learning so much about themselves at the Washington Press Corps annual spoof?

Sometimes, what might have started out to be playful mimicry can no longer be considered "play." What happens, for instance, when mimicry turns to mockery? Repeating what another person has just said—gestures, tone of voice, and all—leads to extremely unpleasant confrontation. When school-age kids in my office really want to get nasty, that's what they do. They parrot. Their heavy, dark-spirited tone is readily apparent. Their faces wear sneers and smirks—not smiles. Mockery is divided from mimicry by its lack of innocence and lightheartedness. The occasional piece of aggressive impersonation can propel teenagers or adults into mortal combat. In fact, some murders may have been narrowly avoided by that quick but absolutely untruthful excuse "Just playing around." Let us not be fooled, however. Mimicry must promise fun for everyone before it fits our definitions of play.

In adulthood, mimicry teeters between the infuriating act of mockery and total invisibility. Nobody notices a subtle mimic. To play well at imitation, a grown person must have a dramatic streak along with a lightness of spirit. The person should be relatively free from anger. Perhaps that is why we treasure the few great adult mimics we have.

WHEN I watch babies, I am repeatedly struck with how their development progresses from their heads on down. First they are all eyes. Then their mouths come into play with purposeful expressions. Their necks and shoulders come into the game early. And then, their hands. In a sense, I think of this as a kind of neurological staging, one that is "hardwired," or predetermined, for every human child. Our play follows this same neurological progression. Newborns can play actively only with their eyes. Later, their mouths become sources of play, and by about four or five months, their hands begin to play as well. By about five or six months of age, babies can bring up a toy with either hand to their eye level. And then they can subject the toy to a good tasting. Within another month or two, the knees and thighs come into the action. And by the end of the first year, feet and toes join the party as well.

As infants, we humans are remarkably helpless when compared to some of our fellow mammals. Consider the example of the African wildebeest, for instance. If a newborn wildebeest does not get on its feet and run within a few minutes following its delivery, its mother is impelled to go on with the herd, abandoning her newborn to the clutches of a waiting predator. From birth on, animals such as wildebeests are fully able to cavort—that is, if they ever have the spare time or the safety.

Animals with more advanced functioning than wildebeests take much longer to get on their feet. Young crows, kittens, and puppies spend days to weeks after their births rooted to their nests or to their mothers' bodies, totally unable to do things on their own. We find—ironically in a way—that these helpless baby animals are from the very same species that turn out to be the most interesting players in the animal kingdom. In other words, a slow start—and one that progresses from the head on down—may discourage wildebeest-like cavorting for a long, long time. Yet this same slow start allows for a great deal of playing with eyes, ears, mouth, and eventually, wings, forepaws, hands, feet. In the long run, slow-developing play becomes the most sophisticated play.

Once they have the capacity to manage objects with their hands, human infants become dedicated object-players. In fact, the only intellectually normal babies that I have found who cannot play with objects by six or seven months of age are those babies who were profoundly abused or neglected early in life. These "failure to thrive" infants, who are underdeveloped, undernourished, and serious-looking—they hardly, if ever, smile or make a sound—frequently keep their hands clasped together at the chest or tummy. They do not use them, one at a time, to play. Pediatricians call this hand posture "praying-mantis position" and consider it a symptom of growth failure. In psychiatry, however, we think of this as a temporary failure of the developing mind. In the hospital, with tender loving nursing care, the condition may correct itself within a few days.

Shortly after I first became a psychiatrist, my colleague Scott Dowling and I made films of such babies at Case Western Reserve University Medical Center. Within hours after they were admitted to the hospital, we unsuccessfully attempted to induce a half dozen of these infants to play with objects, such as keys or rattles. They could not separate their hands. After slowing our films down, we realized that these infants were making tiny finger gestures indicating that they did indeed want to play. But they were not able to move either hand independently enough to grasp any of the objects we were offering. These untended youngsters had temporarily missed an important neurological opportunity and hence could not develop object play, one of our great links to the rest of the animal kingdom. If their abuse, neglect, or starvation kept on, they would not move forward effectively with their development. By the second half of the first year, Scott and I had learned, human babies clearly need more than instincts, warm bodies, and mimicry to play on. They need to "cavort" with their hands.

The changes in human children between the ages of one and three are astonishing to me. So much happens that I remain continually amazed. Brain structures having to do with verbal memory, such as the hippocampus, become fully functional; and nerve tracts through the brain and down into the spinal cord become fully insulated and effective. All of this makes a toddler able to speak in phrases, jump, run, explore, and coordinate the hands, fingers, and thumbs with increasing dexterity. During the toilet-training and early preschool years, children develop the capacities of play that, most biologists concur, comprise the full mammalian repertoire: locomotor play (cavorting or using large-muscle groups just for the fun of it), object play (pulling a toy, rolling a ball), and social play (playing alongside and, later, with a peer). That's a great deal of play development within a relatively short time.

Cavorting play is more difficult for humans than it is for other animals. Yet with practice, human tots can learn to jog, race, skip, jump, climb, swim, dive. But because we humans do not instinctively cavort, we invent all sorts of tools to help us to play in this fashion. For our children, we buy slides, swings, bars, rings, so that they can play in the mode of the monkeys. For ourselves, and in order to play the way that the porpoises do, we purchase surfboards, belly boards, Jet Skis, inflatable rafts. We cannot naturally run the way a cheetah or a deer does, and so we children and adults alike use well-built athletic shoes, Rollerblades, skateboards, bikes. If a grown-up wishes to climb a hill or a canyon wall like a goat, he or she brings along ropes, pitons, crampons, picks. We seek the experiences of animals at play and take our risks to achieve these. To do so without killing ourselves or someone else, we obtain the safest available equipment, take lessons, talk to experienced players, take care.

I find it fascinating that each of the great infantile play forms that we have considered up to now involve play "on the edge." Each establishes a balance between running out of control and getting a good grip on things. And each, for this reason, carries considerable ongoing appeal into maturity.

ALTHOUGH WE are closely allied to our animal kin, we humans are capable—almost from the beginning of life—of certain kinds of play that are entirely human. Take symbolic play and language play, for instance. Have you ever found an animal that could pretend? Or that "gets" plays on words? Other than in a few old newsreels and a few recent TV commercials, do any nonhumans talk?

The first great symbolic form of play, and one with rules of a sort (making it a "game"), is introduced to a human infant in the second half of the first year. Peekaboo is based on symbolism about separation and reunion. It is a social game that requires a second player. The older child or the adult initiating this game covers the baby's eyes. In a couple of seconds, the child's eyes are uncovered and the words necessary to the game are intoned. "*Peekaboo!* I see you!"

Babies do not recognize material objects as permanent. In other words, when they play peekaboo they think for an instant that their fellow player has disappeared. They are experiencing a real loss.

With the words "*Peekaboo!* I see you!" however, infants experience the intense emotional rush of reunion. Such quickly engendered and powerful emotions create an involuntary start, a laugh, and then, uproarious happiness. The baby gestures "Again!" better prepared this time for what will happen in the game. Once more, happiness and relief are almost instantaneous.

On an airplane once, I saw a mother play peekaboo with her toddler's bear and blanket. As they sat across the aisle from me, the mother hid her little girl's stuffed animal behind her blanket, then started a low growl that gradually increased in intensity. A couple of seconds later, the bear popped out. "*Peekaboo!*" The little girl laughed so hard I had to put my book down. Nothing is as infectious as a good old game well played.

Attachment and loss are primary themes in the emotional life of any infant, of any person, in fact. As children, we have all had to wait for our parents, no matter how good they were at reading our hunger signals—or, for that matter, our signals for wanting company or being tired, irritable, or sick. When we had no caretakers around, we sometimes took our comforts at the corners of a quilt or around the plushy surfaces of a teddy bear, making mental substitutions for our absent parents or guardians.

The mid-twentieth-century English psychoanalyst D. W. Winnicott set his theory of human creativity and play around these transitional moments in an infant's life. Being alone while feeling sure that, if needed, somebody would come, is the best state for plays of the mind, Winnicott said. In Winnicott's view, those people who as infants are able to handle gentle separations by indulging in solitary mind play are those same people who maintain playful attitudes throughout their lives. Winnicott was smart enough to realize—before anyone else seemed to—that play is not just an activity. It is a state of mind. Yet, out of the tougher separations, caused by infantile neglect or abuse, there comes just the opposite, the inability to play at all.

A young child's handling of separations and attachments becomes one of the basics of his or her life. But do adults go on to play variants of peekaboo? It's not as obvious as what anyone might observe in the presence of bear, blanket, mother, and tiny airline passenger. But I find that many of us travel to annual meetings connected with our professions and businesses, and this presents a number of play activities built around separation and attachment. We, of course, go to our meetings to find out "what's new" in our fields. But more meaningfully, we have a yearly chance to visit with old colleagues and friends. Once we're back in touch, all the fun breaks through. It's time for a drink, for a talk, for a laugh about old times.

Yearly retreats, class reunions, meetings of fund-raisers and planners for the ol' alma mater—all of these represent adult variations of the peekaboo game. After feeling cut off, separated, from key people for long periods, we show ourselves, changes and all, to our long-standing colleagues and friends. That song "Auld Lang Syne" beautifully expresses peekaboo symbolism. On New Year's Eve we sing it, holding hands—and we might sing it again at family get-togethers, alumni camps, weddings. Some of our universities make a ritual of peekaboo with their every-five-year reunions for alums. In fact, I know two Princetonians who measure their lives during June every half decade. Seeing ourselves within a larger frame of reference is powerful emotional medicine. Considering our lives in the context of other lives allows us to place outside realities side by side with our inner experiences. We feel an emotional high when sensing this connection.

I believe that the psychoanalyst Erik Erikson's work on the phases of play development has some relevance to this old infantile game. Erikson believed that play moves in infancy from being entirely solitary (or, in his words, "autocosmic") to being shared on a small scale (or "microspheric"). Peekaboo is probably the first evidence that a child is able to socialize while playing. Later, according to Erikson, play comes to involve the larger worlds of the child's school, neighborhood, and town ("macrospheric" play). The idea of social movement during the phasic development of play is important. As with the other early developmental theories, however, specific examples can be found that partially disprove the theory's generalities. For instance, Ludwig van Beethoven's play, solitary as it was, reached what many of us feel to be the heights of maturity.

Peekaboo shows up in all sorts of ways within adult play. For instance, one of my adult patients recently miraculously recovered from a rare cancer that his California doctors considered fatal. He had said good-bye to almost every one of his close friends and family and had then come to ask me to help him to die with grace and dignity. I promised him that I would help, but I advised him first to go on the Net and find out if anything else could be done about his kind of cancer. On his computer, he learned about the East Coast operation that eventually saved his life.

Once he'd survived surgery and its hair-raising aftermath, Phillip came to my office. "Now you're going to have to help me to live!" he said. He did not realize that he had already found the way himself. As he recovered from his operation, he had spontaneously begun planning a series of family reunions. They were hellos rather than good-byes. They were a healthy adult variant of the baby game of peekaboo.

LANGUAGE PLAY is a very human form of play that, like peekaboo, starts in late infancy. I can think of no discernible animal analogies, except for the chirping of birds or the beeping of whales. No person I am familiar with has intercepted and interpreted any specific animal language. (I guess Saint Francis of Assisi would come the closest.) We can teach animals our sign language, by the way, and some of our easier computer languages; but nonhumans still are entirely unable to teach us their own modes of communication.

Have you noticed that when human infants use their first words at about twelve months of age, and later, as they begin to use phrases and sentences, they frequently, perhaps constantly, make particularly cogent observations or commit amusing errors? These "right on" efforts and silly mistakes make everybody laugh. The youngster then laughs, too. Suddenly words are fun. And nonsense is fun, too. Words—in and of themselves—become early modes of play.

Double meanings, soundalikes, tongue twisters, and metaphors come in later—and by the time a child reaches adulthood, a huge panoply of word- and language-based play forms are at hand. When talented adults play verbally, I find them irresistibly charming. And much of this fun can be traced back to early in life when a child first learns to fiddle with language and thereby gets or gives a good chuckle.

Some adult word frolics harken almost directly back to our first exposures to human language. One man from the old TV commercials sticks in my mind in this regard. Every time he broke into his superfast, superfluent double-talk, his almost out-of-control sounds reminded me of those that once took my two- or three-year-old fancy. Danny Kaye's rhyme-talk tickled me back then ("The vessel with the pestle has the pellet with the poison. The flagon with the dragon has the brew that is true"). In 1997, the Nobel Prize in literature went to a master of satirical doublespeak, an Italian named Dario Fo. In a one-man play he wrote, *Mistero Buffo* ("Comic Mysteries"), Fo took on both politics and religion, using a nonsensical language that he called Grammelot. When Fo won the Nobel Prize, a number of scholars were critical. Was he serious enough? Deep enough? Again, as occurs so many times, adult play is almost automatically undervalued as too light, too superficial.

But language play can accomplish wonderful things. It often offers gifts to society. One retired professor of English literature from the College of Staten Island, E. Mason Cooley, has spent the last thirty years or so making up bons mots, such as "The time I kill is killing me" or "Self-analysis always cheats" or "One cannot look forward to becoming a virgin." Recently, Columbia University Press decided to record all of them. Who knows, in another fifty years or so, Cooley's epigrams may find their way into Bartlett's *Familiar Quotations.*

The story of a Chicago kindergarten teacher comes to mind in this regard. Miss Elaine Martin was a consummate master of rhyme. An unusually petite, olive-skinned brunette, she mesmerized little children into learning to read by the time that they finished kindergarten. Remarkably, no matter what Miss Elaine's student's background was, that child would be likely to read at the late-first-grade level by May of the kindergarten year.

Because of Elaine Martin's amazing record with reading, the school district sent out a group of experienced teachers and consultants to analyze her techniques. How did she do it?

The experts caught on quickly. They could tell that Miss Elaine regularly started out her school day in rhyme. "Hello, Johnny, how's your mommy?" "Little Cher, can you reach the chalk over there?" "Teddy, quickly, get ready! Be steady!" Youngsters learned how to play with soundalikes, based on the spellings of their names. Students' names were posted in large letters in obvious places all about the room. The group learned to recognize words with similar spellings. The kindergarten teacher and her class were reading by playing with words.

By ten o'clock, however, the reading specialists were feeling a little uneasy. Miss Elaine did not seem to quit her rhymes at midmorning. "Sam, if you don't come this minute to your place, I don't want to see your face"; or "Jeanine, I want you to draw a big circle. It won't hurt'l." The children continued to giggle over their teacher's rhyming couplets. They couldn't get enough. But the experts were now wondering whether there was anything else to this class besides rhyming. Did the kids ever get to arithmetic? Manners and sociability?

By ten-thirty Elaine Martin was using nonexistent words. "I think I see a pink *moraff,* below our daily temperature graph." "Did anybody go to the *meroo* yesterday? We must go in May, I always say." Everybody chuckled. Everybody had fun. And after recess, everybody went on to their number studies and free play. The rhyming eventually extended to social concepts and a bit of geography. It never stopped.

I don't know exactly, in fact, where Miss Elaine Martin's story stops. I did hear that she left the Chicago school system—maybe to get married, maybe to go somewhere else. I know that Chicago lost a great teacher when they lost Miss Elaine.

Most of us grown-ups eventually center our linguistic play on the delivery of one-liners. Or, as Fran Lebowitz and David Letterman have demonstrated to us, we construct funny word lists with one or two items out of sync. We can make up sane-sounding answers that match loony questions—as Johnny Carson did when he went through his "Carnak the Magnificent" routines. We word-players also exaggerate as a matter of course. "My uncle, the famous diabetic," one of Woody Allen's lines, has always tickled me. Some of us love to tell and retell jokes—and a number of us do it very well indeed. We also trade on puns. I remember one, the first "dirty" joke I ever heard, understood, and told. I was six years old:

"What happened to the Indian who drank twenty gallons of tea?"

"He drowned in his teepee."

For some people, wordplay is their favorite recreation. They invent codes, languages, new words and expressions. William Steig, for example, wrote and illustrated two hilarious books, *CDB* and *CDC,* which are based on letters that stand for whole words. (*CDB* means "see the bee" and *CDC* means "see the sea.") Years ago when he was incarcerated at St. Elizabeth's Hospital in Washington, D.C., for allegedly traitorous wartime activity against the United States, the poet Ezra Pound sent out postcards to his friends in that very same letter-language.

Crossword puzzles are obviously popular enough forms of adult wordplay to fill regular departments in airline magazines, newspapers, and Sunday editions. Not only do crosswords offer us the chance to fit words together, find synonyms, spell, and guess information, but they also include a number of puns, anagrams, and soundalikes. Business enterprises depend on these same sorts of plays on words. Among San Francisco coffeehouses, there are such pun-filled examples as Has Beans, Wild Awakenings, Shaky Grounds,

Muddy Waters, and the Morning Due Cafe. Barbershops and beauty salons include A Cut Above Castro, Alley Cuts and Colors, Carl's Barbery Cutter, The Clip Joint, Have Shears Will Travel, Upper Cuts, Bush-Wack Shear Madness, and Long Overdue.

I could tell more tales of wordplay here—of the musician who made up so many puns that he often interrupted good conversation to tell another one, for instance. Or of the judge who could fast-talk almost as quickly as an auctioneer. But I'll expand no further. Most of us play with words just enough to be considered good talkers, amusing wits. Wordplay is part of good conversation and writing. When it's great, it makes for something fabulously smart, such as Joseph Mankiewicz's screenplay for *All About Eve*. When it's less than great, it's still fun. And it's always strictly human.

So you see, you can begin life with play that is so babyish it's almost entirely forgettable; and yet you can end up with derivatives that are as sophisticated as the Sunday *Times* and *All About Eve*. Infantile play finds a number of expressions in our adult lives. And I for one find that kind of long, backward plunge to be intensely pleasurable.

3

Biological Reasons We Pick Certain Playgrounds and Ways of Playing

I know a solitary jogger named Will. He owns a successful leasing company that rents out bulldozers, road levelers, cement mixers—whatever a road-building contractor needs. Will's work depends on careful coordination between those who sell the leases, those who deliver the equipment, those who get it back, those who charge and maintain accounts, and those who keep the equipment looking nice and working properly. To accomplish full cooperation among his team, Will schedules twice-yearly retreats for his employees in places like the Grand Teton mountains or the Gulf of Mexico beaches; and he runs a sociable group back at the office. All of the company's retreat-going and spirit-building require a great deal of sociability from Will. And he can do it. But at heart, Will is a loner—always has been. He is a quiet man who doesn't enjoy social chatter. I've seen him stand up abruptly from dinner tables, apparently at the first moment that he feels the need to get away. Will maintains a happy marriage with a jogger, yet he consistently jogs by himself. Even though his wife likes Will's company, she doesn't push to come along. Will openly states that, in running, he escapes. And running is Will's daily form of play.

Down the street from Will lives a woman named Irene. For exercise and play, Irene walks. A chic, trim divorcée, she goes out walking with three women. Two of these women covertly dislike each other, so that either one may accompany Irene on a given day, but not both. Irene has managed to avoid open conflict between the two women for months by "playing" past their mutual dislike. Irene phones one or the other the night before a scheduled walk and leaves the message that there will be an excursion the next day. Actually there is a turn about the neighborhood every day. But Irene keeps it all straight; and depending on the message that she leaves, her next morning's cast of characters is set. A fourth woman, Daisy, is acceptable to any of the other three, so that whenever Daisy feels up to a vigorous walk, she just comes along. Neither Daisy nor Irene mentions the previous day's outing, unless the same group has gone on it. This tacit understanding spares each of the two alternating walkers the pain of realizing that she actually misses half of the morning exercises. A complex arrangement for a simple style of play, but it works. The group, thus, appears to be a group of three, but in truth, it is a foursome. And Irene is its leader.

Irene's walks are not only for exercise or to view the neighborhood, but are complicated social exchanges. Irene seeks sociability in her hikes, holding meaningful conversations with her friends while moving up and down the gentle hills of San Francisco. She plays another and more serious game, too—Avoid the Conflict, we might call it. Most likely this avoidance is largely genetically determined, but it was also set up by Irene's parents' behaviors while Irene was growing up.

You see, neither of Irene's parents could stand having unpleasant words with their only child or with each other. They were innately social people, but afraid of any sort of confrontation. In fact, they might have picked each other because of their similarities, both psychological and genetic. As Irene matured, her parents consistently tried to read her mind and her moods so that she and they would always be placid. Irene developed trouble expressing her feelings—she had learned from her parents to expect others to know without her saying what her true feelings were. When she married, Irene could not express her needs to her husband. She assumed that he would know or could guess. As a marriage game, Avoid the Conflict did not work for Irene and her mate. But as a walking game, it work perfectly.

Biological differences account for a number of the variations in our playgrounds and our styles of play. Even though we are raised in certain ways, our shyness may first become evident when we are toddlers—or even before. And our ability to get along with other people usually shows up early as well. These are early basic ways of being that often determine our later actions. One could say that shyness and sociability are components of our temperaments. And our temperaments control our choices of play and of playgrounds.

As an example of how temperament affects play, we might think about the contrast in the size of playgrounds chosen by the temperamentally dissimilar American tennis players Andre Agassi and Pete Sampras in their September 10, 1995, United States Open Men's Tennis Championship match. Agassi, the 1994 winner, was extravagantly outgoing, and Sampras, the 1993 champion, was reticent and shy. The length of their walks to the stadium court in 1995 illustrated the sharp distinction in their inherent ways of being. Sampras came onto the tennis court the way most everyone else who plays in the U.S. Open does—from the locker room, where he had been awaiting the beginning of the game. But Agassi paraded through a crowd of TV reporters and cameramen in a two-minute walk outside the stadium that, for him, extended the playground for a couple hundred feet. Here, you could come close to measuring the two men's innate differences in paces.

The crowd loved Andre—he certainly won the cheering contest that evening; and that, of course, was a kind of a game in itself. But Pete Sampras won the 1995 U.S. Open match in four sets.

WHAT MAKES us play the way we do, our natures or our nurture? It is too early to come to any definite conclusions, but certain innate ways of being undoubtedly figure in creating an extraordinary player. Pete Sampras's pediatrician pronounced Pete an extraordinary athlete when Pete was only nine. The only question was what playground Pete would choose—the baseball field? the tennis court? Sometimes parents tell me that they just *know* their child is going to turn out a certain way. They feel all they can do is to influence it a bit. That's the way Ab and I felt about our little David's affair with mathematics. We could introduce other things to him, but David would inevitably fall back to his one true love. David was hardwired for math. Nothing environmental could take that away from him.

One clue as to how, genetically, we pick our favorite places to play was disclosed in the professional journal *Nature Genetics* in January 1996. In it, two separate research groups, one from Israel and one from the United States, published accounts about having located a gene that determines novelty-seeking behaviors. This gene, located on chromosome eleven, encodes instructions for receptors of D4 dopamine, an internal brain stimulant. People who described themselves to the researchers as novelty-seekers had a longer gene than people who described themselves as reserved and deliberate. With more room on their gene to make a protein that would respond to dopamine, the novelty-seekers were distinct from the rest. According to both the Israeli and American research teams, the longer gene actually enabled these people to form more extroverted, impulsive, exploratory personalities. Although one of the research team leaders, Richard Ebstein of Jerusalem, cautioned that other genes beside the recently discovered one might have to do with this very same style of being, the general enthusiasm about the groups' discovery was enormous.

Here is one factor, then, despite any of the ways that our parents raise us, that impels us to play in our own fashions. Even if our parents are both relatively cautious, we may have inherited our novelty-seeking genes from our great-great-great-grandfather Isaac, the pirate. Or from Mother's aunt Maudie, the bush pilot. How much novelty we seek bears directly on how we play.

Years before the American and Israeli genetic experiments were conducted, a fine researcher, the psychiatrist Robert Cloninger of Washington University in St. Louis, predicted—based on his team's comparison studies of twins—that dopamine would eventually be found to be a basic factor in human temperament (and, therefore, in human play). Cloninger has theorized that four behavioral building bricks—novelty-seeking, harm-avoidance, reward-dependence, and persistence—are essential to the formation of normal human temperament. Children are born, he has said, with various combinations of these four basic ingredients. These combinations endow youngsters with natural, inborn ways of being.

As I understand it, Cloninger has picked out four interior brain chemicals (out of the more than fifty that have already been discovered) that he feels are the prods for inborn qualities of temperament. These are dopamine (for novelty-seeking traits), norepinephrine (for harm-avoidance), acetylcholine (for reward-dependence), and serotonin (for persistence). These chemicals are regulated by cerebral genetic activities. And these cerebral genetic activities are probably accountable, in part, for what playgrounds we select and what ways we eventually come to play.

I would guess, however, that the genetic story behind the ways that we play is far more complicated than we can now hypothesize. Other basic temperamental components will also eventually show up and be proven. And these components may have a strong bearing on how and where we play. To make up a person's physical type, about which we already have considerable genetic information, it takes more than just a few building bricks. Instead, separate genes determine small things, such as the space between our two front teeth and whether we have hairy ears. I would propose that the same kind of enormous genetic variety will eventually explain the variety in our styles of being, and along with it, our preferred styles of play.

MOST OF the traits feeding into our play are smaller and more precise than any overall temperamental leanings we have already considered. Human talents are often specific—a talent for the clarinet but not for the piano, for instance, or a talent for clock-making but not for engine building. David, my son, loves to play with the real numbers of advanced mathematical theory, yet he shuns the *x*'s and *y*'s of algebra. The story of Kevin O'Neil comes to mind here. Kevin has *always* been a mechanic. But it looked all through his junior high and high school years as though he'd never get to be one.

Kevin was born with a tremendous propensity to fix things. As soon as he could use his hands, they were dedicated to pulling apart toys and trying endlessly and patiently to get them back together again. Kevin screamed whenever some piece impossible to assemble was finally taken away from him. At eighteen months, he was entirely invested in pulling out electrical plugs. By two, he was fitting them back into their sockets. Anything electrical was an object of delight to Kevin O'Neil. Anything mechanical was the most fascinating of puzzles. By age five, Kevin was fixing his broken toys. By ten, he was fixing the family toaster. Without question, he would grow up to be a mechanic. Sluggish coffeepots, stuck windows, broken venetian blinds—Kevin could handle them all.

But then, the hazards of preadolescent life appeared in Kevin O'Neil's backyard. Most of his friends were pot users by the age of twelve. Alcohol was high on the local menu, as well. Kevin's father was virtually out of the picture—he and Kevin's mother had divorced when Kevin was a year old; and his father was devoting himself to making and breaking one more marriage and three more live-in relationships. Mom worked long hours downtown. By the time she arrived back home in the suburbs, a lot of damage had been done. Grandma and Grandpa tried to help, but nothing like Kevin had ever happened in the family before. As a teenager, Kevin became well-known to the juvenile authorities—driving fast, beer in cars, parking-lot brawls.

By his third year of high school, Kevin's grades were beyond hope. He barely spoke with his concerned mother and grandparents. He grouchily nursed the wounds he sustained in various fights on various ill-lit streets. He was barely approachable. But Kevin could still be asked to fix an electric lawn mower, repair a boom box, recondition a typewriter. And he eventually signed up to take high school auto mechanics. With straight D's and F's in every other subject he took, Kevin received B's in auto shop (he couldn't make an A because he skipped too many classes). Kevin's teacher recognized that he had a mechanical genius on his hands—someone who instinctively understood and who instinctively loved the guts of anything made by man. The boy, troubled as he was at this point, was a better mechanic than the teacher. He was a natural.

After high school, Kevin sat around for a year or so, unable to figure out what to do with himself. Then one of his old friends from the neighborhood phoned him from Los Angeles to say that he had started working for an airline company. His job, a boring one he said, was to repair seats. Did Kevin want to come south and join him? There were plenty of jobs to be had. Why not? Kevin thought. And so he went to L.A. to be with his friend.

Kevin suddenly found himself in a naturally sober environment—the airline company randomly drug-tested all personnel. Alcohol was forbidden. He sobered up quickly and found himself in the incredibly boring and routine job of changing reading lights, adjusting fans, repairing reclining seats, and fixing plugged-up toilets. He had been assigned to "interiors," the dungeon of airline mechanics. And he would have to prove himself for at least two years before he could be considered for anything else.

Well, Kevin did prove himself. And he brought his mother and his girlfriend on a number of inexpensive trips to Los Angeles in the meantime. But of course, Kevin wanted to be an engine mechanic, and that took some planning. His high school auto shop teacher knew a person in engine mechanics at another airline company. He wrote the man. And Kevin's boss in interiors wrote, too. Kevin was accepted into engine mechanics training with another major airline.

Now, a few years later, Kevin O'Neil works exclusively on experimental jet engines for one of the great aviation design companies. After getting away from interiors, he has done nothing but play. His mechanical play, natural with him from the moment that his genes lined up, finally propelled him past his drug and alcohol problems. Kevin has never felt entirely free from the pull to indulge in one or another addictive substance. But his play has helped him to combat it—along with the regular and random screening that his employer maintains. Kevin took a childhood hobby and made a career of it. Because that was possible for him, he was able to straighten out his life. He is now married and has identical twin girls. And he attends a night college in engineering because he wants eventually to design an airplane motor himself; now that his play has become his work, Kevin's scholarly career is going just fine.

WHEN WE look at humans as a huge biological group, rather than as individuals, we can discern that our play has evolved from that of the other animals. Understanding how this evolution came about occupies the minds of a number of ethologists and evolutionists who put nonhuman play high on their lists of interests. One of the first fascinating things that these scientists found was that certain animals do not appear to play at all. There are a million or more animal species on earth, in fact, and only a small minority play. Almost all of the players are birds and mammals.

A few exceptions have been cited, however, and these may be important as far as the biological evolution of play is concerned. Two scientists, for instance, wrote about an alligator that they thought was playing with an object. And an evolutionary biologist wrote that his pet sea turtles flipped their flippers for no obvious reason—in his view, this was a rudimentary play form, like that which young mice apparently do in flexing and extending their limbs.

Why are biologists so interested in these few exceptions from the truism that only birds and mammals play? Because the evolutionary development of play through the animal kingdom is not yet fully understood. Amphibians apparently evolved millions of years ago into the reptiles. And reptiles eventually evolved into the birds and mammals. We should therefore be able to find some traces of play in these lower amphibian and reptilian forms.

Curiosity and play are considered by biologists to be entirely separate and distinct qualities in humans and in the other higher forms of animals. But animal curiosity may actually have been transformed into play during evolutionary history. Gordon Burghardt, an evolutionary biologist at the University of Tennessee and a practiced observer of the behaviors of reptiles, has written that mammalian and avian play originated in reptilian curiosity. He pointed out that at their most rudimentary, both curiosity and playfulness produce similar physical movements in some animals (reptilian flickings of the tongue [curiosity] or repeated movements of a rodent's appendage [play], for instance). Animal curiosity and play also produce the same delayed benefits—more vigorous and effective motor activity and more intelligent uses of the environment.

Here again, as with Piaget's assimilation and accommodation schemes, we see two theoretically opposed qualities apparently bringing about the same practical result, play. Gordon Burghardt went on to theorize that birds and mammals originally developed their play out of boredom. Old instinctive behaviors, which in the reptiles were extremely vigorous at one time, were put to use by bored mammals and birds in the service of their own amusement. Curiosity became converted to play. Some mammals and birds had the time for it. Some had the safety for it. Some could relax and enjoy themselves.

Unrelated to either sex or survival, play appeals to those animals with a few moments to spare and the inclination for it. If you watch for play, you'll be surprised by how many animals have the time. Of course, we can teach our dogs and cats to indulge in almost human forms of play—and pets are great fun, and not at all boring, to have as playmates. But sometimes in the wild, you see sparring or wrestling, reversal of roles in a chase, or sharp reversals of direction that catch your eye and your imagination. Here, the "aesthetics" (the nonsex, nonaggression) of evolution grab you.

One late-summer afternoon in Truro, Massachusetts, for instance, I watched three smallish birds and one crow play out a chase high above a marshy piece of land. Silhouetted against the sky, the play battle veered from three-on-one to one-on-three, with shifts from chasers to chasees ensuing so quickly and without any warning that my uplifted face swiveled as if I were watching a tennis match. The chase continued past the point when I had to leave. It has lasted even longer in my memory.

MOST OF US are well aware that innate gender differences are a hotly debated subject between social scientists and geneticists. But many of us do not realize how intensely this debate focuses on play—and especially on the play of chess. But before we venture out to a chess club, we must pause for a bit to examine what we know about the influence of sex chromosomes on gender choices in play. Is it the chromosomes or our socialization patterns that make women enjoy themselves differently from men?

Certainly women have shown us over the years that when given the chance, they can play a fabulously hot game of basketball, a terrific match of tennis, a quick-paced, hard-fought hockey game. But this is not the rule for most women. The ratio of shoppers-for-fun to ballplayers-for-fun among my sex is still overwhelmingly high. Along these same lines, one of the great challenges that the computer-game inventors have faced and have not yet mastered is how to interest girls in these kinds of games. I have always thought that if you could study young children of both sexes at play, per-haps you might pick out those factors in the gender equation that are strictly "nature"—inherent ways that girls, as opposed to boys, prefer to play.

This, in fact, is exactly what the eminent infant psychologist Michael Lewis of New Jersey attempted to find out experimentally with a group of babies. Along with his associate, Susan Goldberg, Lewis set up standardized play sessions for thirty-two American infants-turning-toddlers who were equally divided as to gender. The researchers found "striking" differences between the play of the thirteen-month-old boys and girls. As these youngsters indulged in standardized free-play sessions in their mothers' presence, for instance, the girls were more reluctant to leave their mothers' laps than the boys. Girls sat. Boys moved about. When the investigators put up a small barrier between the infants and their mothers, the girls stayed still and wept in frustration, motioning for others to come and help them. The boys, on the other hand, got up and investigated, trying to find a way around the barrier.

What Lewis and Goldberg found in these thirteen-month-old infants looked as if it might begin to prove a basic biological difference in how boys and girls would play. But at six months of age, when the very same infants and their mothers were first put into this project, the babies appeared to be treated dissimilarly by their mothers, depending on whether they were girls or boys. The mothers of the girls tended to keep their little darlings closer at hand. They spoke to them more often and at greater length. At as young an age as six months, the genders were clearly being treated dissimilarly. There was no way—even at this early time in life—to clearly separate the babies' nature from their nurture.

But Lewis and Goldberg did not think that these maternal behaviors at six months could have fully accounted for the babies' marked gender differences in play at thirteen months old. Behind infantile modes of playing are inherent, gender-specific traits, they concluded. And most of us concur that something as basic as a chromosome must account for certain tastes in boys or girls for certain-sized playgrounds and for certain ways of playing.

Chess is a form of play that over the years hundreds of enthusiasts have claimed to be the sole domain of men. And a biological one, at that. Chess champions and grand masters have almost universally been male. Chess is a game played at boys' schools, men's clubs, parks—in fact, girls rarely play chess in a public park. Of the 225 members of the Manhattan Chess Club in December 1996, 12 were women. Of 450 grand masters worldwide, 6 were women. At that time, in fact, only one woman, Judith Polgar, was rated among the top hundred players in the world. And in 1996, she was beaten quite handily by the world champion, Garry Kasparov. I ran through 288 headings of chess publications in the 1996 computer list from the various Stanford University libraries. Only four obviously female names stood out among hundreds of male authors. This was a strongly unbalanced interest level, it would seem.

One could easily argue that without social encouragement, women do not develop an early genius for chess. Mothers do not tend to teach the game to their girls, whereas fathers often teach it to both their sons and daughters. A number of other sociocultural factors may also stop women from playing. There have been few women grand masters to emulate. Some women compete with and measure themselves only against other women. Women are also frequently raised to be less independent and more considerate of others, qualities that remain unrewarded in the game of chess. Then, too, the social meaning of chess is the reenactment of war— and that may not be a subject of great appeal to girls.

Despite the obvious sociocultural factors hindering women from playing chess, however, a number of people claim that strong underlying biological tendencies are at work here. In a 1979 summary of what they considered to be the hardwired gender traits that influence chess, two psychologists noted that males are generally superior to females in spatial abilities, embedded-figure tasks, mental rotation problems, solid-geometry tests, maze learning, and map reading—each of these, they said, essential to the game. (Interestingly, studies in the 1990s indicate that girls are moving up in these abilities, when compared to boys.)

In the past, chess writers and chess champions have made their points about inborn gender differences with contempt. The French psychologist of intelligence, Alfred Binet, for instance, wrote in his 1893 book, *Mnemonic Virtuosity: A Study of Chessplayers,* "The best woman [chess] player in Paris is no better than any mediocre amateur." The former world champion Bobby Fischer stated it even more boorishly in a press interview: "They're all weak, all women. They're stupid compared to men. They shouldn't play chess, you know."

If one listened uncritically to these men, one would think that something fundamental prevents women from playing a good game of chess. But perhaps females *should* and *can* play the game. One woman, Joan Arbil, is an excellent example. Since October 1996, Joan has been the assistant chess director of the San Francisco Mechanics Library, a private downtown institution that was founded in the mid–nineteenth century for the lifelong education of working people. The women's chess champion of Turkey in 1980 and 1981, Joan was sixty years old when she returned to her childhood home, the Bay Area, and took over the day-to-day operations of the extremely active Mechanics Library Chess Club. "It feels like being born again!" she said of her job.

I study and write on the mezzanine of the Mechanics Library most Wednesday afternoons; but before interviewing Joan, I hadn't ventured up to the fourth floor where the chess players arrange themselves in a spacious old room with wood-shuttered windows to play out their miniaturized wars. Intensely curious about how a woman gets to be a good chess player, I talked to Joan in a musty, dark fourth-floor office—and that was so that we wouldn't disturb the games in progress. Joan usually works in the chess room itself. I peeked in before we retreated to our little enclosure—no, there were no women playing chess that day.

Joan had moved to Turkey upon marrying a fellow University of California graduate who had always expected to run his family's cotton business back in his hometown, Izmir. Joan gave birth to two sons and a daughter and raised them to eventually work in industry (the sons) and at a university (the girl). Today, Joan's three adult children live in Sweden, China, and Turkey. In 1993, Joan's husband died of a heart condition; and because he left her a small income, she was able to move back to California and to take her relatively low-paying job.

Joan does not believe she was, as a child, what most people would think of as a "chess natural." She was not mathematical, and, in fact, after being assigned to a "bad math teacher" in the third grade, she "didn't want to have anything to do with arithmetic again," she said, lifting both of her hands for emphasis. She hates math, she told me. "People assume that since I've been a chess champion, I'm a good mathematician. Not true. Not a bit." Then she softened and smiled. "But my daughter turns out to be extremely good with numbers. She teaches the math side of business administration at the college in Izmir. And we do logic problems together whenever I visit Turkey."

So despite what Joan said about her problems in math, a few arithmetical genes must be operating on her behalf. Joan's father was a truck driver and her mother, an "uneducated housewife." Neither particularly appreciated intellectual feats or demonstrated great innate abilities. No one knew chess. But a certain biologically determined spatial sense was alive and well in little Joanie. She has sculpted, she noted, for "as long as I can remember." As an adult in Turkey, she was even given a one-woman show of her paintings and sculpture. Her mother told Joan that when she was six months old, she would consistently turn around upside-down books so that the letters were oriented correctly. At this particularly early age, baby Joanie's motivations for turning those books around may seem debatable; but Joan stated it was no exaggeration that she could read prior to going to nursery school, and that when she was six, she was skipped to the third grade because her reading was so fluent.

Paradoxically, Joan's obvious brightness did nothing to encourage her to be a scholar or an expert at something. At fourteen, she even "acted so dumb" that she required a psychotherapist. Playing stupid was a "sort of game" for her, she said. At eighteen, she was shown how to play chess, but it made little impression on her. Shortly thereafter, Joan dropped out of high school. She quickly made up the work, however, and eventually qualified for UC Berkeley.

When Joan contracted infectious hepatitis in Turkey from her son, she was doomed to spending several months in bed. After a week of lying around, she received a gift from her husband, the book *Petrosian's Best Games*. "Chess was beyond my understanding until I finally realized what the plan was," she told me, looking back at this almost mystical experience. "The reason for one knight to move suddenly seemed to be the most beautiful thing that I had ever seen. Just incredible. I kept a chessboard in bed with me and I learned the notations and went over the games in the book. When I saw that one, single knight move, something slipped into place in my mind, something I was looking for all my life." Joan Arbil's life's joy, despite her being a woman, was to become the play of chess.

Joan's husband set up a Turkish chess club for her as her game began to take off. Her children felt resentful because she often left home on chess-related pursuits; thus, they absolutely refused to learn the game, even into their adulthoods. The game "took a lot of physical stamina," she said. "The energy equaled six sets of tennis. That king becomes *you*. It is *you* who is being pursued. I'd lose myself so completely in a chess match that I'd have to be led off the floor afterward—like a yogi after he's been in a trance. If I was playing and someone mentioned a steak or something, it was like a shock to my system. I'd actually jump."

Women chess players, Joan felt, are maligned and discouraged by the men in the game. They are basically just as able to play. "Someone told me once," she remembered, "that a woman couldn't keep quiet for the four hours that it would take to play. He was a man." But Joan was not so sure that all women have the killer instincts for chess. She regretted that she herself does not have these killer instincts. She believed that she plays chess out of enjoyment—for the logic and the beauty of it all.

"A few women I know do have killer instincts," Joan said. "But it does seem to be a more regular part of a man's equipment."

We were suddenly interrupted by a neatly dressed, middle-aged man who rushed into our little room. "Mr. Karasoff says he's going to kill me," the man, Mr. Kukor, reported, his face dark red. "Then I told him I'm going to kill *him*."

Joan Arbil left the room. She was gone about five minutes. "I told Boris, the drunk player, that he must leave *now!*" she informed me upon her return. Which of the two men—Karasoff or Kukor— was the drunk player? I never got it straight.

"Will they come back tomorrow?" I asked her after peace had resumed.

"Sure," said Joan. "Yesterday, the other Russian guy almost threw a chair at his opponent and I had to stop them and kick *him* out. That's the thing about men." She looked admiringly, almost wistfully envious. "There are men who just shake, they so badly want to win at chess. The idea of crushing somebody—absolutely flattening somebody's ego—it's just not in me. I don't like the battle part of chess. I don't have that killer instinct. I play the board, not the person."

So this was it, perhaps. Maybe the true biological contrast lay in being willing to commit murder on a game board. "Is that what it is that women chess players are missing?" I asked Joan. "Being killers?"

"Well, I know a few killers among the women."

"No, this can't be it, then," I thought.

"One woman killer lives right here in San Francisco and is kind of crazy," Joan went on. "Another one lives in Turkey and was our female champion in the nineties. The woman in Turkey is a mathematician with the drive to win. Once, she made a stupid move and lost a match to a female player much below her in the rankings. 'I am destroyed, completely destroyed,' she screamed, lying down on the tournament floor.

"I took her out of the tournament hall to get her some fresh air. 'It's just a game,' I said to her as we walked up to a lemonade stand. Then she hit the lemonade stand. Again and again she hit it.

" 'Tell her to stop!' the lemonade man yelled at me.

" 'It's just a game,' I told her again, not knowing what to do.

"Then she fainted right there—out on the street. Fainted dead away. Her trainer came outside and found her lying there on the ground. The trainer eventually got her to stand up and to walk back into the tournament hall. The woman saw the tournament winner in there accepting congratulations. 'She shouldn't have won,' she believed. So she approached the winner, threw her against a wall, and beat her up."

"My lord," I said to myself, picturing the absurdity of all these histrionics. But that was not at all how Joan Arbil took the incident.

"That woman loved the game more than I do," Joan murmured with obvious regret. "She had what it took to be a great champion."

What does it take to be a great chess champion? The fact that the Hungarian women Judith Polgar and her sister, Susan, are currently enjoying successful careers in New York chess circles is encouraging. All the facts are not yet in, however. Only now, in the past few years, are women being the least bit encouraged to enter this twenty-five-hundred-year-old, all-male enterprise. The crux of the matter lies in who really enjoys the game. That's what play is all about. And there is no question in my mind that the woman I met down on Post Street in that beautiful old fourth-floor chess room, Joan Arbil, is truly cut out for the game. She loves it. It fits her nature.

Joan has a new manfriend, a chess master, she confessed to me with a shy smile. Every time they get together, they play a timed, ten-minute game of chess before they do anything else.

AT THIS point, I need to note the many superior skills that are typical of the female gender. Young girls test out better in reading and are generally more expressive with words early in their lives than are boys. These skills, probably inborn ones, explain girls' greater aptitudes and preferences for verbal games. In studies of how the genders play, conducted by Brian Sutton-Smith and his colleagues in Philadelphia, girls were found to prefer and to do better than boys in creating poetry, fantasy enactments, theatrical productions, songs, and costumed pretend. These forms of play, like chess, probably depend to some extent on innate gender differences.

It does appear through evidence collected in a number of non-Western societies that there are discernible, chromosomally linked differences in play. Rough-and-tumble activity, a play form evident in children by the time they reach age three or four, for instance, eventually becomes so powerful in boys that one little lad of five, rather than pretending with me in my consulting room, insisted on engaging my rabbit puppet in a back-and-forth chase game of tag with his lion and raccoon. There appear to be striking gender differences in how much jostling children will indulge in by the ages of five, six, and seven. Boys like it. Girls no longer do.

In a 1973 study of Kalahari San (Bushman) children (ten boys and thirteen girls) versus London children (ten boys and eleven girls), the anthropological researchers Nicholas Blurton Jones and Melvin Konner tried to determine how much of this observable gender difference in tumultuous play was cultural and how much was biological. The observable boy-girl differences in play chasing and fighting among the Bushmen children were not as extreme as they were in the youngsters raised in urban England. London girls were far less willing to indulge in play scrambles than were Kalahari San girls. We know that Western children hear social proscriptions against "unfeminine" play. However, even in the Kalahari San culture, Blurton Jones and Konner found observable sexual distinctions between the boys and the girls. Males were noticeably more vigorous and enthusiastic than females in their play fighting. Most likely, these differences reflected something innate, something hardwired.

Gender mix-ups in theater and film reflect how much pleasure we adults take in playing around with our almost unspoken expectations about how the genders are innately supposed to be. Shakespeare's comedies and Mozart's operas contain a number of examples of girls playing at being boys and boys playing at being girls. Gender twists, such as those in *As You Like It* and *The Marriage of Figaro,* allow us to laugh and to play with the emotions and dilemmas of the opposite sex. In Shakespeare's time, an audience might easily have enjoyed watching a boy actor play the part of a girl named Rosalind, who then disguises "herself" to be a boy in an ironic "double play" on gender. Today, in *The Marriage of Figaro,* we watch a mezzo-soprano sing the role of a boy, Cherubino, who then dresses "himself" up to be a girl—another of those double gender mix-ups.

These scenarios are funny, pleasurable, and broadening—as is gender play itself. Cary Grant, awkward and uncomfortable in a feathery peignoir; Dustin Hoffman, anxious and embarrassed with curlers in his hair at a female sleepover; the young Elizabeth Taylor, bound up and tucked in so that she can race horses by pretending to be a boy—these play images are highly entertaining. Not only do they impress, but they may also civilize us. We broaden our contexts as we picture the other gender's point of view. We in the audience can consider our own sexuality in a larger format. Stress is dissipated. We grow in empathy. Perhaps some woman out there beyond the lights rethinks the hard line she originally took on whether she would ever retire near a golf course; perhaps some man reconsiders whether his wife should ever get started on those graduate courses that she keeps talking about.

THE MOST striking case I ever saw of innate gender preferences in play came to me through an unusual East Coast to West Coast referral. One spring, I psychiatrically evaluated a young man named Gabriel who, though he lived in New York City, was brought to my office by an older cousin, who resides in San Francisco. She wanted my opinion about a sensitive problem in Gabriel's life. A year before, the young man, who had started his training for the priesthood in a suburban New York religious seminary, had been forced to resign because an administrator accused him of homosexuality. Although he had never been caught in any sexual activity whatsoever, Gabriel was told by a faculty representative that he was too short, had too high-pitched a voice, and was too easily teased and bullied to become a priest. Gabriel's heart was broken. He had wanted nothing in life but to enter the priesthood. He had always been celibate, a natural condition for him, he told me. In his spare time, he had done a great deal of thinking about man's relationship to God, and his own relationship with God was now threatened. He was currently making his living in Manhattan as a bank teller. And he was miserable.

After seeing him a couple of times, I realized that Gabriel suffered from an undiagnosed biological problem with gender. Not only was he short with an unusually high voice, slightly webbed fingers, and a slightly webbed neck, but he also had had several surgical procedures as a teenager to correct for undescended testes and overly large breasts. Gabriel had no sex drive, he said. He had never needed to shave.

I sent Gabriel to an endocrinologist in my area who specializes in the hormonal abnormalities of males. He diagnosed the young man as suffering from Noonan's syndrome. Gabriel's sex chromosomes were the normal X and Y configuration of the male gender, but his dysfunctional genes had severely limited the masculine side of his growth and development. His intelligence, heart condition, and facial appearance were normal—something that, unfortunately, is not always true in boys with Noonan's. But Gabriel would require testosterone injections for life.

It appeared that Gabriel would also require antidepressant medication. But I soon came to realize that he needed something even more pressing—a reassignment to a good, scholarly seminary. I wrote to the cardinal who was serving the New York metropolitan area, explaining Gabriel's medical situation and asking him to reconsider the Church's actions of the previous year. The young man suffered from a lifelong, but never previously diagnosed, endocrine disorder that was treatable. As far as I knew, he would make a fine priest. The director of vocations for Gabriel's diocese wrote back saying that he realized they had erred. The young man would be allowed to begin his training at another seminary, but they would like to see Gabriel have an entirely fresh start. Did he mind repeating his first year? The diocese truly regretted what had happened.

And so Gabriel went off to his new seminary that September. He went with his prescription for testosterone injections, a few months' worth of Prozac, and the names of a few of my New York City colleagues. Gabriel's story soars from there. But I will pause for a moment before I finish it, in order to fit him into our current framework: the biological basis to our preferred playgrounds and modes of play.

Ordinarily, a number of masculinizing hormones are at work long before a lad ever enters pubescence. These hormones operate, in fact, in utero. Gabriel didn't have enough of these hormones. And these hormones—or, more precisely, the lack of these hormones—influenced his childhood play. Even though Gabriel had a he-man father who wanted his boy to go fishing and to shoot birds, Gabriel was never interested in those pursuits. Although his mother believed that her boy should be out there roughhousing with the neighborhood kids, he could never bear that kind of play. Both parents were deeply disappointed. Gabriel had been biologically bound to go in a different direction.

But Gabriel always was a player. It was important to him. "Even in kindergarten, I felt different," he told me. "I looked like a baby. The teachers took me under their wing to protect me. . . . I was out of the picture when it came to sports. I was never even picked last for a team; no one picked me at all. But I always had fun. My neighbor Jack was my age, and he'd come over and we'd color together or watch TV. When Jack got into track and field in our high school years, I got ready for the priesthood. But before that—like in second and third grade—I'd take a dictionary outside at recess. Or I'd walk around with the teacher who was on yard duty. Sometimes I'd play Barbies on the playground with three girls I liked—I felt accepted by them. I'd be their 'Ken.' Or I'd be given the Kiddles that the girls had brought to school and I'd cook their food and put the Barbies to bed. Sometimes I'd yell, 'Nee, nee, nee, troll!' and get everybody's attention on the playground. I guess it wasn't such a great way to get attention. At home with my sister and her girlfriends, we'd play house. I'd always be the daddy. I liked that.

"In the third grade I started Catholic school, and I enjoyed that a lot. The kids there called me Holy Joe—they knew I was religious. I loved the stories of the saints. Loved the nuns. Once at recess everybody was out playing—you *had* to play at that school—and I went into the outfield and said the rosary. The kids got excited and said, 'Look, Holy Joe's praying for our team!' I let them think so. But I really took my rosary more seriously than *that.*"

Looking sad, Gabriel went on, "When I returned to public school in the sixth grade—I left parochial school 'cause another short guy was teasing me nonstop in order to try and get himself into the in-group—I was not allowed into the boys' group at all. I found another outsider who became my recess comrade. We wound up playing hopscotch and jacks with the girls. It was funny. I was a kind of leader. But I simply could not do sports."

Male hormones, an antidepressant, and a few sessions of psychotherapy helped Gabriel immeasurably. But, of course, what helped him the most was working toward his life goal: being a priest. He was an outstanding seminary student and a leader among his peers. In the seminary, it did not matter if he could play tennis, shoot a pheasant, sink a basketball. Once in a while, during a summer vacation or over Christmas, Gabriel would visit his cousin in San Francisco and I would see him. His transformation was formidable. His voice had landed an octave lower. He had developed a five-o'clock shadow. And he admitted to a newly developed sex drive—it was harder now, though not impossible, to live the celibate life.

So how does Gabriel play today? Did testosterone make a difference in the way that he chose to enjoy himself? Well, Gabriel plays in the same way that he always did—except that hopscotch and Barbies were discarded along with childhood itself. Gabriel continues to consult dictionaries, but now he reads them in English, Spanish, and Cantonese. He enjoys studying languages. He travels for fun, and he continually plans from one trip to the next. A travel brochure was on his desk when I phoned him in New York to talk about his current play. "I like to plan trips," he told me, "even if I don't get to go on all of them. I like to go to the movies and the theater. I enjoy reading, talking with my friends, going for a walk. But I could never achieve a thing in sports—I was always uncoordinated. I don't even try anymore. I guess I'm kind of envious because I was never a good sportsman. But I watch others play. And now that I'm a priest, I go to as many of my church's elementary and high school games as I can. I like it. As long as I can be a spectator, sports are great."

Early one year not too long ago, I received a formal invitation from the School of Theology, the Archdiocese of New York. Gabriel was to be ordained a priest, and the ceremony would take place in

St. Patrick's Cathedral on Fifth Avenue. The presiding official would be the cardinal himself. By happenstance, I was in Manhattan on the chosen day, and I attended. By the time that Gabriel marched up that long, beautiful aisle, my eyes were awash with tears.

Gabriel serves a largely Hispanic congregation now—he prepared for this as a high school boy by learning Spanish and thinking a great deal about God. And from what I can tell, for the first time in his life, Gabriel is truly popular. His hormones, his looks, are amazingly changed. But his habits are not. What started Gabriel in life, his biology, pushes him even today. Despite all of the medical corrections that have assisted him, Gabriel goes where his genes initially propelled him. And he goes where he felt most comfortable as a child. Along with our upbringing and social exposures, our biological inheritance helps to determine what behaviors give us the most pleasure.

4

Play Built on Fantasies About Aggression or Sex

If you're going to play on a theme, there's a good chance that your diversion will rest, at bottom, with a personal fantasy. Yes, it's entirely true that toddlers and preschoolers wrestle and jostle one another with no apparent fantasies in mind. And it's true, too, that nonhuman animals tumble about with no fantasies that anyone is able to demonstrate. But by the time that a human child starts to run around the house, chasing the cat or tackling a playmate who hasn't yet shed his galoshes, the chances are that an idea, a simple wish, lies at the root of all that play. Achieving dominance? Yes. Being loved? Yes. Being seen and heard? Yes. Being beautiful? Yes. Becoming important? Yes. Growing up? Yes. Winning in a competition? Yes, yes, yes.

The earliest mutual, socialized amusement in humans that expresses aggression, or the drive for individual survival, is rough-and-tumble play. After going through much of the professional literature on play, I would say that this early form of enjoyment must be the most heavily researched one of all. Scrambling or

jostling is relatively easy to spot and carries important implica-
tions, as we've already seen, about the biology of recreation. Play
wrestling and play chasing begin deep in the toddler and preschool
years. The child's behavior mimics serious aggression, but it is
accompanied by laughter, occasional screaming; and the participants take turns being aggressors, going on and on, rather than
breaking up and dispersing, the way that a true fight would end.
When I spot the laughter and back-and-forth movement of an
immature wrestling match, I know that this is "play," not something more dangerous. Even though some peril is inherent in any
run-of-the-mill play melee, children enter into it voluntarily and
seemingly unafraid.

Nonhuman animals in the laboratory show us by analogy what
aggressive play in our own childhoods may do for us. In one rat lab,
for instance, the juvenile rodents were kept from ever playing
aggressively. Other young rats (a comparison group) carried on as
usual. As adults, the rough-and-tumble-deprived animals turned
out to be relatively inept at judging if, where, and when to feel
threatened by other rats. At times, they were wildly overaggressive.
At other times, they were wimps. Failure to play on aggressive
themes as a juvenile rat created failures in recognizing true aggression in maturity. One might begin to analogize from this kind of
research that aggressive play in human children prepares human
adults for recognizing and handling aggression in themselves and
in others.

Human children get their first play-fighting, play-chasing experiences with us, their parents and caretakers. This starts once our
youngsters begin to ambulate. For example, one of us might play-
chase our own stumbling, awkward toddler who has recently
learned how to walk. Upon sensing the chase, the little kid
screams—and then he or she quickly gets up and chases us back. At
this age, in particular, it is crucial for both the adult and the child to
clearly signal their intentions to play. "Play faces," marked by smiles
and relaxed facial muscles, and the sounds of laughter say, "No, this
is not a real war. This is play."

Run-of-the-mill, pretend aggression is available to every preschooler, regardless of gender. And in preschool, both boys and girls indulge. Although considerable play fighting appears to be fantasy-free, the importance of pretend in play fighting has been observed in cultures far different from our own. A group of Kalahari San (Bushman) children, for instance, were observed by the ethologist Melvin Konner to be play attacking a young person who was willingly playing the part of an animal. In a Western society, a cadre of tiny Batmen, let's say, might be fantasizing an attack on a child who has elected to take the role of a Joker or a Penguin. We may see the same aspects of pretend, in a way, in our adult games. Take Monopoly, for instance. A couple of players may pounce on a third player and drive that person to bankruptcy. Like a Kalahari San child waiting to be jumped on, the unlucky Monopoly player may temporarily serve as a passive recipient, whether or not this player is aware of aggressive fantasies being fulfilled around the table.

When I think of little Batmen and Jokers running about, I remember having coffee one weekend afternoon with my sister-in-law, Ibby, at her house in Cleveland. As we sat down in Ibby's kitchen to talk, her tiny, four-year-old son, J.J., and two of his same-age friends came flying through the back door. Each wore, tied at the neck, a cape made out of a bath towel.

"Who are you?" I asked one of the minuscule fliers.

"Superman," Max, a neighbor, answered.

"And who are you?" I asked his redheaded sidekick.

"Superman."

I turned to the host of that afternoon's tumult. "And who are you, J.J.?"

"Superman. We're all Superman!"

Their brief stop to talk to me made the three of them itch to get at their play once again, and so they flew out the door to scramble over one another in the backyard. Taking a new direction every couple of minutes, the three Supermen vied for power with smiles on their faces and with reasonable care not to hurt one another.

"Doesn't it bother them that there are no designated villains?" I asked Ibby.

"No, I don't think so."

"And don't they see the illogic in three different boys being exactly the same superhero?"

"Oh, no, not a bit. They can live very well with the idea of three Supermen."

SINCE rough-and-tumble play carries some potential benefits into adulthood, it may help us to understand how it can be promoted among children. Peter Smith and Kevin Connolly, two British play researchers, studied children in a number of English preschools. They varied the sizes of the playgrounds for the three- and four-year-old youngsters of both sexes. And then, later, they also varied the availability of toys, doubling the number of kids who would have to share one. Play fighting was more frequent whenever a bigger play space was available. The sparring frequency also increased whenever fewer playthings were available. Other factors encouraging this kind of play were a fairly large, same-age group (ten or more), and a permissive "free-play" atmosphere at the preschool. From Smith and Connolly's research, it appeared that rough-and-tumble was a natural form of play for both boys and girls of preschool ages; but it also appeared that this kind of false fight depended upon a number of social factors.

Despite any attempts to promote free-for-alls, however, girls drop out almost entirely from the chasing and fighting scene by the time they reach kindergarten. We have already discussed how London lasses let go of their aggressive play more completely than Kalahari San girls do; but most girls, except perhaps for a few tomboys, lay off play wrestling as they reach school age. Along with this laying off, girls gradually develop a misunderstanding of what this kind of play really is. By the time they are adults, many women believe that jostling, tumultuous games indicate real fighting. In this regard I found one Pennsylvania study to be particularly instructive. The investigator showed preschoolers of both sexes fourteen short videotapes of playful aggression around toys, including war toys. The four-year-old subjects in the study thought that only two of the videotapes were examples of real aggression. But a group of female college students who were shown these same videotapes rated them differently. While the adult males rated the tapes the same way that the four-year-olds did, the females believed over half of the tapes to be examples of true fighting.

This study demonstrated to me that while, at age four, both genders exhibit similar points of view about how to tell serious aggression from play, over the next fifteen years, young women change. Perhaps something innate in female development alters a girl's viewpoint about aggressive play. Certainly, however, the way that girls are raised exerts considerable influence—girls are generally brought up to reject naked aggression.

Girls I have known in my child psychiatric practice tend to pull away from playing at war with boys at about the age of six or seven. Young lasses say that the lads are too tough, too hurtful. The aggressive, competitive games that boys prefer cause them pain, girls say. Little misses have complained to me for years about the game red rover, for instance, where children stand holding hands in two lines and a player from one side runs as hard as possible at the weakest position in the opposing line in order to break it. Boys consistently run at the smaller girls, if they are playing. (I wonder if this game derives from some terrifying medieval siege.) Dodgeball is another aggressive game that young females often dread. Children who have grouped in a circle throw a ball at the few "its" who are running around in the center. It stings their bodies to get pegged hard, girls tell me, a little pain still lingering in their voices. And the boys may purposely throw harder at them than they shoot at one another, the girls say with perhaps justifiable suspicion.

Girls of the early elementary school ages are relatively pain-avoidant as compared to the boys. Physical jolts are not well tolerated. Perhaps the fact that their daddies don't feel comfortable wrestling little girls down to the ground makes a contribution. More recently, possibly, the stranger-avoiding behaviors that we teach our daughters for their own protection may bear some influence. Schoolgirls end up being stuck as "its" overly long in the middle of circles of ball-peggers. Without small pains as part of play, and without the quick turn-taking that characterizes pleasurable play-chasing or "it" games, girls begin to misinterpret what real aggression is. They become afraid and avoidant.

Without question, a number of social forces discourage young females from exhibiting overt aggression in their play while encouraging young males to go on playing on overtly aggressive themes. Along these lines, the University of California, Berkeley, sociologist Barrie Thorne discovered two entries that she, as an eight-year-old, had put into a journal that she kept for her third-grade class in 1949–50. These entries reflected on the aggressiveness that youthful fellows in particular were allowed to show in midcentury elementary schools within the bounds of their play.

In the first entry, recording an afternoon at a class picnic, young Barrie wrote, "Some boys found water snakes and scared the girls. After that, we went home." In the second entry, she jotted down a few words about a playground cleanup day and then added, "Gerald teased the girls by putting earthworms down our necks, and as soon as all the weeds were out, we went home."

As an adult, Thorne interpreted her two journal entries as "gender scenarios," showing how easily, while she was young, she accepted the culturally promoted category of "the girls." This almost automatic categorization is another factor that makes it difficult for girls to play aggressive games or sports with "the boys."

Critical mass contributes in an interesting way to these culturally based gender movements toward or away from aggressive play. If a boys' group at a school is not quite large enough to sustain an ongoing jostling jamboree or a full-scale game of handball, for instance, then, more often than not, the girls are invited in. When both genders play together in small school settings, the boys' tastes prevail. It is rare indeed for a mass game of jump rope or four-square to ensue. Instead, it is usually red rover or dodgeball, or some milder sport such as handball in a bow to female sensibilities.

These small mixed-gender groups, however, have in no way been the rule in our contemporary American public schools.

Boys eventually drop their play chasing and play fighting, too. They just do it later than girls do. But once they drop rough-and-tumble—in late elementary school—those lads who continue to play in this fashion are the unpopular ones. Anthony Pellegrini of the University of Georgia led me, through his research, to an understanding of this darkening play progression. In a group of seven-year-old boys, for instance, Pellegrini found that those young men who were still playing aggressively also knew how to play cooperative games with rules and tended to be well liked by their peers. Their play fighting did not help them to establish dominance over others (measured by asking each boy, "Who's the toughest in your class?" and then, "Who's the next toughest?"). For those few lads, however, whom Pellegrini found to be still playing in tumultuous styles when they were eleven years old, the interpretation of their play by others had changed. These subteens, like their seven-year-old counterparts, were not considered dominant or tough by their classmates. But unlike their peers, they were highly disliked.

So, even as a boy, it's not cool to play rough-and-tumble games after you've turned ten or so. Play fighting loses its meaning, its playfulness, and/or its other benefits in preadolescence. In an interestingly analogous finding, the Alaskan animal researcher Robert Fagen demonstrated that when animals just short of adulthood play rough, these animals are usually seeking to exploit other animals. We all know that the idea of rough-and-tumble play eventually tempts some pubescent humans to try to victimize weaker children or adults. This "dark side" of play is usually hidden behind the attitude "just playing." But it accomplishes something far more menacing. And here is where we need to remind ourselves that everyone must agree to play before an act can really be considered "play."

So overtly aggressive play goes underground as we near adulthood. Where does the fighting spirit really go? I think it moves into competitive fantasy and into small-scale replications of rough-and-tumble that are recognized by all of us to be play. Some grown-ups attend gymnastics classes. Others pick up kung fu. We jostle and wrestle with our children. On company picnics and beach outings, we play touch football with one another, chase our coworkers around with soccer balls, try one-on-one basketball, beach volleyball. These spontaneous games may take on the aspects of small wars. Fantasies of winning, of competing heroically, accompany this play. But sometimes, the physical labor is so tough there is no fantasy at all.

Not only do we revisit our old childhood enjoyments of play fighting at our adult picnics and days at the beach, but we are able sometimes, when we feel particularly weak, to reempower ourselves through a reacquaintance with rough sport. Amateur karate and judo classes, for instance, have turned out to be helpful for the victims of violence. People who have previously been overwhelmed feel better when they learn to jostle and fight. Although I do not know of any female martial-arts student who ever seriously used it later against a man, this style of play helps many women to feel empowered. Just knowing that she can use it, if she needs to, restores heavily injured pride. I once heard on national television news that the nuns of St. Anne's Convent, located in a dangerous area in Madras, India, had been given karate lessons after they suffered a series of street attacks. This helped the holy sisters to reestablish their sense of well-being.

It's also healthy and restorative, I find, for a weary or stressed adult to take in a good action movie. Here we grown-ups vicariously experience our old satisfactions from rough-and-tumble play, but without the play faces that children and animals inevitably wear at home and in the wild. Take a Steven Seagal production, for instance, or something with Chuck Norris or Bruce Willis. The villain establishes himself as formidable and dominant by killing several people straight off. This is more like a true animal fight—the dominant beast simply bites or claws the victim, and it's all over. But when Seagal gets into it, then the ultimate fight—at least the final one of the film—is given to us play-chase, play-fight style.

Seagal gets strangled. But he simultaneously locks the villain in a wrestling hold that eventually forces the villain to give way. Now the roles change. And again and again. It might take fifteen minutes for such a crucial struggle to be resolved. What about Robert Shaw and Sean Connery fighting to the death on the Orient Express? While watching *From Russia with Love,* we so closely followed each change of attacker to attackee that it must have made the more serious screenwriters among us die with envy. Movie fights are play chasings, play wrestlings, play shootings, done by play actors. We adults remain as fascinated with the process as we were when we were children. And it relieves us.

DURING THEIR sixes, sevens, and eights, girls stop playing with boys. This probably takes place for biological reasons—in the animal kingdom, especially among primates, adult females don't play with adult males unless the males invite themselves in. But by the onset of the elementary school years, strong cultural and social elements, as well, are behind this important gender shift. Teachers call out, for instance, "Boys over here, girls over there." Spelling bees take place—"the girls against the boys." Even in unisex schools, the arbitrary separations that teachers sometimes make throw kids into confusion. I remember my own daughter being confounded in preschool when her teacher instructed, "Brown-eyed girls in this circle, blue-eyed girls in that circle." Julia has green eyes. She suddenly became aware that she belonged to neither category of girl.

The California sociologist whose third-grade journal I quoted earlier, Barrie Thorne, writer of the book *Gender Play,* has been particularly interested in how and why boys and girls become so tightly grouped by gender as they play. She studied two elementary schools, first watching the younger children, and later observing the older children, to see how aggressively and how separately the two genders carried on during their recesses and lunch periods. Among the older groups, Thorne found that the boys had clearly won the battle for play space. Whereas the girls clustered close to the school in a small area for the jungle gyms and pavement games, the boys successfully commandeered all of the larger spaces for their sports and games. This enabled them to play far more aggressively.

Not only did the available space affect the ways that the two genders played on aggressive themes, but shame and embarrassment entered in, as well. Throne observed that older boys appeared to feel mortified about playing with girls. Among second graders, an occasional boy might join the girls once in a while in a jump-rope or hopscotch game—if he was generally popular, this did nothing to his standing. But by fifth grade, a boy would be teased if he played in this manner. Interestingly, girls who chose to be tomboys and to play with the boys were not shamed. They were not universally accepted, however, by either the boys or the girls.

Also, in terms of finding and keeping a favorite playmate in the neighborhood, shame about picking the opposite sex seemed to seep into the equation. A study by the Illinois psychologist John Gottman, in which two Urbana neighborhoods were canvased in order to learn of children's favorite playmates, showed that about a third of children's favorite playmates at ages three and four were cross-gender. But by the time the kids were seven years old, the number of cross-gender favorites had plummeted to only five single situations. These five girls and five boys had been "best friends" when they were younger; now they played happily and easily at home, but at school, they no longer openly acknowledged their relationship.

How do we expect adult heterosexual couples to play with each other regularly when the whole idea is so humiliating, painful, and "not done" among the vast majority of grade school children? Well, it's noticeable to me that for an afternoon of play among a group of eight or ten adults, the women are more likely to go shopping or sight-seeing, and the men are more likely to locate the local golf course or, one at a time, to settle into a place like a hardware store. Just like elementary school. By themselves, however, numbers of American heterosexual couples play together—both will jog or bike or walk, or both may develop a hobby together, such as antiquing, museum going, bird-watching, dancing. Compromises must be made—somebody may not be in the mood for a vigorous workout or for studying the merits of a certain Victorian chest, but both will still go along. The patterns set up at ages seven, eight, and nine, marking out the sharp divisions between the sexes, must be broken down to accommodate courtships, marriages, and families.

One way to overcome the obvious obstacles against such couple play is to emphasize activities that were not contaminated earlier by those old elementary-school-playground attitudes. Travel is a good, mutual source of play, partly because it is not ordinarily touched during childhood by the strict gender divisions that were so often applied on the playground to "the boys" and "the girls." The non-aggressive sports, such as biking and skiing, and the sports that young children hardly play at all—tennis, golf, and racquetball, for instance—all work for couples. If both sides of a couple can enjoy a hobby—chamber music, collecting something, ballroom, ethnic, or historic dance, hiking—this, too, breaks down the old social barriers that were constructed in elementary school. For the sake of our relationships as adults, we must relearn how to play easily and well with the opposite sex.

PLAYING AT being the best may appear to accomplish negligible ends, yet this kind of aggressive pretend is often an important source for our adult play. Not only do we compete with others, but we compete with ourselves. We collect certain kinds of objects—stamps, CDs, facts—and this gives us a sense of uniqueness, improvement, dominance. Consider, for instance, a southern Californian I will call William who exercised a number of his special qualities—and some of his aggressive urges—by conducting little art and sculpture quizzes at his Westwood home.

Let's say, for instance, that a group would be invited to brunch. (A few Sundays when he knew I was visiting Los Angeles, William graciously asked me to join in.) As his caterer squeezed oranges in the kitchen, William, a widower, would almost certainly show a beautiful, matted photograph of an artwork to his guests, who were beginning to take seats in the living room. "Who did this piece?" A few people would know. "But what medium was he using?" Well, somebody might come up with the right answer again, let's say "gouache." And William would be complimentary in response: "That's brilliant of you!" he'd say, pleasure lighting up his face. "But what period in the artist's life does this come from? What private or public collection owns it now?" By this time all of the guests would have arrived and begun to participate in William's game. William's central position in his little quiz and his clear authority would be established. He held all of the questions and a verified set of answers.

Another professional-quality photo would come around. A sculpture. A black-and-white glossy of a relatively unknown work. But William might skip the issue of who had crafted the piece and, instead, ask a question about the artist's gender. "Who is the sculptor—man or woman?" Now, a "blind" guess-the-gender poetry, art, or music question is sort of fun, but it requires a hard look or listen. Too much time, in fact, for a prebrunch guessing game. William, bursting with enthusiasm and geniality, would be eager to get on to the next photo. He'd tell the group the answer, and one or two scattered guests might offer their applause. How brilliant was the question! How intriguing the answer!

At this point, our host would pull out yet another picture to pass around. From a quick count of his stack, it seemed clear that he could not get to them all. The caterer was about to call the guests out to flower-laden tables on William's patio. Was there to be another round of gaming after brunch?

"Take a look at this one last photo," William might coax. "It's one I took last year at a museum show in Chicago. Just think about it as we eat. I'll ask a question later."

William would smile and beckon his friends out of doors. "Don't forget to think about that photo," he'd remind them. In reality, however, all might likely be forgotten in favor of the delicious food, the lovely garden plantings, the news about William's adult son's recent successful foray into professional journalism, and the unfamiliar, interesting faces. An old friend turned up once at my table, and that was a treat. William's "art quiz" was discarded until the next brunch—probably because of everybody's evident ignorance about that last prebrunch photo. William would offer us the one final question and answer of the day and conclude the party by giving a few lucky guests one of his wonderful photographs.

A talented architect, William Hart does not need his little Sunday-morning quiz games to achieve business success, social status, recognition, respect. But his aggressive play carries high stakes for him all the same. Yes, he most likely turns a few people off. But yes, too, he has gained a large cadre of admirers who love the way he looks at painting, sculpture, and architecture. William's quiz shows give him a sense of well-being. His friends occasionally come with a gift for him—a photo, of course. He exhibits about his home a fine collection of work by other photographers. For a man who, within himself, has never been able to accept any guarantees of safety, such little reassurances must mean a great deal.

William has no foreign accent now, but as a boy, his name was Wilhelm and he lived in Munich. His father, a successful industrialist, began to suspect Hitler's general plans for the Jews, and as a result, he put the ten-year-old lad, under the name Guglielmo, into a good boarding school for boys outside of Milan. The child's parents warned him to be discreet, never to "show" too much. As Guglielmo entered adolescence, the war broke out. The Italians were allied with the Nazis, but Guglielmo stayed safe in his school—after all, the school officials had known him for "so long" that his racial and cultural origins were not suspected. His Italian was perfect. And for a while, Guglielmo's parents remained safe, too, in Germany. His father's technical industrial knowledge had made him necessary to the Nazi government—at least until they could educate and train his replacement.

One day Guglielmo's father showed up unannounced at the boarding school. The two of them would be leaving at once, he said. Guglielmo's mother had been picked up by the Gestapo and sent off to a camp. Guglielmo's father had escaped only because of a sudden, unannounced business trip and a timely warning from a friend not to come back home. The boy and his father would have to tell a number of lies to make their way safely north to the border and into Switzerland.

The plan was scary, but it worked. Father and son stayed for a while in Lausanne, where Guglielmo became "Guilleman" and learned French along with the artworks of Delacroix, Degas, and Rodin. Then, when they received permission, the pair immigrated to the United States, where the boy was called Bill. He consistently studied—there were not many diversions in his routine with his father, and he could not fully mourn his mother, although he was convinced that she had been killed (she was). After a year of solitary preparation for college, Bill was accepted at Swarthmore.

Now "William," "Bill," "Guilleman," "Guglielmo," "Wilhelm," who had never had the chance to excel at an enjoyable and perhaps trivial pursuit, who had never been able to "show" himself too much at his Italian boarding school, found himself, for the first time in several years, fully able to play. Only at Swarthmore did his old but excellent German camera and his young but excellent eye allow him to make, not just look at, art. William's one-man photography exhibition at the college library was probably the high point of his life. His already excellent knowledge of German, French, and Italian perfectly positioned him to enter a prestigious graduate architecture program—and, as well, to take a number of art history classes, which for Bill were entirely "play."

Although, as an adult, William favors several different styles of play, including his active social life, his writings, his philanthropies for his alma mater, his love of music, art, and the languages, he expresses his frustrated boyhood assertiveness with his brunchtime quizzes. And he expresses an intense adolescent wish to compete successfully with his father, who not only served as his savior, but functioned as a successful industrialist in Germany, and later, in America. The informal art quiz has consistently been one of William's favorite forms of competition. It is aggressive. Showy. And slightly odd. Although it involves people, William remains strangely removed from them as he plays. This unique mode of recreation allows William to feel separate and different, as if he were hiding in an Italian boarding school, while expressing an assertiveness that he could never show while he was young. As if to make up for a secretive, frightened childhood, William developed his unique adult game with its own rules, rules that completely suited him.

In reading this story, you might wonder how anybody could accept a second invitation to one of William's brunches. But behind his little quizzes, one always senses a shared playfulness and considerable emotional excitement. The art he shows is consistently interesting. The questions carry challenge and intelligence. Then, too, William is a lovely person. And so, William's friends—without knowingly recognizing his fantasy—indulge him and enjoy it. And many of them come again and again to brunch. In fact, one of the *Los Angeles Times* art critics attended both times I was there.

WE OFTEN pretend while we play. Sometimes our pretend is so simple that we don't even realize that a fantasy is involved. But many wishes are in effect as we amuse ourselves—wishes to be loved, wishes to conquer, wishes to be dominant, wishes to improve the world. And many of these wishes boil down to aggression or sex—but in locales far away or into the future. Our games of golf, checkers, Monopoly, help us to win turf, kingdoms, real estate empires. These games can be small wars, though they are usually played out in good spirits. Our ongoing games with friends—be they unisex poker games every Thursday night or couples' bridge—take on the meanings of a tournament. (If the Joneses win this time, the Smiths say they're going to "win them big" the next time.)

When I write that fantasy, pretend, is alive in these games, I mean that the sense of overcoming, of being the best, lives while a person competes. And it is in the realm of this ultimate possibility that play does its work for us. Yes, a great speed skater who failed to win in two previous winter Olympics *can* win the next one. (As a matter of fact, he did it in Lillehammer in 1994.) Yes, we, too, might meet the better player, the smarter player, the younger player, the bigger one, the better-conditioned one, and at least once achieve a victory. The hope is there. The possibility is there. All play rests on possibility.

Does hope help us to win? Oh, yes, it does! Playing in and of itself clears the mind. But winning confirms that the possible can and does actually happen. Play is mainly about the present and the future. And so much of the rest of our lives is about the past.

Play metaphors mean a great deal to us, long after we adults might scoff out loud at the idea of "pretend." Pretend play eventually moves us into the realm of daydreams. Like our more overt play, our daydreams deal with the present and the future—perhaps just the future of this afternoon after school, but perhaps, also, a much more intriguing "What if?" question. Pretend scenarios carry many people through their lives: "What if this?" "What if that?" It is a private form of mind play that generates pleasure, and sometimes, a special idea, even a breakthrough idea.

For example, a surgeon I know got the idea, at the age of sixty, to enter a marathon. It was, I suppose, a "What if?" assertive fantasy for Michael McGuire at first, a piece of pretend. But it started him daydreaming about becoming a runner. To be a sixty-year-old marathon runner somehow struck Michael as personally meaningful. His twin sister had suddenly died of a heart attack the year before. Her death got Michael thinking about his own mortality. Then, too, he'd always seen himself as his sister's protector—and as his wife's and as his kids'. But now he wondered if he could protect anybody. In fact he developed such an acute fear of flying that he could no longer travel on planes. All of this was hard on Michael. He was a surgeon, after all.

Michael practiced running for six months. And then he made his move. He signed up for a marathon race that wasn't too crowded, wasn't too highly publicized, and he got a number and ran. That was all. He just ran. He finished the race, not too high in the rankings, not too low, definitely not the last. And it helped him. It was a victory against himself. A victory against death. Completing his self-imposed challenge became a boost to his morale. His sense of control immediately improved and has continued to improve since then. Now Michael runs at least one marathon every year.

Michael showed me a letter that he wrote to his favorite aunt after a 1996 race. Because it expressed an adult fantasy, a daydream built on pretend about assertion and overcoming, I asked if I might copy a couple of paragraphs.

> To marathoners, running is far more than physical. There's something spiritual about it. It's like—there's a place in every marathon at which you're depleted of energy, completely fatigued to the point that you *know*, you're absolutely convinced, it's impossible to finish. You can't run another step. But through the agony, you deliriously keep putting one foot in front of the other, each step inflicting its own measure of pain.
>
> The satisfying part is that on a good day you may finally cross the finish line. And then, you see that you've done something impossible. It's real. You actually did something that seemed impossible. So in that way, a marathon can be more than a simple test of endurance and will—it can be almost like dying and being reborn, a reaffirmation of the human spirit.

Michael's pretend has propelled him into more and more playful pursuits in recent years. He started writing—short stories, a novel (about a marathon runner), a couple of screenplays—and he has been singing with a men's chorus. On Friday nights, Michael sometimes plays jazz piano at one of the really good restaurants outside of San Francisco. Parenthetically, as a surgeon, Michael has been known for years to be one of the best.

When we fantasize in our play, we usually express both our drives and our defenses. "Displacement" (moving the wish and/or its object one or more steps away) is the most important defense used in pretend. While any fantasy may express itself abruptly, directly, without any transferring of feelings—as in "I like my history professor; I want to have sex with her"—a fantasy commonly expresses itself in more distant, more playful, more metaphoric terms—in other words, with the defense of displacement. "What if an eighteenth-century Philadelphia newspaper printer was able to go to college for the first time—because his friend Benjamin Franklin gave him the money—and he fell in love with his history professor, who happened to be the first woman professor in America?" Now the fantasy expresses the same wish ("I want to have sex"), but it is far more distant and easily elaborated.

Displacement moves us away from ourselves—away in time, away in place, away, even, in gender. Particularly in four-year-old to eight-year-old children, displacement may move the protagonist altogether away from humanity and into animal or space-creature form.

From the time that children reach preschool age, they spend much of their play time creating fantasies. Fantasy play is "pretend," and among other things, it expresses sexual and aggressive feelings, hopes, and terrible frustrations with past or present realities. With pretend, we can express hopes and dreams for what we want to be and want to do. A. A. Milne's poem "Nursery Chairs" expresses meaningfully how ordinary preschool fantasies play out. In it, Christopher Robin sits on various seats in his playroom, changing from the leader of a band of Amazon Indians to a huge, caged lion to the captain of a ship and back to himself. When Christopher returns to his six-year-old self, he is somehow smaller, less powerful, more vulnerable.

Not all children express as elaborate or as well-stated fantasies as A. A. Milne's poetic little fellow. And here, preschool girls appear to be more adept than preschool boys. Their fantasies incorporate more detail, more narrative, more complete instructions for the cast of characters. Girls' great and early knack for pretend may be, in fact, one reason that they back off so early from rough-and-tumble play. Their pretend conveys elaborate scenarios and can express the same aggressive themes that they might have lost by failing to indulge in play fighting. Pretend also frequently expresses the generalized wishes for sex—not sexual intercourse in any sense of the word, but closeness, meaningful relationships, "grown-uppedness," families, romance. Girls prepare themselves for family life by playing house, school, princess. They corral their younger brothers and their preschool male friends into such play, as well. Just about everybody prepares for sex and for love, in a sense, with such pretend scenarios.

Surprising as it may seem, pretend can be studied in structured research projects. And what we learn from some of this research is how wide a range of sophistication exists in children's pretend. Pretend runs the gamut from simple statements of situations to plots as complex as historical novels. The developmental psychologist and play researcher Greta Fein, for example, studied twenty-six middle-class preschoolers (half of them were boys) from two East Coast child-care centers near a big city. Each youngster was seen for two days in a row. On the first day, the child was handed a set of family dolls, including a dog and a baby. On the second day, a problem doll, an alligator, and something not usually considered a toy at all, a piece of string, were substituted for the dog and the baby. When playing with the family set of toys, the vast majority of the preschoolers produced an extremely low level of pretend play, being able only to list their cast of characters. The next day, with the problem set of toys, 62 percent of these same children offered significantly more complex scenarios.

In all of the pretend play that Fein's team elicited in this study, the themes were aggressive—none were romantic. This, however, may well have occurred because an alligator was inserted into the toys. You don't usually make up a love story about a swamp monster. If a young prince and princess had been inserted into the toy box instead, something very different might have emerged from the minds of these children.

Immature pretend sounds funny to our adult ears. It sometimes consists of a list of people or events, for instance, "Mama, Papa, baby," or "school, picnic." Nothing else. Often, the characters do not act on the events: "Who went to the picnic?" for example;

"Nobody." Sometimes the events do not intersect: "Did the school have a picnic?" "No." Or the plot may have an end, but no proper sequence leads up to this conclusion: "Mama, Papa, and baby went home," for instance. "Where were they before they went home?" "I don't know." Some children keep recycling their stories. The tale seems to end, but the problem instantly reappears, and another end must occur: "The baby bit Mama, so she put him to bed. So he bit her again, so she put him to bed. So he bit her . . ."

As adults, we expect stories to include characters and plots with beginnings, middles, and ends. But in early childhood, no such expectations exist—unless, of course, the child's parents have been actively listening to the youngster's narrations about how the day went, or asking the child to relate the plots of movies and of the things that have happened down the street. Parents or teachers help their young children's stories find their introductions, middles, and conclusions. Narratives are an important part of kindergarten show-and-tell or first-grade talking time. Those children who are able to develop tales of personal adventure also develop more advanced styles of pretend play by the age of seven or eight or so. And they may eventually become the best storytellers among us.

In many of our adult lives, elaborate schemes of fantasy and pretend do not stay prominent, visible, conscious, or even commanding. Instead, simple wishes around sex and aggression are played out over sexual foreplay, flirtations at a party, enthusiasms about sports, a Saturday golf game, a juicy piece of office gossip. Sometimes our adult preoccupations are loaded with playful qualities. Other times, all sense of play is lost. Many of us care a great deal whether our local sports teams win. If we can find a friend who is rooting the opposite way, it becomes fun to argue, parry, bet. Sometimes the thing takes on the dimensions of a personal contest for dominance. And that becomes a sort of play.

Much of our adult play has to do with winning at sexuality. Contests for admiration, profit, somebody, something, challenge and amuse us. In adulthood, flirting is play that, if done well, marks a person as charming, and if done badly or excessively, marks a person as a "tease" or a "dirty old man." Two young men I once knew flirted quite differently and created entirely different impressions. One always joked, always teased. You could barely tell if he was serious at all. He made girls come to him; he wouldn't extend himself beyond a nice smile. He could barely dance. But he was uniformly chased by women because he had mastered the art of the gentle tease, of the inviting one-liner. The other fellow, a headhunter for corporations and for himself, practiced what he called, and what everybody else calls, a line. His come-on did not vary. Girls could quote in advance what this man was about to say, and he'd fall into their traps at once. All the practice in the world couldn't give him a perfect line. This man could dance. He was handsome and intelligent. But most women thought he was a jerk.

As I've thought about adult play, I've realized that much of a mature person's skill at play has to do with the person's success at subtlety. The aggressive video games that some kids play, concerning who can dismember the most electronic opponents and cause the most blood to flow (Mortal Combat is one such example), are so overt and obvious that they may actually kill a child's ability to value subtlety. Some of the sexual games that Jane Goodall described among young chimpanzees in the West African Gombé colony lack this same smoothness. Female chimps, for instance, pick up a stick and then take turns tickling their genitals with it. Young males carry around small rocks, set them onto the ground, and thrust the lower halves of their bodies into them. Our human children, when they get some practice at pretend, can sand the rough edges off such overt kinds of play. In human childhood, we do not have to be as direct as a young chimp. We can master the art of fantasy. We can use displacement, a healthy defense. In our adulthoods, some metaphor, some wit, makes our play charming. Human play is set aside, removed from stark reality. We need our fantasy to civilize us, to make ourselves more subtle. In a sense, we need to stay in constant touch with the pretend side of ourselves in order to maintain tastefulness along with a lifelong sense of play.

In miniaturization—in watching a football game of twenty-two men shoving and tackling one another far below us on a brilliant green field—we may avoid having to express ourselves with full-scale armies. In spinning out romantic fantasies and in trading one-line witticisms over cocktails, we may be able to keep from going at our bodies, as Jane Goodall's chimps did, with sticks and stones.

ADULT sexual games and fantasy aid marriage. When unstated or extremely subtle, pretend makes encounters with the opposite sex all the more interesting. But like everything else, this play sometimes goes too far. An attractive, successful forty-year-old man, an innovator in creating worldwide computer networks, came to consult me a while ago because a game that had always worked before for him and his wife (a restorer of old houses) had gone awry. Their pretend, Quinn told me, was totally out of control. He and his wife, Germaine, were becoming obsessed with it. Quinn could not see a way out. He and Germaine had been playing a sexual bit of pretend since the year before their marriage. Each had told the other many times that their sex life was fabulous. And neither had been unfaithful. But they were beginning to let their pretend move toward reality, and this was making Quinn extremely uncomfortable.

The game had consisted, at first, of telling each other their favorite sexual fantasies. One fantasy might give them sexual pleasure for six months or so. Once in a while, they would act it out. Usually, they would just talk about it and picture it. About two years prior to his visit to me, however, Quinn began experiencing demands from Germaine for more enactments, less talk. For example, in response to some animal stories that they had told, Germaine had confessed to Quinn that she would like to include their female rabbit, a large, fluffy, white bunny, in some of their sexual encounters. Quinn felt squeamish about it and protested. But Germaine became more and more insistent. Luckily, he said, the activities did not go beyond some nuzzling, and he was able to live with that and to perform sexually despite his discomfort. After several months they eventually banished the rabbit from their bedroom.

Germaine found that the animal was shedding too much white fur on their hunter-green carpet. The whole thing, in fact, had become "old."

A year ago, however, Quinn had made a serious mistake, he felt. He told Germaine a sexual fantasy about a business associate, an athletic, tall, unmarried woman who often played volleyball with Quinn's group after they had finished lunch. The woman seemed to be, though Quinn couldn't be sure, heterosexual. The married couple began having exciting sex over Quinn's office stories, and Germaine insisted on more and more of them. Then one day, Germaine, without any warning, showed up in Quinn's lunch room. Afterward, Germaine played a hard-fought round of volleyball along with the usual group. She and Lori, Quinn's coworker, said hello and chatted for a few minutes. Germaine was at her most charming. After that, Germaine began telling erotica about Lori to Quinn. Lori was hiding, she said, watching them from behind their bedroom curtains. Lori wanted to have sex with Germaine and then with Quinn. Then, maybe both at once. The volleyball player was going to leap from the net into their bed at any moment.

For the first time in the marriage, Quinn began to lose his sexual interest. He did not like the idea of triads. Sex became a chore where previously it had been a high point. And sometimes he could not perform at all. When Germaine told one of her office volleyball tales, it pointed to homosexual leanings in her that Quinn found distasteful. He could have lived with these stories alone, if he could have been sure that they would go away within a few months' time. But now Germaine was pushing things toward action. She had come to the office for lunch one day earlier that month, looking fabulous and bringing an equally fabulous bottle of sports cologne for Lori. A couple of weeks later, she invited Lori to a late supper at their house—and the young woman would be there the next night! That, in fact, was why Quinn had chosen that particular day to come to my consulting room. That was why he had taken, what to him was, the drastic step of visiting a psychiatrist.

It took Quinn most of an hour to bring his story to the point of

Lori's impending visit. Now it was time for me to give him some-thing—a piece of emergency medical advice.

I told him that if enacting something sexual with Lori and Ger-maine was absolutely off-limits, he needed to tell that to Germaine immediately. If then, during the dinner, his wife chose to disregard his wishes and invited Lori to stay, he might consider leaving the scene and spending the night somewhere else. I felt that Quinn needed to express plainly to his wife that the homosexual side of her impulses held no appeal; and although he could still listen to her stories, he was no longer willing to convert any of them to action. I also suggested that he tell Germaine that he deeply regret-ted their past episodes with the rabbit. Fantasy was one kind of play, but enactment was something very different.

Well, that was a hard prescription to fill. Quinn told Germaine only a part of it, mainly that he would allow nothing to happen that evening. He came back to see me a couple more times. Ger-maine had ignored what Quinn did manage to say and was contin-uing to escalate their contacts with Lori. The three of them had had dinner at a small Italian café, and Quinn had caught the two women staring at each other. Lori had spent a holiday-Monday afternoon with Germaine, having lunch and trying on clothes at a couple of boutiques. By then, Quinn had told Germaine a number of things about his sexual likes and dislikes. For the moment, he had completely blocked any encounters à trois, but he felt unsure and jealous of his wife's relationship with his business associate. What would happen next? He wanted me to guess. But I spoke to him instead about his passivity and the importance of fully stating his position.

Quinn stopped calling and coming to my office. I would not have learned a thing about what happened to him and Germaine if not for an odd little coda. Ten years passed. I was on an airplane and picked up an in-flight magazine. The feature story was about Quinn. It included a fact that I found particularly illuminating. Quinn and Germaine had moved away from the Bay Area during the spring of the year that Quinn's company went public. I later checked and found that this was the same spring that Quinn had come to see me. The move was sudden, and it was based, the author believed, on Quinn's overnight success in the international computer market along with California's slow recovery from a recession. Quinn and Germaine now had homes in Boston, Hawaii, Martha's Vineyard, and Grenoble. They appeared to have left San Francisco once and for all.

I could now make an educated guess about what had happened to Germaine and Quinn that last spring in northern California. For this married couple, pretend that had originally been play had heated up so intensely that it was about to explode. And that was probably why they fled San Francisco and Lori. Actuality was impinging too strongly on fantasy. The subtlety and potential innocence of their play had been lost.

I wish that I could talk to Quinn now—find out how he engineered that move, whether he was ever able to tell his wife how he felt about her lesbian tendencies, whether he was able to fully recover his sexual abilities. You see, Quinn and Germaine were far more adept at words spoken as pretend than they were in speaking about their real feelings. In fact, while they lived in San Francisco, it had been their play that had taken enough of an edge off their pressing emotions to enable them to function so well so much of the time.

5

Rules of the Game,
Tools in the Game,
Fools for the Game

Have you ever seen a film where someone is murdered because he's not playing a game correctly? I'll bet you have. When you play a game, you are invariably playing by a predetermined set of rules. In the card game gin rummy, for instance, the rules say that you must hide your hand until someone wins. But you can also play a similar game, called rummy, where everybody is to put their completed three- or four-card sets on the table. So, if you were playing rummy and were caught with a finished set in your hand, you would be seen as cheating—or at the least, as naive or mixed-up about the game. The hand would be voided and everyone would have to start all over again—if anybody still wanted to play. Players become disgruntled when such a thing happens. A rule has been broken, a game ruined. If they played rummy in western movies, a fella might just get shot.

Speaking of the movies, a number of interesting ones offer us characters who indulge in games about which we, in the audience, are left entirely unaware. Without realizing that "this is a game, this

is play," we see their film situations as suspenseful, perhaps auda-
cious, while really, we learn later, the characters were just having a
bit of fun, with rules conceived in advance and then played out on
film. We in the audience are tricked and befuddled because knowing that "it's a game" is, after all, the first rule of any game.

Consider the films *Shoot the Piano Player, The Right Stuff,* and *Nina
Takes a Lover,* for instance. In each, a man approaches a woman (or
vice versa) and launches into an outrageous seduction. We, the
viewers, are titillated and amazed—how can such a character be so
smooth, so nervy, while dealing with a total stranger? While the
protagonists are already married in these scripts, they are not yet
known by us to have any such special relationship; and in *Nina Takes
a Lover,* in fact, the marriage becomes evident only at the end. So the
audience sees a here-and-now seduction, but the actual game is,
these people were seduced a long time ago, and they have simply
agreed, as a kind of sex play, to entice and re-entice each other for
life. By being concerned for them, we, the audience, have been
entirely taken in. We did not perceive the surprise until the party
was over.

The writers of this kind of screenplay toy with us by failing to
tell us the rules of their game. But then, do we, as "voyeurs," have
the right to know the rules? Like naive rummy players caught with
our completed three- and four-card sets still hidden in our hands,
we feel confused and guilty. We have walked into a game for which
we were not prepared. Even when a film is all about games—for
instance, *The Sting,* which centers on a group of confidence men and
their plays at filching—we can easily be fooled if we fail to pick up
one of their schemes. Near the end, when the two *Sting* protagonists, played by Paul Newman and Robert Redford, are shot dead,
we viewers may feel perplexed, even responsible perhaps. Was all
this comedy ultimately aimed at tragedy? Was all that previous
laughter somehow inappropriate? No, we learn in just a couple of
minutes when the two fellows rise up from the floor, good as new.
They were just fooling. It was just another game after all.

Once in a while, in real and tragic life, a police officer kills a teenager who happened to be playing somewhere near a crime scene with a toy gun. Here, one person trifles while the second person fails to see anything trifling in the act. It is highly problematic to walk in on a contest already in progress. All players are far better off being there from the start.

The way a game is entered is an extremely important factor in its success. Nonhuman animals are adept at this preliminary phase of gamesmanship. They put on a play face and then bow before starting to play. We humans have to say things like "Let's play," for instance, or "What are we going to play?" Of course, in some games already in progress, one can simply join in. But to start a match takes a little forethought.

One of the most interesting things that the mid-twentieth-century British play researchers Iona and Peter Opie observed was how much and how avidly children tried to avoid being picked as "it" at the beginnings of their little meets. Among elementary schoolers, it often took as much time to pick an "it" as it took to play out the contest that involved the "it." In England, "it" was also called "he," "het," "on," and "on it," depending upon what region the players came from. Children seemed almost uniformly unwilling to volunteer for the position. I have noted myself that considerable scapegoating, jeering, and teasing rests on being "it"; but in addition to this simple observation, the Opies pointed out that a number of folklorists consider the position of "it" to represent an evil, perhaps supernatural, force.

Once in a while, a psychiatric case begins to prove an idea like this. Being "it" may relate to somebody who has already committed a devilish act. I treated three children from a church that took in, fresh from prison, a paroled pedophile who had confessed to a couple of the priests that he wished to mend his ways. As a kind of rehabilitative effort, the clergymen let the man supervise the congregational children. In their extraordinary naïveté, the priests did not take into account how highly repetitive pedophilia is.

Every Sunday following services, while their parents lingered over their potluck lunch, the congregational children would run up a set of stairs off the dining hall. The parolee waited for them there. As the result of an entirely separate incident, this man was eventually arrested, convicted, and sentenced to a long prison term for trying to abduct a child from a South Bay playground.

The church parents soon learned about this arrest and began putting two and two together. They knew this man! He had been baby-sitting on the church stairs while they all ate lunch. And their children had been indulging in strange sexual behaviors and making inexplicable sexual statements for several months. The man had been dressed, when they saw him, like a clergyman. He must be a devil. An Antichrist. A satanist. By the time they got to me a year after their discovery, a few parents really believed this.

The three young children whom I treated following the church debacle told me that the man on the stairs had operated within the rules of a hide-and-seek game. He often dressed in a clown suit and chased them into little rooms, half-up, half-down the stairs. When he hunted and found a child, the penalties were so "yucky" that the children could hardly remember them.

Who controlled this game? Who frightened and harmed these children? Well, of course, it was the self-designated "it." One five-year-old boy from the church told me later, intense surprise registering on his young face, "We never had to figure out who would be 'it.' He *always* was 'it.' No matter what game we played, he *wanted* to be 'it.' "

Even if only a few pedophiles acted this way through history, one could still see how the idea of "it" might come to be tinged with evil. Some childhood tag games carry rules based on the idea of dirtiness, grossness, and contamination—what children on American playgrounds call "the cooties." Whoever is "it" in such a game must carry the extra burden of being supposedly germy. Children have invented all sorts of rule-based antidotes for these tag-transmitted contaminations. But many a child becomes upset if he or she has to leave such a game still being "it."

Here is what a fifteen-year-old boy, Paul, a relatively sheltered only child, wrote in a high school essay about his fourth- and fifth-grade exposures to such contamination-style games. They still bothered him, it was clear:

> When a sort of personal cooties game was played on my elementary school playground, I always got the worst of it. Paul Germs was the name of the game. It was conducted under the premise that I was the source of the "germs." If I touched somebody, then he was the carrier of the dreaded bacteria and he had to rid his body of the polluting filth. This was done by touching someone else, who then became a disease carrier, repeating the cycle. Transmission of the germs could be embellished by such strict criteria as "no backsies" or the even more severe "for keeps."
>
> I thought that the game meant that everybody at school hated me. I had no idea why. I hadn't done anything to them. I suppose I showed my resentment over the game too much, because Paul Germs was played until I left that school. Did they play it later after I left? I'll never know. I can't help thinking, though, that the game was specially designed for me.

Since nobody wants to be an "it" in any game—cooties or no—and a ritual of deciding who is to be the first "it" of the game must be initiated. Here, Iona and Peter Opie went to work. They found that children often play a new game, sometimes a complicated one, to pick the "it." With fists they do "One potato, two potato, three potato, four." With pointed fingers, they intone, "Eenie, meenie, miney, mo." With hands they alternately grab a baseball bat until no more room remains for the "it" to lay on hands.

It is clear to me that these choosing rituals survive into adult life. We, too, open our games through the process of elimination, picking our "old maid," perhaps, by pulling names out of a hat or drawing straws. In Chaucer's *Canterbury Tales,* his pilgrim characters drew straws for the unfortunate position of being the first person to be on the spot and tell a story. Today, our adult choosing rituals retain the ceremony but have lost many of the negative connotations of being "it." In watching television, for instance, I see huge choosing rites being played on enormous stages for the almost exclusive benefit of adults. Nothing, even in childhood tag games, could be more complicated than how a racing car gets to take a certain track position in the Indianapolis 500. On Super Bowl Sunday, picking the professional football team that elects to kick off or receive can be as complex as anything that little kids try to do on the playground. Throwing out the first baseball of the season, celebrating the opening day of the Olympics, any of these fresh starts to an important contest has a tendency to develop into a separate rite of its own. At times like this, it is easy to spot the alignment between ritual and play that Huizinga wrote about so enthusiastically.

MUCH OF our human play is completely unrestricted. But by definition, our games, a subset of play, come complete with rules. We begin playing games when we are infants and are first exposed by our parents and guardians to such prescribed activities as pattycake and This Little Piggy Went to Market. By the time we are late toddlers, we can be trusted to play our old infancy games in a family room with a younger sibling or neighborhood child, without having some adult at arm's reach to make sure that we do it right. The rules of the games keep most of our spurious behaviors in check, even when we are only two or three years old. But the real heyday of childhood games arrives between the ages of six and twelve. During that time, games take on great interest and extreme complexity.

By the time children reach early elementary school, they begin to play games outside with their peers—on the cul-de-sac, in the yard, in a vacant lot, on the street. At this point, while pretend and pell-mell rough-and-tumble are still the chief contenders for a child's attention, organized games begin to command considerable time and energy. At first, a six-year-old might just run around in a large chain of children out on the playground, saying, "Join our line. It's fun!" The child might play such simple board games as

Candyland, Chutes and Ladders, or Sorry! But by the age of eight or so, children are excellent and complex games players. They can use strategies and planning as they play. By the time they are about ten, while pretend has moved inside their minds to become an important internal process, games are out in the open and acknowledged to be in top position out on the street.

As I was thinking about the significance of the games of children's elementary school years, I was drawn again to the work of Iona and Peter Opie, who spent most of their professional lives observing, recording, and commenting on how youngsters played in Great Britain. The Opies believed that the real "homes" for children in mid-twentieth-century England were not the houses in which they lived, but the streets on which they played. There, the Opies found children interacting in an entirely unaffected and natural way. In 1969, in a book called *Children's Games in Playgrounds and Streets,* they published their observations of how young people went about their games. They described with great gusto the rules of such matches as kick the can, relievo (called statue tag or freeze in the United States), and hide-and-seek.

The Opies made the point that when youngsters were under adult supervision on school and community playgrounds, they tended to play rougher, more violent games than what they played when they were away from authorities. Children tended to contest more imaginatively in the relative privacy of their own streets and culs-de-sac. Robert Louis Stevenson once said that cricket and football were colorless, hardly play at all, when compared with the romance of the game hide-and-seek. I guess he had been out on one of those old Scottish streets that, years later, the Opies loved to watch.

Iona Opie spent enough time observing children on her hometown playground in Liss, England, that she concluded that school-age children with time on their hands could almost always be counted on to be in some sort of contest. Consider this statement from her 1993 book, *The People in the Playground:*

I soon realized that any child with a look of concentration on his face was likely to be part of a game, even though he might be leaning against a wall with his hands in his pockets.

Young children, whose sense of organization and rudimentary logic has just begun to crystallize, do not dare to tamper with what they consider a "right" and "fair" game. When an eight-year-old plays, he or she is enamored with the rules—the child is an absolutist, a stickler. In fact, if the child has the chance to make up some rules, these guiding principles will be detailed and impossibly restrictive. Like the new religious convert, the eight-year-old "believes" in the gaming enterprise. In this regard, for instance, we might think about this list, mistakes and all, for the governance of a tree-house club. It was composed at my request by a half dozen eight- and nine-year-old San Francisco girls in their third-grade class:

1. No boys!!
2. Siblings are only allowed if they are over eight.
3. All cute furry pets, allowed.
4. You have to be kind, helpful, nice and no arguer to enter the club.
5. No talking about the treehouse at school.
6. No matches alowed.
7. Every one should help to ceep the clubhouse clean.
8. No groaners allowed.
9. You haf to bring a junk food snack every day.
10. No fighting.
11. No cheating on games that we play together.
12. Come to all the sleepovers.
13. When the club has a sleepover, you can't wake somebody up without permission.
14. Every time you go to a club meeting you have to bring something to share with the club.
15. You can't be mean.

16. You can be silly, but not out of control.
17. Have cookies and lemonade sales.

Third-grade boys are just as rule-bound as girls are, but their rules for the governance of an imaginary tree-house club were racier, braver, and less mutually cooperative. Boys are also slightly less verbally adept at the age of eight or nine, as compared to girls, and so their rules flowed less smoothly. Here are their tree-house rules, mistakes and all, as composed for me at the same school by six young San Francisco lads:

1. NO GIRLS !!!
2. NO ADULTS !!!
3. There has to be a password for strangers.
4. You have to be a member to come in.
5. New commers must pass test.
6. You can bring anything apropiet to meetings.
7. Must annoy parents.
8. Non-membership card pay five bucks if they want to join.
9. You can't be a geek.
10. Anybody caught letting a non-member in the clubhouse will be severely punished.
11. Leader of the club decides everything except the basic rules.
12. Each club member must bring Unhealthy food to each meeting.
13. Some meetings will be on friday night at twelve in the graveyard.
14. Every time someone pays five bucks, it goes to get a pitt-bull for the club.

By the time a child is eleven or twelve, that child can handle the governance of games with more fluidity and improvisation. In the eleven-year-old mind, the main points of a game attract, but the fine print often slips away unnoticed.

By the time we reach adulthood, especially in playing solo games such as solitaire or pinball, the rule book can almost—but not entirely—be dumped. Consider how we adults cook for fun, for instance. Some cookbooks are set up to teach us principles and then discuss the ways we might improvise. When people really love to cook, they grasp the dictates and then play entirely on variations. This is one place, I notice, that the saying "Rules are meant to be broken" applies. The new discoveries of good cooks frequently go past regulations. The same can be said of what fine gardeners do. We green thumbers order plants that, by the book, are not recommended for our growing region. Yet, for the fun of it, we watch these displaced plants thrive, fare so-so, or collapse. Once we are particularly adept at a certain game or hobby, we can have the satisfaction of consciously finessing a rule, or a couple of them, and then waiting out the suspense for the outcome.

CERTAIN game regulations are written. They might be considered the "ethics" of the game. And here, even the most organized of sports vary in how much leeway they allow us. Pinochle and basketball, for instance, give us far more room for rules interpretations than contract bridge and horsemanship. Take the rather loosely interpreted sport of prizefighting, for example. On October 30, 1974, in Zaire, Africa, the clever Muhammad Ali was given enough latitude for improvisation—for demeaning talk and for leaning back against the relatively slack ring ropes—so that he was able to wear down the World Boxing Champion of that time, George Foreman. In his memoirs, *The Greatest: My Own Story,* Ali relates that he told Foreman just before they started the fight, "Chump, you're gonna get yourself beat tonight in front of all these Africans." Ali talked all through the fight. In *The Greatest* he says, "Where does it say in the rules that fighters can't have an orderly discussion while they work as long as they perform properly? Where does it say that they cannot discuss some personal problems or world problems? . . . If [the ref] expects me to be quiet on the day I'm supposed to die, he's mistaken."

Through each round of this fight, Ali lay against the ropes, letting Foreman pound and pound him until "near the end of each round, I come to life just when George thinks my life is over." Ali's now-famous "rope-a-dope" trick exhausted Foreman as he punched himself out. Ali talked Foreman into overextending himself. "Hit harder! Show me something, George. That don't hurt. I thought you were supposed to be the best." But Ali did not set the slackness of the ropes himself. Nor did he see to it that anyone else did. The prizefight was conducted within the rules for fighting.

Ali found a great deal of leeway within the rules that festive day in Zaire. But he never stepped over the line. The ethics of a sport or game are usually covered in the rule books—what's not there is usually okay to go ahead and do. In Zaire, Ali improvised in the mode of the most accomplished of adult players. George Foreman admitted in Thomas Hauser's book on Ali, published seventeen years after the fight, that Ali's tactics had never occurred to him while they were boxing. But they were tactics nonetheless, not moves intended to sabotage the game. (Foreman was knocked out in the eighth round.)

In certain adult sports and games, trying to make your opponent anxious becomes standard. Though not written into the rule books for such sports, psychological play is considered ethical and expected. Take chess, for instance. Odd behaviors toward an opponent and peculiarities about the way that you deliberate before making a move, the time you arrive at your match, how or whether you ever look at your opponent—all of these are allowable and expectable. Psyching out is one of the great weapons in chess. Yet if you're playing tennis, as Venus Williams and Irena Spirlea did in the U.S. Open women's semifinals in September 1997, you don't purposely bump into your opponent, as Spirlea—or Venus?—appeared to do, while you're changing sides. That's just not done in tennis, even though there's nothing about it in the rule books. Football, maybe. Hockey, yes. Tennis, no. In some sports, mental warfare is an integral part. In others, "it's just not cricket."

Psyching out may be a good strategy, depending upon the game. But as a rule, unethical actions and lowered standards of excellence hurt a game. That has happened with professional wrestling and Roller Derby. Now that these games are considered exhibitions and have ironically exchanged one audience for another, they allow for plenty of blood, histrionics, mellifluous announcing, and phony championships. But we don't have to take it all too seriously. To see real wrestling, we head for the high schools, colleges, and the Olympics. And to see real roller- and in-line skating, we head outside for the urban streets and parks.

As jaded as we are today about the lives of our best games players (along with the business and educational institutions that back them), we still carry inside ourselves a hope that people will play "fair." We identify with our heroes at games. And in identifying with them, we vicariously enjoy their victories and suffer their defeats.

When we learn that a sports star has broken our deep, largely unspoken moral codes, our own vicarious games are stymied. Our whole lives have to be questioned internally. The "morals" of games do not come from the rule books or from the ethics of a certain kind of play. Instead they are a more internal matter, an issue of conscience. Everything that we have learned at home, at school, and at church feeds into the moral aspects of play, aspects that go far beyond any printed decrees.

When our mothers say, for instance, "Don't poke the baby in the eye," this applies to every game that we will ever participate in, every sport that we will ever watch. We adults become uncomfortable when this kind of moral boundary is violated. And here is the place where many of us become absolutists about our play, long after the time that we pass into our majority. After all, if somebody gets away with using drugs to enhance his play or with doing something deliberate to injure another player, then we have to rethink our whole lives. Maybe we should have cheated. Maybe we *did* cheat. The Tonya Harding story inserts itself here—into the question of adult abuses of morality in play.

Tonya's sport, ice-skating, has never been particularly fair in the global sense—especially to a person who doesn't fit in. Tonya came out of a rough, blue-collar background, unusual for an ice queen.

She had five stepfathers. Her mother was in no way the typical, eager, and committed "skating mother." Tonya was lucky enough to find a female coach who paid special attention to her and who also paid most of her skating expenses. But as the child grew into adulthood, she did not become either delicately statuesque or daintily petite. Her blond hair refused to fall in silky cascades down to the shoulders. She was no ballerina, nor was she a team player. Then, too, as she came into prominence on the skating circuit, she had already been married—unusual for a young skater working up to her first Olympic Games. All things considered, Tonya Harding was not the kind of skater to whom competition judges like to give high marks. She was atypical.

But Tonya worked hard. She mastered the triple-axel jump, an extremely difficult maneuver that most top-level women skaters cannot do. And because this feat merits a higher number of points, the rules of skating tend to protect the skater who can accomplish such a move. Despite the downside to her prospects, in early 1994, Tonya Harding was a serious contender for the American championship and for the Olympic gold medal. We saw her as a gifted athlete and a persistent player. Her triple axels could easily land her in first place.

Then the event that many of us remember took place. Nancy Kerrigan, Tonya's main rival for both the U.S. championship and a berth on the Olympic team, was attacked by a couple of thugs as she finished skating at Cobo Arena in Detroit, Michigan. The pair of hooligans nearly destroyed Nancy's knees with a wooden bar. Miraculously, no bones were broken. Although Kerrigan missed the U.S. national competition, she suffered no permanent damage, and a position on the Olympic team was held for her. The investigation of the Kerrigan attack led to a trailer park at the eastern outskirts of Portland, Oregon, where Tonya Harding and her ex-husband, Jeff Gillooly, were living. The men who had attacked Nancy Kerrigan knew Jeff and told authorities that Jeff had paid them to ruin Nancy's legs. Eventually, the chain of "Who knew about this?" was traced back to Tonya herself.

Winning at any price attracts us. Underdogs attract us. Those outside the norm attract us. And immorality oddly attracts us, as well. Americans found Tonya Harding utterly fascinating. Nancy Kerrigan eventually won the Olympic silver medal, and Tonya, who skated poorly in Lillehammer, did not place at all. Tonya was eventually banned for life from all U.S. figure-skating competitions and from teaching or coaching. And retroactively, she forfeited her U.S. championship. Following all the hullabaloo, she gradually dropped out of sight. But for a while, Tonya Harding was the biggest show around. And when, in 1997, she briefly considered moving to Norway to skate competitively, her ice play—unconscionable as it had turned out to be—sparked national interest once again.

Tonya eventually hired an agent to represent her to any circuses willing to ice up a ring or to any hockey teams that could use an offbeat intermission show. Tonya might have been a difficult person to "sell," but her agent told the press that Americans love a comeback. He said that Tonya had the guts to take a few boos and that she had already lost fifteen pounds readying herself for first-class performances. Tonya's agent put a spin to the Kerrigan attack that, for an instant, would make anyone wonder why we need any rules, ethics, or morals in order to play. "There were a lot of benefactors to this injury of poor, unwitting Nancy Kerrigan," he told the *San Francisco Chronicle* in 1997. "The microsecond the collapsible baton hit her knee, it catapulted the figure-skating industry to a position second only to the NFL. For better or for worse, the best thing that ever happened to Nancy Kerrigan was Tonya Harding."

Winning at any price, fascinating though it may be, contradicts the ultimate goal of play, to have "fun." When a cheater wins—as Tonya did when, for a few months over the winter of 1993–94, she became the number one woman skater in the United States—then we are all unconsciously forced to reconsider our own moral development. What would have happened if we had been able to foul our siblings out of their rights? What would have happened if we could have won the oedipal contest, gotten through school without ever studying, beaten up our competitors at work, dragged home a mate by the hair? With the same fascination that people feel about Al Capone and Jesse James, we cannot help but think about players such as Tonya Harding while inadvertently considering a number of reverberating, barely conscious motifs. Tonya set up a kind of titillating mental pretend, and for a while, we couldn't get enough of her.

WHEN CHILDREN reach the ages of seven to twelve, they begin to develop the tools for their games. These tools, or techniques, come through practice. Many elementary school children begin with sports that are both seasonal and popular. Tennis, golf, baseball, basketball, swimming, gymnastics, are taken up with great verve at this stage. But many school-age kids also take up musical instruments, dancing, dramatics, singing, and art. And everybody practices.

During this same period of development, children also become enthusiastic hobbyists and collectors. They take up the needle arts, computers, videocameras, the study of coins and stamps, the collection of facts. Some children find individualistic and relatively uncommon ways to practice or to indulge in hobbies. They become "trolley jollies," for example, watching streetcars and buses, while checking and rechecking the changing schedules.

In Western societies, our dominance patterns are established through excelling at something. For the best hoopster on a local basketball court, the best children's-league soccer player, the best dancer, the best musician or actor, there are kudos aplenty and more to follow. The same can be said for the speediest, the strongest, the nimblest, of playground players. Not only do talented children's techniques build, but their self-assurance builds along with this technical competence.

During our years in school, we practice at skills aimed at competition and singular accomplishment. Practice begins to take up considerable time in our preadolescent lives. Sacrifices must be made. And sometimes the scrapes among child peers and coaches rival adult battles over politics. Sometimes practice becomes work, pure and simple. But often our efforts build on talent, on natural propensity. This practice stays play. I know a fourteen-year-old leftie, for example, who has already been scouted by a National League baseball team from the Midwest. He has been practicing his pitching with his father, his coach and catcher, for five years now. If the lad's arm holds up, and if he ever gets enough homework done to merit the grades that he will need for a college baseball scholarship, he may eventually build a significant career. And I know a fifteen-year-old athletic superstar who has been practicing volleyball since she was ten. She broke an ankle when one of her own teammates kicked her (accidentally? on purpose? she never knew). She jammed a thumb while receiving a pass from her own side of the net. Yet, despite all of this, the girl continues to aim for the Olympics. Is her game fun for her anymore? "Yes, when we really play," LaTasha told me. "But all that jealousy and maneuvering and stuff really gets to me at other times."

These children are gifted, and their practice is still enjoyable for them. But other school-age children are not so gifted—they simply want to do something for sociability and to give them a skill to measure themselves by. Can they still make their practice efforts personally meaningful and fun? Consider a child—Mary, let's call her—who has suffered severe concentration problems (attention deficit hyperactivity disorder [ADHD]) ever since she was six and did not, therefore, do well in elementary school. Although Mary was basically a good kid and exhibited considerable talent in art, a few teachers didn't like her. Her inattention irritated them.

I met Mary when she was eleven. For the first time, she began taking the proper medication for her disorder and responded to it well. But Mary still felt cut off from teachers and peers. What could she do about it now? Well, Mary's town had an active swim program, with teams representing the ten-year-olds, eleven-year-olds, and so on. Perhaps if she joined the swim team, if only to practice with a group of girls, she might make some friends. Mary joined, and after a rocky start, she came to truly enjoy the practices. Although she was not as talented at swimming as she was at art, the girls' swimming team did something for Mary that painting could not. It put her into the company of peers and gave her the first group camaraderie that she had ever tasted. What's more, and something quite unexpected, Mary earned a couple of medals. Practicing had helped Mary do better. If the only purpose of games were, as the play researcher Brian Sutton-Smith puts it, to get better at games, then Mary would have been well served by practicing. But Mary, like Rick the handicapped skier whom we met much earlier in this book, was so responsive to her sport that it produced a noticeable effect on her entire frame of mind.

Our skill building in elementary school and adolescence makes it possible for us to play well as adults. I remember my daughter, Julia, studying ballet and practicing the flute for five, six years, taking lessons, playing in little recitals, and dancing in the San Francisco Ballet's production of the *Nutcracker*. Eventually she dropped both the flute and dance—she didn't like either well enough to step up her practicing to subprofessional levels. But all that after-school practice led to an attitude about play—that to be excellent at it, one had to work. Julia transferred this attitude to writing short stories, and later, to making films. She manages a public-access cable-television station now and loves it. For her, all that learning how to play as a child fed into knowing how to play as an adult. I think it would be fair to say that Julia feels that she plays at her work today. And she picked up the tools to do that on her dancing and flute-playing route to maturity.

At some point in adulthood, we usually have to give up active participation in team sports. We lose some of our tools for the game. Yes, bowling goes on into one's sixties or seventies. And I heard about a Florida softball league that includes guys well into their eighties. But a number of team sports require far too much strength and agility to continue forever. One sociable fellow, an attorney named Dan, played baseball and basketball with lawyer-league teams until he turned forty-five. A bachelor, Dan christened the teams he played on with clever names, captained these teams at various times, organized restaurant dinners for the teams, broke an ankle a couple of times in service to his teams, and was elected Most Valuable Player on more than one occasion. When he reached what he considered middle age, Dan decided that he would quit. His teammates were going to miss him, they protested. Couldn't he stay and be coach? No? Oh, well, the team would go on.

Dan decided to practice at a new and more doable sport, a "loner" kind of sport. There was an archery range at Golden Gate Park out near the ocean, and Dan determined to take up a bow and arrow and try it. He bought some equipment, started to practice, and found himself getting pretty good. Then one day he ran into another lawyer from his office at the archery range. It was fun to have some company, and they went out afterward for pizza. The same lawyer came back the next Saturday. A couple of weeks later, another office buddy showed up. Then another. Eventually, two or three of the people from Dan's law office would join him every week. Archery was fun. The practice was both new and challenging.

Dan is an attractive person. People want to be with him. Although he retired at forty-five to a solo sport, he finds now that any sport can be a "team" activity. That is the magic of Dan. And that is the magic of play.

As LIFE goes on, we must keep on picking up new skills, new games. As big, well-fed, nonhunted animals, we have a propensity to become bored. The evolutionists tell us that play was put into our lives to prevent boredom. Older people sometimes need new tools for games. And we need to practice. We can take up dancing, learn more about chamber music, develop skills at hiking or golf, go back to college just for the pure enjoyment of it all. We can go out playing and traveling with our grandchildren.

Those separate retirement communities well apart from families may not be a good stimulant to developing play tools as we advance in age. In growing older, it is important to have a number of play options and a number of healthy ways to continue to practice and have fun. I know a lady who took up Greek in her sixties and earned her master's degree in ancient literature at eighty. She could not have done it tucked away in some semirural retirement community. An older man I know began printing desktop newsletters after he retired. In a senior enclave he might not have been able to gather the computer expertise he needed. And the grandpa I know who taught his grandson how to fly-fish may not have been able to do it at all had he lived in isolation with his fellow grandfathers. Today we have many retirement options inside our cities and towns. Mixed into more stimulating communities, those of us who are now aging may be able to find a broader selection of new ways to play.

SPORTS FANS are "fools for the game." Being a fan is obviously not as active a form of play as indulging directly in the game itself, but most of us sports enthusiasts consider team spirit to be a form of play. We yell, wear T-shirts and hats appropriate to our sport, chant the team chants, throw up our hands and bend our bodies to make a "wave" across the stadium, dive into the program, keep score, comb the Net and cable TV stations and sports pages for statistics and trivia, and talk, talk, talk.

At the same time that children start preferring organized sports, they also become fans. When prepubescent kids discover their favorite styles of popular music, their favorite movie stars, their favorite ways of wearing clothes, they also discover their preferred sports, players, and teams. Preadolescents idolize individuals who symbolize freedom or remarkable achievement. They must look beyond their parents for this kind of role model. It's too tight a fit to turn out to be exactly like one's parents. If a teenager actively competed with Mom and Dad, who knows, the old folks might just win. And so preadolescents make substitutions for their families. And they fall in love. With their heroes and heroines. With the local team.

We adults hang on to these loves. Whole bar and saloon industries hinge on those fans who want to get together with others to yak about their sports. Whole talk-radio shows center on what's doing with the home team. Whole betting and gaming concerns—

legal and illegal—trade on the fates of our favorite sports organizations and idols.

In the eighteenth and early nineteenth centuries, it was safe in polite conversation to talk about the weather, a book, a poem, a journey one had taken a while ago, a new journey coming up, the decor and architecture of a house, the individual sports of shooting and riding, perhaps. Today it is quite safe to speak of all of these things *and* the local team. Being a fan can promote hours of conversation. Women and men alike talk about the Niners, the Packers, the Indians, the Knicks, the OSU-Michigan game. Our talk about our teams becomes a kind of game in itself. Bridge aficionados read the newspaper bridge columns, vicariously replaying the play of others. Chess fans do the same. And organized-sports lovers pore over statistics, world records, history, and autobiographies of star athletes, memorizing those items that will enable them to be good conversationalists and avid though vicarious players.

Are audiences true players? After all, a fan is not moving a muscle related to the actual play of the game. I believe that fans, at least a sizable number of them, truly play. We indulge in this kind of vicarious activity strictly for the fun of it. While some indirect players may have more complicated motives—profit, gaining power or prestige, gaining a date or a mate—many fans do what they do because the game is separate from the rest of their lives. Going to a game can be enjoyable, mind-clearing, a chance to see friends. In this sense, fans play. This does not mean, however, that every family-room lounger whose eyes follow the sports on TV is actually playing. Play depends upon activity—conversation, scorekeeping, rooting, exhortation, thought. A watcher who does not vicariously play the game along with the team does not meet our definition for play. One must exhibit a certain kind of concentration in order to play. One must do it actively.

By taking the time to actively observe, by moving onto the playing field of our minds, by finding heroes and antiheroes to urge on to victory or defeat, we fans join forces with the great athletes of the world. Upon coming home again from the game, be it from the

arena or the TV set, our minds have been emptied of pressing concerns. For a while, at least, the air was brisk, the walk was healthy,
the hot dog, peanuts, beer, apple, and ice cream bar tasted good.
Watching games at the stadium is as close to a full-scale Huizinga-
style play ritual as one can come—pom-pom girls, drum majors,
brass and reed music, certain foods that are eaten primarily *there*.

When we go to the theater, attend a concert, sway to the sounds
of a rock band, we are playing as spectators. Sometimes we are
unable to get into the action—something keeps us from letting our
minds go and being there. It may be the quality of the play itself. It
just isn't good enough. Or it might be us. We're not in the mood. In
either case, we become unable to play because we cannot lose ourselves. But if the play is good and we are in a good enough state of
mind to let go, we will slide into the action without realizing it. Our
minds become cleared. We can then perceive how much play
accomplishes for us, even when our play is entirely vicarious.

Fools for the game do play. But I must say there is more to playing than just sitting back and watching others. Some of what we do
for play should be active. The story of Charlotte Brent, one of the
most ardent sports fans I ever met, illustrates a couple of my points
here: first, that it's never too late to start playing actively, and second, that active play is most likely more ultimately satisfying than
being a fan.

As a preschooler, Charlotte was probably sexually abused by a
man or men who hung around San Francisco's Ocean Beach, where
her family lived and worked. I say "probably sexually abused"
because Charlotte retained no waking memories of this and mainly
suffered from cycles of vivid, horrifying nightmares of hiding from
a man as a preschooler or toddler. She maintained incredible prohi-
bitions all of her life against any kind of sexual activity. And when
she relaxed a little in her first and only relationship with a man, she
behaved strangely, as if the only sex that she knew came from childhood exposures to a pedophile.

These frightening childhood experiences made Charlotte afraid
to let go and play. She did not play with other children. She could

not pretend with others, probably because whenever she did, she reactivated a few shards of horrible memory. She could not play games at recess because she felt inferior to the other girls at school. In her view, she had been deprived of her own controls, while they had never experienced that sort of thing. She felt less than human. She automatically assumed that they would be better than she at play. So she rarely tried.

When Charlotte reached adulthood, she was hired as a secretary and began to respect herself more. She began to play, but only as a spectator. She became deeply involved in the Giants and the Forty-Niners, joining their fan clubs and signing up for such things as rooter luncheons and pep talks. She bought as many single tickets for the home games as she could, and she began having some fun. She remained too afraid to venture out on her own to play, but as a fan Charlotte had the best times she had had up to then.

Charlotte was well into middle age when her mother died and she began seeing me for psychotherapy. Cut loose from the closest relationship of her life, Charlotte realized that she would have to begin taking trips and discovering pleasures beyond spectating. It was difficult for her; and a number of vacations that could have been pleasurable for others turned out to be too demanding and fear-ridden for her. After thirty years as a member, she quit her fan clubs, but kept going to the games. Gradually, her vacations became more enjoyable. She cut her psychotherapy down to once a month. But she did not quit.

At age sixty-two Charlotte retired from her job. She was fully vested in her company's retirement plan because of all those years that she had worked in that single place. What could she do to keep herself busy now? She responded to that question with the most playful and active gesture that she had ever made. She began buying and selling old things. What did Charlotte specialize in? Carnival memorabilia, amusement-park souvenirs, Disneyana. The hobby made sense to her because these were the things that she had known as a child of the beach—things that she had enjoyed in San Francisco's old-style oceanfront amusement park, now long gone.

In retirement, Charlotte could collect, hold, eventually sell, memories. It was all play, self-initiated and unnecessary to the achievement of power, prestige, or personal sustenance. The first really creative play of Charlotte's life, it was empowering. And it began when she was sixty-two.

I asked Charlotte how she saw the difference between her old play, being a fan, and her new play: picking, holding, selling, and keeping old objects. "Being a fan was okay," she said. "I had lots of good times. But there is something else that I get from what I'm doing now, especially now that I know what I'm doing. It holds me for longer. It takes up more of my time. It makes me feel strong. I can travel as part of it. Vacations are more fun because I always make a point of picking up some old stuff wherever I go. I can keep whatever I particularly like. There's no real money in the whole thing. I shovel all of my profits back into what I buy the next time. But there's a big difference from being a fan. I mean, I still love Joe [Montana] and Bill [Walsh]. But I like my life better now. I don't have to live only through idols!"

For me, Charlotte Brent was a particularly meaningful example of the move from passive to active play because I could watch her develop her play capacities right under my nose. Her progress from being a fan to being an active, more creative player was uncomfortable for her at first. But when she became more adept at it, she seemed brighter, fresher, younger. Something new had happened to Charlotte Brent, and you could see it on her face and in the way that she walked.

6

Adolescent Turning Points in Play

Late one August before she starts high school, my niece Sarah and her family visit my home in San Francisco. An excellent student and an adept pianist, Sarah has recently been given bad news. Her piano teacher has told her that she must double her practice hours. Before, it was one hour a day; now it must be two. She is getting older. She must strive to be better.

Over breakfast, the fourteen-year-old mentions her dilemma to her parents. Shall she go on playing? Sixty minutes was easy enough to manage. But the additional sixty? Where will they come from? Sarah likes to hang out with her friends for an hour or so after school. She will not give this up. No way. Then, too, there is the hour she practices after school, and there's homework. Her extra practice hour has to come at the beginning of the day, she concludes. There isn't another obvious route out of this maze.

The monologue has ended, but nobody says much.

Okay, Sarah again starts tossing around possibilities. Right now. Aloud. Another monologue. While her parents silently take their last few bites of toast, she says, "I'll get up at six, shower and wash my hair, and start playing at six-thirty while my hair dries."

"Oh, no you won't!" Her father's sudden, intense response surprises us all. "We sleep till seven."

Sarah looks confused. How can she groom herself, practice, and keep from waking everyone else up? How can she be with her friends? How can she get all of her homework done? Yet how will she be able to develop good enough skills to play a piano concerto? If she really likes playing, she will have to fight for it now. Or compromise.

Sarah has reached a typical adolescent turning point in her play. As my daughter, Julia, realized a few years ago about her own practice, Sarah will have to accept the increased load of work required to play at an advanced level, or she'll have to bow out.

Something had better happen soon, I think from my vantage point at the kitchen sink. Sarah pauses as she tries to decide. Does she dare to be a better player? I watch her.

"Okay." Her face settles. "I'll dry my hair until seven and practice till eight. How's that?"

"Okay," says Dad. "A deal."

In this way, Sarah passes a test. As she moves beyond this moment, she will be able to be a better player. She feels committed enough to work it out, or better put, to play it out. She has reached an adolescent milestone and is about to jog right past it.

I phone Cleveland a few weeks later. "How are things going?"

"Great!" says Sarah. "I like high school, I've made some new friends, and I'm practicing more. I think you'll be able to tell the difference, next time you hear me play!"

"Are you waking up the family?" I chuckle, thinking of her parents' sacrosanct morning sleep.

"Not at six-thirty! My hair is so long now that it takes me at least fifteen extra minutes to dry it. So I'm really busy before I start practicing. And nobody sets their alarms anymore. The sound of me at the piano at seven-fifteen is an automatic wake-up call."

*   *   *

PLAYING IN adolescence is a major marker of that phase. But unlike the play of the elementary school years, adolescent frolics don't come so easy. Adolescents are under tremendous pressure to give up playing and, at the same time, are being counterpressured to cavort dangerously or to waste too much time at it. The combination of temptations to quit and to go too far place a healthy adolescent into a play dilemma that may not resolve until the early to mid-twenties.

We want our older children to keep on playing. Their chances for a balanced life and a sense of well-being rely partly on their ability to keep on conjuring up fun for themselves and for others. Yet some of these pathways to mature play resemble trails through swamps. We want our teenagers to try football, for instance, but then they get injured. We want them to drive to their teams' away games, yet that means that they have to drive back home again—after a defeat or, more dangerously perhaps, after a win. They go out on their own to a local hamburger joint, and they run into somebody dangerous. They go off to college and meet scores of kids who have been practicing harder, working harder, playing harder.

To sort through all of these influences, both good and bad, an adolescent must develop a life theme, something to live by. The kid of fifteen or sixteen has to believe in possibilities and in his or her abilities to bring these about. In some ways, adolescence is all about power—the control of burgeoning physical powers, the development of mental powers, the harnessing of sexual powers, the willingness to accept powers bigger than the teenager's own. In adolescence these powers are all bent toward potentials that may or may not be achieved.

The psychologist Brian Sutton-Smith has written extensively about the possibilities and powers inherent in play. At the end of 1996, he retired after forty years of studying how we, especially as children and teenagers, enjoy ourselves. When he ended his career at Penn, Sutton-Smith wrote a memoir about his own play. Obviously a lover of games who devoted most of his life to playing them, watching them, thinking about them, Brian surprised me as to what an active and chance-taking youth he had been. I was impressed with how hard he went on to play as an adult—how competitively, dangerously, completely. But I felt most admiring about how he had as a teenager overcome a significant roadblock to his ventures into sports. The researcher himself serves as a prime example of what adolescents must face and surmount in order to go on playing throughout life.

When Brian was a child, his psychological spur toward sports was his superathletic older brother. The firstborn Sutton-Smith was bigger, stronger, and faster. Whenever Brian tried to take his brother on in some contest of strength or agility, Brian invariably lost.

Brian, his brother, and their parents lived in suburban New Zealand, where his dad served as a postmaster. Particularly influenced by the males in his family, Brian listened carefully to his dad's wistful statements about scholarship. Rather than be a government worker, he would have much preferred an academic career, his father said. Okay, one possibility for Brian would be academics. You see, the boy believed in possibilities; if his father had missed a life at the university, Brian might create one of his own.

Before he reached puberty, Brian daydreamed a great deal. He says that he always loved this style of solitary mind play and indulges in it still. In daydreaming you can *be* anything, *do* anything. You can be the central person in your daydream, in a power position in which you choose your own story, style, and role. But Brian also came to believe—from elementary school on—in holding power positions in groups, central positions especially in sports. A natural athlete, he loved being captain of the team, a strong offensive scorer, a mighty force.

His favorite game in adolescence was rugby. His brother had been a rugby star and Brian wanted to be one, too. He practiced with determination. And Brian did get to be a high school standout in this rough sport. But during his teen years, Brian suffered in short order three serious concussions on the playing field. He faced a choice. He could continue playing rugby and perhaps suffer permanent brain damage, or he could quit. If he quit, he might still have a chance at a career in academics—his father's unfulfilled love. If Brian stayed with rugby, he might have a more glorious high school record than his brother ever did.

Brian was prodded throughout his development by his competition with his older sibling. Now as a teenager with three concussions, he'd have to reconsider the entire course of his life. Young Sutton-Smith decided to quit rugby. But rather than giving up on play altogether, his will to continue contesting prevailed. He took up soccer, basketball, baseball, and prizefighting. The direct aggression that had characterized his attempts to compete with the image of his all-powerful brother continued to characterize his actions in these new games. During college, he was offered a prestigious upper-level scholarship in physical education. But Brian remembered his old intellectual competition with his father and still wanted to be a scholar. He turned the offer down in order to earn his way through a more academic program and to work particularly on the psychology of play.

Throughout his life, Brian Sutton-Smith has been willing to accept a challenge, and his chance-taking has made his work an ongoing kind of sport. In 1966, for instance, he debated Jean Piaget about what Brian saw as the Swiss psychologist's tendency to let his theories about childhood cognition dominate his observations of children's play. Whatever Brian Sutton-Smith did about the psychology and folklore of play in his forty-plus academic years, he did with almost swashbuckling daring. That adolescent thrust toward indulging wholeheartedly, whole bodily, even dangerously, is strongly evident in his life story.

ONCE YOUNG people attain adult-sized bodies and the thinking and planning capacities that go along with them, they can use their burgeoning abilities to take risks. Taking chances characterizes adolescent life, and sadly, it also characterizes a number of adolescent deaths. As part of teenage play, daring may lead to tremendous accomplishment and, of course, as Brian Sutton-Smith teaches us, to the achievement of power. However, teenage challenges may lead, as well, to disaster. Parents fret, and rightly so, about their older children's safety during their times away from supervision. Yet without these times alone and in small groups, juveniles may lose that thrill of playing, of creativity, of attainment. In many ways, we must continue to be brave all of our lives. But as a specific form of play, "the romance of risk" belongs primarily to adolescence.

Daring teenage games are often a response to a peer-initiated challenge ("I bet you can't climb the wall behind the school"). Fads, such as Russian roulette, arise, quiet down, and start up all over again. Sometimes, as when boys lie down on highway lane markers following the premiere of Walt Disney Studio's *The Program,* dangerous dares are part of copycat syndromes. Until the studio removed that scene from the film, some lads found its siren call to action irresistible. Tragically, a few teenagers were run over and maimed or killed.

Kissing games are specially constructed play routines that meet pubescent needs for sexual risk and experimentation. Teenagers don't need games of smooching when out-and-out sexual experimentation is available to them. But in the 1950s when the sexual mores were prim, kissing games were extremely popular in teenage America. A study by Brian Sutton-Smith's group in the 1950s revealed all sorts of local variations on kissing themes in various Ohio towns. By college age, almost every single Ohio teenager interviewed had been exposed to a game like spin the bottle or post office. Interestingly, now that the sexual habits of early adolescents have again become less overt and experimental, play around kissing and hugging is regaining some momentum. A twelve-year-old girl recently informed me that she had turned down an invitation to one of her school's in-group parties because she had been warned that they were planning kissing games.

Older adolescents in racy, chance-taking moods try strip poker or truth or dare. Younger ones make play rituals of their love for certain musicians and movie stars. Many eventually create games over going to concerts or films, tie-dyeing their shirts, coloring their hair, growing or shaving their hair at various levels of their scalps and faces, applying temporary or permanent tattoos, and going for other startling effects. The occasional adult plays games of daring as well. In 1991, the pop star Madonna made a documentary of a short period of her life, *Truth or Dare,* which reflected the dramatic risks involved in the teenage capers behind her film's title. Though far removed in time and space from high school when she made the movie, Madonna opted to insult the popular film actor Kevin Costner by rolling her eyes into the top of her head, adolescent fashion, as Costner, a fan, visited her dressing room. While they were filming, I doubt that Costner realized what kind of pleasure Madonna was experiencing at his expense.

Adolescents easily go too far with their on-the-edge play. Often, in fact, this kind of sport does not meet our full definition of "play" because some or all of its participants remain ignorant of the full agenda to be enacted. And although a number of high schoolers look and sound superbly confident, they may actually feel terrified of what might happen in their games. As parents, we stay up late at night, eaten alive with anxiety over how our kids will ever endure their gambols in the dark. The "toys" for the risky play of adolescence are huge—cars, trains, trucks, mountains, canyons, lakes, far-flung city neighborhoods, weapons, roadways. Most important, fully grown, but vulnerable, adolescent bodies, perhaps under the influence of alcohol or drugs, are the enactors of these dangerous frolics.

Brian Sutton-Smith calls this kind of juvenile behavior "the dark side of play." Robert Fagen has found analogous activities among almost-mature nonhuman animals. Young people experiment with risky games because it feels important to them to forsake their parents once and for all as potential lovers, sources of competition, even as lifelong caretakers. Among themselves, teenagers almost invariably put down their parents' warnings as old-fashioned or ignorant. They suspect their mothers' and fathers' advice as being based on impotence or envy. They critique the older generation as being simultaneously hypocritical and naive.

One recent example may help illuminate the intrigue, learning potential, and dangers behind these adolescent games of risk. Three slightly chubby tenth-grade girls entered into a private competition, a "contest" they called it, to see who would lose the most weight in the shortest time. Each swore the others to secrecy. For a time the game consisted only of diet and exercise. The girls lost their first five pounds fairly quickly, but there was no clear winner. The trio, unsatisfied with their successes thus far, decided to start playing rougher and dirtier. They doubled their exercise. One used laxatives. Two tried vomiting. One girl—let's call her Girl C— knew about the singer Karen Carpenter's death. C's parents had mentioned it when she was around eleven. When her friends tried to teach her how to make herself vomit, Girl C silently dropped out of their game. She celebrated her gain—she had shed eight pounds (hurrah)—but she mourned her loss of two best friends and the loss of the joy and camaraderie of an ongoing escapade. Girl B stayed in the contest for a couple more months until her parents inadvertently came across the traces of her after-dinner purging. B's family ended the game by decree, by supervision of all of her evening meals, and with a child psychiatric consultation. The two dropouts from the weight game eventually resumed their friendship. Sadly, however, Girl A continued her contest entirely on her own. What had previously been daring teenage play moved toward solitary illness.

There is nothing shocking about such stories; we happen upon them every day. Until something along these lines occurs in the life of an adolescent we actually know, though, these tragic teenage tales remain much too remote. But we inevitably hear about tragedies closer at hand as we raise our kids. On a lark, a girl from our son's eleventh-grade class turns over the keys to her family car to a boy she is dating. Both are killed. After a party, four classmates of our daughter's break into a professional office building and sniff a dentist's nitrous oxide. One suffers mild brain damage from insufficient oxygen. On a dare, two thirteen-year-olds from our children's junior high school shoplift at their local mall. They are caught—a good cautionary tale for preadolescents, one might think. But one of the girls is so humiliated by the store detectives that she never quite recovers her self-esteem.

These teenage tales of risk and tragedy require airing around our houses. At the table, our children can bear sad stories, if told with care. If the fables do not eventually revert to "That's like *you,* Mark" or "That's the way *your* crowd behaves, Lucy," these tales can be digested right along with dinner.

Another way that we can discuss play risks with our teenagers is to go to films together. Movies allow for plenty of talk about *those* on-screen people, *those* on-screen forays into danger. By discussing film protagonists, we can easily bypass our own adolescents' defensiveness. Over after-the-movie pizza, considerable back-and-forth talk can take place. To keep such conversations moving along pleasantly, we must keep our moralizing to a minimum. Remember old Aesop of *Fables* fame? He was able to teach his life lessons in just a few words. For most adolescents, the lessons to be gathered from these darkest forms of teenage play are self-evident. Young people just have to drop their denial long enough to be able to "see."

Of course, we must also supervise, check on, appropriately ground, and otherwise punish our adolescents if they are ever to emerge alive and well at the other end of this dangerous time of life. And, of course, day-by-day, week-by-week communication among families is needed, whether or not there are cautionary tales to tell. But it was particularly heartening for me to learn a month after the tragic *Challenger* explosion of 1986 that virtually every teenager I interviewed had been trying to obtain more information about *Challenger.* It was just as heartening to learn that an almost as high percentage of parents had already discussed *Challenger* with their kids. If we were able to talk a while back about that almost unspeakably sad event, we can talk today about more local and immediate tragedies. In doing so, our teenagers may emerge into light from the denser shadows cast by their play.

BESIDES daring, another diversion perfected during adolescence is solitary play. Although it has its origins in the crib when an infant discovers ten strangely distinct toes wiggling above the blanket, solitary play becomes its most elaborate, complex, and creative in the teen years.

Children's pretend reaches great complexity by the ages of seven and eight, but by preadolescence, it appears to subside. Rather than give up these moments of shared fantasies, however, a child's daydreams move mentally indoors to a more private place. By adolescence, kids write out fantasy-based literature, poetry, and journal entries. They draw, sketch out, and computer-generate fantasied creations. If one looks broadly at this preadolescent and adolescent transition from communal pretend to more private pretend, one can see that often, internally, the sense of play is retained. "I'm just toying with an idea," the teenager answers, stopped by a question like "A penny for your thoughts?" Or, "I'm just wandering about in my mind." The college freshman on winter break says, "Oops, I'm sorry, I wasn't really here." And those of us long past attaining adulthood drift off, as well. Solitary mind play is pleasurable and relaxing and may even be accompanied by a subtle smile.

For a few lucky adolescents, solitary plays of the mind—for instance, writing, computer tinkering, videotape making, film-making—become the seeds of fruitful adult careers. But even more promising for a greater number of adolescents are the entirely mental scenarios that they invent—of courtship, for instance, or of a courtroom fight against a parent, or of an op-ed piece against the high school administrators. As opposed to the "What if?" question, which promotes a mental picture, "How would it go?" promotes a mental dialogue. I call these playful internal conversations "scenarios."

Just as a dream is an experiment of action while the body lies partially paralyzed and asleep, the scenario is an experiment of action while the body remains motionless or otherwise monotonously engaged. Scenarios are entirely safe at the same time that all sorts of unsafe social exchanges are being planned, reviewed, implemented, and completed. This type of solitary adventure may seem to be useless, but it leads toward the establishment of better social

judgment and decision-making. And all of the time that an internal
dialogue ensues, it feels pleasurable. Nothing is actually ventured
or lost. Everything is gained. And it is safe.

We adults continue to dawdle inside our minds with "What if?"
and "How would it go?" questions. Such mind plays enable us to
see another person's point of view. They help us to strategize personal actions, including those actions we might take following the
various tacks that someone else might take. Solitary mind play
empowers us. Within a minute or two, we adults usually develop a
plan—a "game plan," we call it in common parlance. And it usually works better than what would happen if we acted purely on
impulse. We can also share such fantasies with those with whom we
are particularly close.

Along these lines, "hanging out" becomes one of the more regular and highly developed forms of adolescent play. In hanging out,
the teenager indulges in solitary mental plays in the company of
others who are like-minded. An excuse is found for getting
together—"We both like rap music," "We stop at Barbara's after
school 'cause her house is on the way home for all of us," "We're the
only three cigarette smokers in our class, so we don't bother anyone
else's lungs when we get together." The group meets somewhere,
and hanging out is accomplished.

Hanging out involves scattered conversation. It involves a
shared place—the corner café near the junior high school, the
high school band room, the journalism classroom, the YMCA gym,
the street, the supermarket parking lot. It involves an activity that
serves as the excuse for getting together—viola-section practice, a
quick turn at one-on-one basketball, an afternoon on skateboards,
an early evening at the mall. Much of the time that adolescents
spend together is actually spent with minds on idle. Thoughts come
and go. Pictures flit in and out. A one-sentence secret is shared.
Acquaintanceships build. Quiet ensues. Lasting friendships take
hold.

Some of us adults are lucky enough to hold on to our hanging-
out habits. A number of us do it at health clubs. Others do so at

bars. Some manage a few leisurely moments at the corner coffee shop, Bloomingdale's, the local antique store, the barbershop, a certain park bench, an espresso machine, the grocery store on the next block, the newspaper stand, that teetery step on the front porch of the old general store. Hanging out makes friends. It allows a person time for the newspaper and coffee. It allows time for a good look-see, a chance to smell the smells or to register the sounds. It puts the mind at rest. It just might create an idea or two. Most of all, hanging out builds a sense of pleasure. It's a good way to start a day. And it's a good way to finish one.

ADOLESCENTS must learn about one final aspect of playing before they decide whether or not to play at all. And that's how to handle the politics of play. Teenage players must discover how they will balance their drives for individual excellence with the general needs of their teams. They must learn how to handle prejudiced racial, religious, gender, and otherwise malicious attitudes. They need to remain tactful and considerate as they play, despite their intense emotions about the games that they play in. Sometimes it becomes impossible, and a teenage player also needs to realize when impossibility is at hand. This is the primary reason I like the story of Ramon Marquez so much. As an adolescent Ramon was a naturally politic player. But when he perceived that an impasse had arisen, he made his move, a courageous move, and I admire him for it.

Ramon was a sixteen-year-old high school soccer all-star who was born in Nicaragua. Shortly after his mother died, the two-year-old Ramon and his father immigrated to the United States and settled in the distant Bay Area suburbs, where Ramon's dad opened a ladies' hair salon. From the time that he was a preschooler, Ramon, his father, and a few Central American friends of his father's played soccer on Sundays. The lad loved the game and the game loved him. Though basically a normal kid, he needed to see me in his midteens after witnessing a boy run over and killed at his bus stop.

Early in my acquaintance with Ramon, I learned that his high school soccer-league team caused him some problems. Ramon was perfectly bilingual, but his English was marked by Central American intonations and inflections. His soccer style looked "South American," too, to the other boys and the coach. His beautician father was also derided by the team. "Son of a Spanish-speaking faggot," the boys called Ramon. And despite two fistfights on that score, Ramon's teammates kept needling him.

One day shortly after he started psychotherapy, Ramon told me of a cheer that his all-white team made sure that he heard at practice—the last straw in a valiant attempt to stay on and play. The cheer—or jeer, to better characterize it—included insults about Ramon's dead mother, slams at his father's work, mentions of Proposition 209 (a referendum passed in November 1996 that ended California's affirmative action programs), and allusions to Ramon's manhood.

Upon hearing the cheer for the first time, Ramon turned toward the coach, who had heard it, too. The man was silent. A small smirk lingered at the corner of his mouth. No one was about to stop this team from turning on a fellow player. "You must have done something to offend them," the coach said later in private.

"I quit!" said the boy, and he walked out. He didn't consult with me on this. Ramon did it first, talked with me later.

I believe that Ramon Marquez knew exactly when he had to quit his team. He recognized utter impossibility when it loomed before him. He perceived stubborn prejudice. He realized that this team and this coach had never wanted him. Despite his previous year's successes—the team had won the league championship and he had made the California High School All-Star list—the coach had given special praise to two other players at that year's awards banquet. Never once did the head man mention the best player on his team.

Immediately after his son quit, Pedro Marquez told me he was considering moving to San Francisco, with its greater cultural and racial mix of soccer players. But this would entail a long commute for him to his salon. Mr. Marquez also wanted to report the coach to the soccer league. But Ramon wouldn't let his dad do this. He was hoping for an athletic scholarship to college. How could he get one if his dad made a public fuss about a coach? Ramon quieted his dad down. The lad was the better politician of the two.

Ramon then found himself facing a crucial decision. Everything about moving his play from adolescence into adulthood hinged on it. He carefully reflected on his choices. He could quit soccer forever. He could move to San Francisco. Or he could join another team close to his school (an "only fair" one, he told me). This team practiced just down the bus line from the other team, and the new soccer coach was promising to pick him up at home every weekend that there was a distant match. This third possibility sounded to Ramon like the best—despite the relative inferiority of the team. Ramon petitioned his league for an immediate switch. He was learning the politics of play the hard way.

The soccer league was known to be particularly slow and reluctant to respond to players' requests. But with Ramon's written quotations from his old team's cheer, the authorities allowed this young man to change squads within a couple of weeks. And so, Ramon sacrificed little playing time. Losing him made the old team drop one or two games toward the end of their season. Getting him made his new team finish with its first winning record in three years. But nobody realized in this short period what the teams had lost and gained. And, of course, Ramon didn't make the High School All-Stars that season.

This current soccer season, Ramon's adopted team has won their first four games. It is a little early to tell if Ramon can win an athletic scholarship to a top-level college, but it seems likely because a couple of smaller schools have already shown considerable interest in him. Daring to quit a bad playing situation temporarily put Ramon Marquez's play in jeopardy. But the right decision enabled him to continue playing into the future. And the kid figured out all of the politics himself. He grew from this understanding.

*   *   *

IN ADOLESCENCE, far too many of us give up on our play. The psychologists and psychoanalysts of developmental staging may have been correct in their observation that teenagers tend to stop playing, but by now we can recognize that they were probably wrong in attributing this stoppage to an adolescent's increasing thoughtfulness and maturity. In my view, it takes emotional maturity for a young person to withstand outside pressures to stop playing, and it takes fortitude to make the time for play. At crucial points in life—adolescence, for one, but also after tragedy, illness, retirement, and grave disappointment—it is tempting to quit.

One of the factors controlling whether an adolescent will go on playing is time management. Like Sarah, my concerto-playing niece, any teenager has homework to do, phone calls to make, friends to be with, home chores to accomplish, parents to fight with, extracurricular clubs to join, and mandatory family activities to attend. Just being an adolescent, enduring it and mastering it, takes energy and time. Play, and along with it the sense of playfulness, can easily be lost in the competition for time.

Then, too, a number of kids stop playing in adolescence because of the ever-increasing and bitter contesting at this time of life. In Western societies, adolescent singers must perform at recitals, dancers must appear solo, actors must participate in dramas and prepare monologues, athletes must be tracked with statistics. Even adolescent Boy Scouts are judged by their progress toward becoming Eagle Scouts. A game can easily turn more serious than fun. And the work that goes into it—bodybuilding, running, memorizing, exercises, deadlines—may overwhelm any sense of enjoyment. An adolescent can easily become tired and dispirited.

Teenagers find themselves losing confidence in their play, too, because of the sometimes merciless self-examination at this stage of life. Every adolescent makes mistakes, and these may occasionally mar a teenager's self-esteem. The drive to go on playing depends a great deal on having an intact self-image. Any good adolescent player experiences an off day. A game or a string of games may be lost because of an error. The good player may also drop into a slump or suffer an injury. At such times, encouraging coaches, teachers, friends, parents, may save teenagers from themselves, their own worst critics.

Additional psychological factors occasionally discourage adolescents from playing. Having to compete with a parent may be an issue, for instance. A boy who recently developed a good golf game might suddenly have his father's greens scores to contend with. Is it psychologically worth it for the young man to revive unresolved oedipal struggles? This time the son might just win. Winning in these circumstances feels extremely stressful. Children of excelling parents are often compelled to look for different modes of play from the ones that Mom and Dad prefer. This is a double-edged sword. Even though the adolescent has inherited the same biological skills for play, the family triangle may feel too formidable, too intense, for any attempt at same-gamesmanship. Sometimes it is the confidence and encouragement of the parents themselves that helps a teenager out of such a bind. Sometimes it is a grandparent's or a teacher's guidance. Sometimes it is the general friendliness of the community at large.

We parents find ourselves in the difficult position of wanting to show our pleasure at our adolescent children's accomplishments, but not *too* much pleasure. It is one thing for young people to feel that we are proud of them, and quite another to feel that we are vicariously living out our lives through them. The sense that we enjoy their play too much may drive our teenagers out of their games. Or it may create enormous internal conflicts over playing.

The Australian film *Shine,* based on the pianist David Helfgott's life, is a moving example of teenage play that created intense psychological turmoil inside a family and, eventually, inside of David Helfgott's mind. After young David, counter to his father's wishes, left Australia for England to study the piano on scholarship, he won a prestigious British contest with a performance of his father's favorite piece, the Rachmaninoff Third Piano Concerto. As he finished playing, the lad's conflict over winning versus defying, over stepping out of his father's shadow while cringing under its authority, caused an acute emotional crisis. The crisis, and no doubt his genetic propensities, drove the young player psychotic.

David Helfgott did not recover well enough to develop a concert career until his father died, he himself married, and he was finally able to determine his own destiny. For a decade in the Australian mental institutions where he was treated, this young man's desire to play stayed cocooned, but not destroyed. He did not reemerge on the concert stage until he gained back his self-confidence by playing piano at a wine bar in Western Australia.

In 1997, with a full concert and recording career developing, the forty-nine-year-old Helfgott still muttered encouragements aloud to himself before he played. For instance, prior to recording Liszt's Hungarian Rhapsody No. 2 early in 1997, he was overheard saying, "Pedal, pedal, I love pedal. . . . I'm pretty good sometimes. I'm pretty good sometimes. I'll play if it kills me. Just keep smiling, just keep smiling. Better keep playing. Better keep playing." Obviously, Helfgott's mental preparations for play were painful for him. But when he could let himself go, the experience of playing was self-healing.

Every teenager cannot win in competitive games, even though he or she may be willing to practice. But one important consolation to all adolescent players is that many youthful modes of play last throughout life. A high school tennis player—if not discouraged by early losses—can indulge in enjoyable tennis all through maturity. A young clarinetist, who never once won a contest, can perform as a grown-up in a concert band, take up klezmer music, specialize in Gershwin songs. Good rock dancers can later learn ballroom dancing. Adequate, but enthusiastic, adolescent cooks develop as they go.

Another consolation is that practiced teenage players become resilient enough to shift their particular play interests as adults. They can move from the swimming team to a spot in journalism or debates. They can transfer their love for rowing into a love for sailing. Through playing, they develop enough flexibility to continue to find other, entirely different, and more age-appropriate modes.

As Brian Sutton-Smith demonstrated through his research and his own life, playing hard and long at one activity enables a person to play hard and long at another. The contemporary Hall of Fame wide receiver Jerry Rice, for instance, will someday become, he says, a golfer. Injured severely at the beginning of the 1997–98 football season, Rice demonstrated the emotional elasticity he had gained over his years at sports by serving as a volunteer wide-receiver coach for the Forty-Niners. Today's nonplayer will have more trouble starting the whole process deep into maturity.

Our teenagers need the courage to keep on playing because turning points show up all over the adolescent map. A band conductor dislikes a kid, and there goes all the pleasure from the trumpet. A hockey team doesn't click. A job or a school schedule conflicts. An injury requires days, maybe months, of rehabilitation.

Discouraged adolescents often garner praise for giving up on their play. "I'm glad you've cut back your heavy schedule," says a headmaster. "Now you can really get to work," says a parent. Yes, much play does not flow automatically into acceptances to good colleges or unlimited career choices. But ongoing play through the teenage years accounts for an ongoing spirit of playfulness. If a person stops playing, there will be an unfortunate change. It is clear to me that we don't have to give up the pleasure principle just because we accept reality. I hope—by now—it's clear to you, too.

THE STORY of Shirley Temple is the tale of a crucial adolescent turning point in play. In her early teens, Shirley suffered a dramatic reversal of fortune. And I believe that this came about, in part, because of a youthful shift in Shirley's sense of fun.

The child actress, born on April 23, 1928, in Santa Monica, California, experienced an extremely successful film career from ages six to eleven. She was America's favorite movie star, ranking number one at the box office for four straight years (1935–38). Adults went to the "picture show" just to see Shirley. She outranked both Clark Gable and Jean Harlow in popularity. Then, in 1939, Shirley Temple fell to the number five position, and in 1940, she could no longer be located among the top twenty Hollywood stars.

What happened? While most child performers don't continue in the limelight as adults, in Shirley's case, her stardom began to dim when the Great Depression began to clear. America in its diminishing misery no longer needed the twelve-year-old lass's optimistic company. Then, too, Shirley had developed a slightly stocky look by the ages of nine and ten—a chunky prelude to a prettier, petite later adolescence. Perhaps she was not as physically appealing. But psychologically the most interesting factor to me was that Shirley appeared to stop enjoying her forays into the movies. Her previously obvious playfulness had somehow slipped away.

At ten or eleven years of age, Shirley hit a silent turning point in her love affair with the motion picture. She could no longer have a wonderful time performing before the cameras. And her audience caught on. The icon "little Shirley" remained forever loved. She is loved today. But the early-adolescent Shirley was a different matter.

Before looking more closely at Shirley Temple's decline and virtual fall in Hollywood by the age of twelve, we should consider her psychological beginnings. The third child and first girl in her family, Shirley arrived to Gertrude and George Temple thirteen years after their first child, George Jr., was born. The couple had met when Gertrude, a frustrated dancer (without ever having had a dance lesson), went out for an evening of dancing to Henry Kramer's cotillion for adults. There Gertrude, just seventeen, met twenty-three-year-old George Temple, a school dropout by the age of fourteen. The short, stocky man and the tall, thin, late-adolescent girl danced with each other enough times over the next several weeks to fall in love and to begin what turned out to be a sixty-year marriage. George became the branch manager of a bank. Gertrude took care of the house and their two boys. The Temples developed close friendships with two other couples, the Isleibs and the Fergusons, each of whom, in 1926, gave birth to a blond, curly-haired girl.

Gertrude Temple decided that she and George must have such a girl, as well. Soon after, they conceived. Although their fetus's sex was unknown to them, Gertrude named it Shirley Jane and exposed it to what Shirley, in her 1988 autobiography, *Child Star,* called a "prenatal blitzkrieg" of music, art museums, ocean walks, and movie matinees. The expectant mother tried just about anything to ensure that her fetus would become a girl—and an actress and dancer, to boot. After Shirley's birth, when the success of Gertrude's regimen had apparently proved itself, there was no letup. Gertrude danced around Shirley's playpen with a tambourine. She played a plethora of radio music. When Shirley was three, Gertrude enrolled her in Meglin's Dance Studio, a place on Buster Keaton's studio lot for starstruck Hollywood "kiddies" to learn the basics for song-and-dance careers. Every Sunday night, Gertrude Temple set her child's hair in precisely fifty-six curls. The little tyke loved it. For her, all the lessons and the grooming were a form of play.

"Discovered" at age three, Shirley Temple was signed by Jack Hays to make a number of one-reel "Baby Burlesk" movies for a company ironically called Educational Films. Shirley was the female lead opposite one "nasty" girl and several boys. They wore diapers with overlarge safety pins. Above their diapers, their costumes mimicked the most sophisticated of adult outfits. These kids sang and acted out takeoffs on the plots of popular movies. *The Front Page* became *The Runt Page. What Price Glory?* was to become *What Price Gloria?* but was eventually changed to *War Babies.* By the time she turned five, Shirley Temple had been set up in a Marlene Dietrich–inspired outfit complete with off-the-shoulder blouse, a vamp-style feather boa, and diapers. She was given a torch song to sing, along with instructions to hug one boy while lip-kissing another. The Baby Burlesk series, which eventually extended to eight films, exploited forbidden adult wishes. These films were *not* for children. Verging on pedophilia and voyeurism, the series, in a sense, foretold what Brooke Shields's mother would eventually allow little Brooke to do in *Pretty Baby.*

Mrs. Temple presented an odd amalgam of underprotectiveness and strict command of her tiny Shirley. While failing to protect the tot from a weird form of exploitation, she never let her out of sight. "I wanted her to be artistic," Gertrude Temple told *Parents* magazine in October 1938. "I was determined she should *excel* at something. . . . When I speak, she minds. There is no argument, no pleading and begging. I have never permitted any impudence, crying, or display of temper. I have also taught her not to be afraid of anything. . . . I began this training very early and it means constant vigilance."

Shirley's first spoken phrase in life was "Don't do 'at!" She wrote that it was probably mimicry of what her mother repeatedly said to her. As a small child, however, Shirley Temple was uncommonly happy. She willingly took Gertrude's directions and amiably went with her mother all over Hollywood for auditions. Her break came when the Fox Film Company hired her to do a song-and-dance number with James Dunn called "Baby Take a Bow" in the vaudeville-style movie *Stand Up and Cheer* (1934). After viewing the child through the camera, Fox immediately signed her to a contract, including an additional contract for her mother as Shirley's acting coach and hairdresser. The six-year-old, repositioned by Fox as being just five, was then lent out to Paramount for her first big role (*Little Miss Marker,* 1934). In returning to Fox, Shirley danced as a leading lady in *Baby Take a Bow* (1934) and, after that, in three or four films a year. In 1935, she won a pint-sized Academy Award. She loved what she was doing. For Shirley, studio life was "play."

In the films made at the beginning of her career—in *Stand Up and Cheer* or in *Baby Take a Bow,* for instance—Shirley clearly gave her viewers the animal signals for play. We can see them today on tape. Before singing and dancing, she smiles and bows, just the way a puppy or a polar bear does. Her play face automatically sets the viewer for the beginnings of something charming, silly, enjoyable, fun. The first-time watcher in the darkened theater probably smiled back and, who knows, maybe even nodded a bow, as well. Those biological signals—along with Shirley's unusually deep dimples, one on each side, and her cute curtsies—could be read and accepted by anyone. "Let's play," Shirley beckoned to the average grown-up. And an adult world, unable to play because of ongoing financial and social catastrophe, accepted her invitation. Without their children in tow, adults repeatedly came to watch Shirley. Like Babe, the Australian pig who enchanted 1990s film audiences of all ages, Shirley Temple carried universal appeal. But unlike Babe, Shirley outscored all other contemporary stars in popularity.

The leading lady of American film had little time to play with her neighborhood "gang." Except for ceremonial visits, such as on birthdays, she was kept from contact with peers. She was given her own studio bungalow and her own private teacher. Through a lack of opportunity, she was forced to accomplish virtually all of her childhood play on camera. And with adults. Shirley described her sensations during her first musical number with Jimmy Dunn as "basking in the pleasure of my new tap shoes." Learning new lyrics during breaks in filming was "exhilarating," she wrote. "What nobody but Mother and I knew was how much I really *loved* to sing and dance. . . . I would gladly have rehearsed all day." "Coming to work in the morning," she said, "I rejoiced. And I sorrowed when the day ended."

In fact, singing and dancing for films were not Shirley's only studio-inspired pleasures. She made up a kind of game for herself in which, by comparing the heat from the spotlights on her forehead with the heat that she felt on her cheeks, she could know exactly where on the set she was to be and at what angle she was supposed to position herself. She became a wonder of cooperation with directors. She also developed another self-imposed game, learning her tap routines not by watching her studio instructors, but by listening to the sounds of their shoes. Her on-screen dances in four films with the great dancer Bill (Bojangles) Robinson were about the best things that the little movie actress ever did. They were play for her. And they have become, over the years, her classic moments. "The smile on my face was not acting," Shirley wrote later of her time with Robinson. "I was ecstatic." Bojangles Robinson became one of Shirley Temple's best friends. To be more exact, he was her favorite playmate.

Gertrude went everywhere with her daughter. The child and mother became isolated in a blanket of privacy. Ostensibly, Shirley's virtual quarantine was meant to keep people from taking advantage of her. But it also reflected Gertrude's way of teaching Shirley not to be afraid of anything by dint of "constant vigilance." The six- and seven-year-old child star exhibited tiny rebellions against her mother, such as forming friendships with adults on the studio back lot, adults to whom she did not owe any duty to behave. She also willfully stole scenes from the famous actor Lionel Barrymore (in *The Little Colonel*, 1935). But with Gertrude Temple, the little girl perpetually behaved as the soul of respect. In fact, the final sentence of the sixty-year-old film star and successful diplomat's autobiography was "Thanks, Mom."

From the ages of seven to ten, Shirley Temple's playful personality single-handedly overrode the increasingly stereotypical plots that the Twentieth Century–Fox studio created for her, tales of a parentless waif who inevitably latches on to the first gruff, single male she can find. The child's love of moviemaking and her natural on-camera playfulness intrigued an ever-growing audience. Any adult watching her was a potential play partner. Her audience, at least in these younger, golden years, automatically wanted to join right in.

However, a devastating ambivalence about play appeared in Shirley Temple at about the age of ten. What had previously been pure fun began to turn in part to drudgery. What had previously been unbelievably easy was becoming hard.

Shirley Temple's first menstrual period occurred on her real eleventh (the studio's tenth) birthday. The year or two before this developmental landmark are particularly difficult ones for girls. Prepubescent and early-adolescent girls' attitudes toward older women, particularly their own mothers, become challenging, sometimes belligerent. At a garden party at Val-Kill, Eleanor Roosevelt's country home, the ten-year-old Shirley purposely hit Mrs. Roosevelt on the backside with a slingshot-propelled pebble. Yet the lass was not reprimanded by anyone connected with the First

Lady—Shirley's personality, up until then, had been that cute, that much fun. Preadolescent girls' behavior toward their female peers becomes competitive, too, and frequently downright mean. In a girl's preliminary quest to establish her own identity, she tends to reject the well-known and the familiar. The self often becomes an object of contempt. Mothers become undesirable role models. Adults are "old" and to be pitied. Boys and men are the objects of intense curiosity and, sometimes, of a strangely mature vampishness. Lolita did not emerge from Vladimir Nabokov's imagination as a unique, never-to-be-duplicated character. Despite the novelist's exaggeration, there was a universal element to her.

Shirley Temple's prepubescent behaviors began to move toward rebelliousness and self-questioning. Whenever she could, she stole into her mother's cache of chocolate. The candy went straight to young Shirley's chin, hips, and thighs. The results were obvious, despite adept costuming. The child became increasingly self-conscious. More than once in her 1988 autobiography, the sixty-year-old Shirley castigated herself for having short, plump legs. A *Washington Post* reporter didn't help in this regard. H. I. Philips wrote, "Shirley's getting matronly, Shirley's getting fat / At eleven all joints creak / Life is just like that." Shirley was actually twelve years old on May 18, 1940, when the *Post* published those lines. But the young actress's crisis regarding her own play—whether to laugh, to smile, to be as optimistic and as tickled with life and with her playmates, the adults, as she used to be—had already come and gone.

Shirley became a different person off the screen at about the age of ten. She had previously been a joy to work with, according to any number of coactors and directors. Now she arrived later and later on the set. In her autobiography, she stated that this increasing tardiness was due to Gertrude's growing concerns about her own middle age: she had to get her makeup on just right and her teeth well scrubbed before leaving with Shirley for the studio. Shirley began refusing interviews with reporters. A tour to the 1939–40 New York World's Fair was suggested by Mike Todd, but Gertrude Temple responded, "Shirley will never do a tour. She's too shy!" The young actress began to snipe at wardrobe mistresses, obvious substitutes for Gertrude, arguing adamantly to one that her costume for *The Little Princess* (1939) should not be shredded and aged from a new dress, but rather, bought from a used-clothing store. She reduced another wardrobe assistant to silent battles with a buttonhook. Asked by a reporter whether Twentieth Century–Fox was pushing Shirley into maintaining the "personality which made her reputation," Gertrude Temple replied, "Yes, but it isn't her personality now."

Shirley's newfound peevishness and competition with adults showed up in her reactions toward adult visitors. Orson Welles, inquiring of the eleven-year-old whether she had listened to his broadcast of H. G. Wells's *War of the Worlds,* received back, "Nelson Eddy was why I listened." Noël Coward came to visit her cottage on the Twentieth Century–Fox studio grounds and briefly sat in while Shirley attempted to do a few fractions. Bored, Coward walked out, saying, "I never could do fractions either." After he left, Shirley quipped to her teacher, Frances Klampt, "He must be over thirty and he *still* doesn't know how." At lunch with Shirley in a New York restaurant, Gertrude Lawrence struck the preadolescent as overly aware that people were watching her. As Lawrence fussed nervously with the elaborate folds at her neckline, the child interrupted, "My, you seem uncomfortable, Miss Lawrence. It must be because your dress doesn't fit you well."

Films started revealing Shirley's newly acquired struggles with play. In *Heidi* (1937), she was asked to do a Dutch song-and-dance number, "Wooden Shoes," that made her look awkward and tired. In *Rebecca of Sunnybrook Farm* (1938), Shirley was asked to sing a couple of her old movie hits once again out of pure nostalgia—"Animal Crackers in My Soup" and "The Good Ship Lollipop." Singing these ditties made the ten-year-old look deenergized compared to the supercharged six-year-old imp that everybody could still remember. In *The Little Princess* (1939), Shirley was supposed to do a ballet number, but the studio discovered that she was unable to get up on her toes. Initial failure to do something in the realm of dance had never stopped this game young girl from trying before, but this time it did. The studio choreographers, rather than let her ballet scene be scrubbed, surrounded their child star with accomplished ballet dancers and had her swoop, twirl, and pivot in the foreground. This was not fun for Shirley, and it shows on her eleven-year-old face.

In the movies she made when she was twelve, *The Blue Bird* (1940) and *Young People* (1940), Shirley appears to have lost her desire to persist in any film-centered play. She looks sullen and unsmiling. She sings a few songs halfheartedly, and the occasional cute little pout has grown into a Brigitte Bardot–like sulk. Although the pubescent girl followed directors' instructions with a practiced actor's obedience, her performances held little joy or spontaneity. The dimples, still there, rarely beckoned anyone to enter a fun-filled world. In *The Blue Bird,* a film based on Maurice Maeterlinck's children's classic, Shirley depicted a more irksome, selfish, envious character than Maeterlinck had conceived. At twelve, she insisted on acting this way. "Gone was goodness," Shirley later wrote, "enter evil. The character appealed to me, a peevish, greedy, spiteful brat, the sort anyone would like to put over a knee and wallop. . . . I remained nasty until far too late into the film for successful redemption." According to *Time* magazine, after *The Blue Bird* "laid [its] egg," Shirley's image was "in tatters."

Gertrude Temple recognized that something must be going wrong for Shirley and rescued her by placing her in the seventh grade at Westlake School for Girls, a demanding but cool setting where Shirley could get a good education and spend more time with peers. However, filmmaking had already stopped being play for young Shirley. She could not make herself "belt out" a song the way the new screen sensation Judy Garland did, even though the director of *Kathleen* (1941) urged and urged her to try.

In her later teens, Shirley Temple's film career was briefly rescued by David O. Selznick, who hired her to costar as a serious teenager in the popular film *Since You Went Away* (1944) and the less popular *I'll Be Seeing You* (1944). But although Shirley made nine additional films for such studios as Warner Brothers, RKO, Twenti-eth Century–Fox, and Columbia, she had few real triumphs. Shirley married in her late teens, partly to try to escape her parents. This first marriage, to John Agar, ended in divorce but yielded a daughter. After 1949, Shirley retired from films to be a full-time mother and to enjoy her second marriage, a happy one to Charles Black, a northern Californian who was entirely removed from Shirley's mother and any connection to her old-time films.

Shirley Temple Black gradually began to "play" at politics and found entirely new enjoyment and pleasure in government and international diplomacy. She eventually served as U.S. chief of pro-tocol, U.S. representative to the United Nations, U.S. ambassador to the Republic of Ghana, and U.S. ambassador to Czechoslovakia.

The roots of this governmental play might retrospectively be found in the way that Shirley's studio teacher, Frances Klampt, was able to arouse the young star's interest in her studies. Whenever Shirley Temple had a visitor—the Japanese ambassador S. Saburo Kurusu, who presided on the day the Japanese bombed Pearl Har-bor, for instance, or three Soviet transpolar flyers, Andrei Yuma-shev, Mikhail Gromov, and Sergei Danilin—Miss Klampt insisted that Shirley study a number of things about that country: its his-tory, literature, geography, and people. It was fun for the little movie star, and this source of early pleasure became the prime source of Shirley Temple Black's rebirth. From what I can tell, Ambassador Black has deeply enjoyed her second career. And she matured into a thoroughly delightful person. She rediscovered play.

7

How Play Moves Through History and Around the World

We didn't always think of childhood and play the way that we do today. The story of a scampish little French prince will help me illustrate this point. By the time Louis XIII of France, the keeper of the King's Musketeers, was a late adolescent, his life was almost half over. But by the time he was an adolescent, he had already indulged in more modes of play than most of us will ever try. This wasn't merely because Louis was a king. Or because he was French. It was because he lived at a certain transitional time in history when children were just beginning to be singled out as special and separate. Along with this newfound position of children came some speedy changes in the nature of play.

Louis XIII was born on September 27, 1601, at Fontainebleau to the elderly King Henri IV and his second queen, Marie de Medici. No dauphin had been born for eighty-four years, so tiny Monsieur's birth (he was not known as Louis until his public christening when he was five years old) was greeted with a hearty nationwide celebration. A special physician, Jean Héroard, was hired to tend to the royal prince. The doctor spent the last twenty-seven years of his life observing and caring for young Monsieur. Héroard kept a journal about his patient's behavior and health that was eventually published as *Journal sur l'Enfance et la Jeunesse de Louis XIII.* Because the good doctor was particularly interested in how the dauphin played, he recorded in his notes, some of them still unpublished today, considerable information about the toys, customs, and age ranges for players that characterized play at the beginning of the seventeenth century.

In 1960, the distinguished French historian Phillipe Ariès used these notes to prove that the whole idea of "childhood" was being born at the time that Louis XIII was conceived. We have seen much earlier in this book that the concept of child development evolved in the twentieth century. But the idea of childhood itself came earlier—with Louis XIII and his contemporaries. Even though Monsieur was unique in being a king-in-the-making, some of the ways that he played almost four hundred years ago will still strike our contemporary sensibilities as unusual, to say the least.

Three aspects of the dauphin's play were uncommon: its mix of babyishness and maturity, its mix of solo and communal play, and its mix of variously aged and socially classed players. Historians tell us that mixes frequently mean that an important change is taking place. Young people had generally been unnoticed from the Middle Ages up to the seventeenth century, but by the birth of Monsieur, they were losing their invisibility. For many hundreds of years, children's lack of specialness had enabled them to rove freely around their environments and to play with all sorts of adults, regardless of age or class. The change that took place during the age of Louis XIII ensured that children would be safer and more lovingly treated. But it also ensured that they would lose their privileges and independence.

Almost from birth on, Monsieur was exposed to an odd combination of child-oriented and sophisticated modes of amusement. According to the British editor and 1929 translator of Dr. Héroard,

Lucy Crump, in her book, *Nursery Life 300 Years Ago,* the French crown prince lived in a special children's palace at Saint-Germain-en-Laye with his staff, his half siblings (children of the king's various mistresses), full siblings (eventually there were five), the sons of great nobles who were sent to live near him to complete their gentlemanly educations, children who served as pages on the king's staff, and children belonging to various adults who staffed the place. Monsieur happily played alone or in crowds. He often frolicked along with adults—maids, soldiers, ladies and gentlemen of the court, his doctor, his nurses. During his infancy, he was given a hobbyhorse, a windmill, and a whirling top, still typical today of young childhood at solitary play. But at seventeen months, he was also noted to play the violin while singing a song. This was young, one might say, to be exposed to such a valuable, easily destroyed, and hard-to-manage instrument, even if the fiddler was a French crown prince and the fiddle, a pre-Stradivarius model.

Monsieur was dark complected, with protuberant eyes and big, puffy cheeks. His behavior was "cheeky," too. Once the two-year-old had a temper tantrum when the king tried to kiss him. Henri became angry and showed the child a rod. "Who is this for?" he asked.

"For you!" snapped the tiny prince. There was nothing to do but to laugh. The child was not handsome, but he was mightily amusing.

At seventeen months, the dauphin was noted to have indulged in an adult game called mall with his father's courtiers. During this game, the boy injured one of the king's party, M. de Longueville, with a "muffled shot." At twenty-three months, Monsieur was taken to his father's apartments, where he danced a repertoire of steps—bourrée, galliard, saraband—to the sounds of a viol. Young Louis performed his dances in the recently developed costume of male childhood—a kind of bib and tucker (a dress that was worn under a robe) and a gown, or robe, that survived from the men's long coats of earlier centuries. Little girls dressed just like their mothers—in miniature adult fashions of the day. Boys were, thus,

just beginning to be dressed in unique, child-specific clothing—
long gowns when young; shorter ones when older. Boys did not
stop wearing this kind of dresslike outfit until the end of the First
World War. Today we still come across old photos of our fathers,
grandfathers, and great-grandfathers clothed in the girlish robes
and tunics of their early childhoods, a special costume, it turns out,
for the specially designated and historically "new" concept of
childhood.

By the time *le petit Monsieur* turned three, he walked the edge
between more babyishness than we tolerate today and more adult-
ness. He could play tennis, something most three-year-old children
today wouldn't even know how to think about. Yet he also greatly
favored "a little carriage full of dolls" presented to him by his
father's state treasurer, Sully. Louis wheeled it all around the castle,
and he was noted to do so for many years, much longer than a
turn-of-the-twenty-first-century child would get away with. Monsieur also enjoyed a miniature cannon and conducted "little mili-
tary engagements with his little lords." He owned a complete set of
child-sized armor, and he often lined up anyone, adult or tot, who
would march along with their costumed prince. A drummer from
the king's own guard beat out the rhythms for the dauphin's mot-
ley band.

Once, at three years of age, Monsieur performed the part of
Cupid in a court ballet, naked as a newborn. Yet, at the same age, he
could make out the letters of the alphabet and was learning to read.
At four and a half, he could write with the help of his father's scribe;
yet he still pretended with his playmates to be a wagoner. He loved
to cut up pieces of paper with scissors. He also loved to paint in oils.
He was immature enough to have to be told that fairy stories were
not real; yet he was allowed to practice archery. During one parlor
game, he lit a candle blindfolded, "as if he were fifteen years old."

At the age of six, Louis joined with older children and adults in
charades, trades (similar to the old TV show *What's My Line?*), and
"cabbages on midsummer day" (kicking the behinds of the participants, teenage pages in his father's court, and receiving plenty of

kicks back). At six, too, he organized a hunt featuring falconry; his party ended up killing a hare, half a dozen quail, and a couple of partridges. He stayed up all night and served as a "bean king" in that year's Twelfth Night festivities. At seven, he formally learned the ways that a proper Frenchman rides and trains a horse. Yet young Louis was still having his troubles forsaking that carriage full of dolls, his miniature army, the dog-pulled go-cart, and pretend, aimed at growing up to be a wagon driver or a cook (an interesting irony, since a wagoner's or a chef's child might more likely play at being king). Louis dressed up as a woman on more than one occasion. Although by six and seven years old he was allowed to watch palace baiting spectacles in which captive bears would maul oxen and dogs, he was simultaneously having his problems "giv[ing] up the games of infancy."

When he reached his eighth birthday, the dauphin was told by his new governor, M. de Souvré, that he was a big boy now and must surrender all childish pursuits. Along with this newfound responsibility, Louis was given permission to wager with adults. Almost immediately, he won a turquoise gem in a raffle. But being invited into the privileges of adulthood didn't necessarily deter him from his more infantile enjoyments. After the deeply saddened and shocked young Louis became king of France at the age of eight and a half—his father was stabbed to death as he rode through the streets of Paris—Louis still played with his toy soldiers and his wagon. In fact, he and his favorite courtier, a young man named de Luynes, who had previously served Henri IV as a falconer, played inside a little fort they constructed in the Tuileries gardens. They did this well after the new king had turned ten and de Luynes had attained majority.

After the assassination of Henri IV, young King Louis was never quite the same. His physical health declined. He became shy. He hankered for a loving, comfortable relationship with a man, the very thing that he had lost with the death of his father. As an adolescent, Louis was dominated by ill-chosen male favorites. As an adult, he was dominated by his ambitious minister, the all-powerful

Richelieu. Somehow Louis did not continue to be playful after he became king of France and began having serious problems at court. Today's historians characterize him as dour. The little scamp could no longer show his enjoyable beginnings. Play effectively fled from his life, as we recognize that it does from so many adolescent and adult lives in contemporary society.

There was little to no acknowledgment of adolescence as a special phase of development during the time of Louis XIII. Until the twentieth century, having an adult body generally meant having to take on adult responsibilities. By the time that Louis was fourteen years and two months old, he *was* an adult, at least in one respect. He was married to the infanta of Spain and that night consummated the marriage, he said to his courtiers, "two times." (Dr. Héroard checked him immediately thereafter and found his penis to be "red.") This happened, however, only after Louis was almost forcibly taken to the queen's, his wife's, bedroom and put into her bed in the presence of his own mother, the queen. In 1615, the boundaries between childhood and maturity still remained unclear.

What is clear to me today, in the Louis XIII story, is how many continuities and discontinuities have occurred in the history of play. We still play tennis at the turn of the twenty-first century. But where is mall? We give our kids hobbyhorses, windmills, and tops. But we don't send them downstairs, undressed as naked Cupids, to meet our dinner guests. Six-year-olds don't stay up all night as Twelfth Night kings. Yet our eighteen-year-olds stay up all night as prom queens and kings. But then, too, what has happened to falconry? Or to the bourrée and the galliard? The history and the geography of play is a story of amazing sameness, yet striking differences.

WE CAN tell from the Louis XIII tale that during his lifetime children began to gain something while simultaneously losing something else. Their gain was for them to become central inside their own families. Their loss was to be kicked out of general society. In the Middle Ages, young people were of little value to their parents because of the high birth and mortality rates and the early ages children would leave home. But those pre-seventeenth-century children who were fortunate enough to survive enjoyed certain advantages. They could mix in multigenerational societies. They could know everybody in town. They could learn about life through experience. They could romp through the same games as their mature counterparts. There were few differences, in fact, between child and adult play.

By removing children from adult society, adults also gained and lost important qualities of life. They could cluster as families and gain the ever so meaningful experience of watching their children grow up near at hand. But young adults also lost their places in community leadership by pulling away from larger society into tight-knit family groups. And their communities lost the impetus to play. After all, if they are about, children impel almost anybody to make merry. But with children penned up in their own houses, whole communities cool their desires to cavort. This is one of the historical reasons, I believe, that play was eventually lost as a key to adult health and happiness. With the children gone, play could be sacrificed without much notice.

We can see from old pictures in museums, especially from the Dutch painters, that before the eighteenth century, middle-class and lower-class children still hung out in bars and on the streets. But as early as the seventeenth century, upper-class families and royalty began grouping together to dote on their children. The idea of "childhood" began as something trendy in the upper classes. It later spread to the urban middle class. Gradually, great communal rites and rituals, in which children had previously participated as equals, and the smaller festivities at inns, marketplaces, drinking establishments, in the streets—gambling, hanging out, dancing, gossiping—became unavailable to the young. Once middle- and lower-class children were enfolded by their families and schools, they became less a part of their towns. Adult rites and games, which had been the property of all, became the province of only a few.

Without whole communities to partake in them, many routines no longer globally entertained. Slowly, these routines settled into the worlds of childhood and of rural life. The old communal rites began to look like games. In fact, they became games.

Phillipe Ariès made the point that childhood play develops out of ritual, that not only are there continuities in play, but that there are continuities from declining rites into rural play and child's play.

Today's children and country folk still demonstrate remnants of old adult ceremonies as they frolic. Ariès was so taken with how avidly children hang on to the old folkways that he said, "Children form the most conservative of human societies." To consider a living example of what the French historian meant, we might think back to the 1958 Hula Hoop craze among adults, adolescents, and school-age children. In earlier times, rings like the Hula Hoop were used in the ritual dances that adults performed on religious festival days. During the late sixteenth century, for instance, a roving Swiss student named Felix Platter (who, by the way, traveled with Jean Héroard's father for a while) described his fascination with the traditional "dance of the hoops," done as part of the Shrove Tuesday festivities in Avignon, France. Young-adult and adolescent nobles and townsfolk took part in this dance, holding gold and white hoops above their heads while they moved rhythmically to the music. Felix Platter wrote, "It was wonderful to see them passing backward and forward under those rings, bending and straightening up and passing one another in time." Phillipe Ariès described watching this kind of hoop dance three hundred years later in the remote villages of the Côte Basque. We recognize, too, that such dances—really writhings of sorts—are practiced today in the turn-of-the-twenty-first-century American preschool. The preservers of the hoop are becoming younger and more remote, it seems.

Speaking of dancing as a remnant of what once involved whole communities, we might also look at the square dance, so currently typical of the summertime American country fair or the suburban couples' club. In one century, square dances moved from whole towns and counties into preservation societies, rural festivities, and the domains of children. Today they are part of the school gym class and the Girl Scout jamboree.

It is interesting to me how during approximately the same period—at the middle of the twentieth century—one historical expert, Phillipe Ariès, reached one conclusion about play while another historical expert, Johan Huizinga, concluded just the opposite. Ariès made a good case in 1960 that play is a leftover from communal ritual and rite. But Huizinga had made just as fine a contrary point years before—that play develops into ritualistic civic and religious activities.

What if both men were correct? What if there has been such a tight connection between recreation and rite over time that either one feeds the other? I think *that* must be what happened in history and continues to happen today. Some play filters down into childhood from ritual. But some play builds into adult institutions, such as the law, philosophy, poetry, religion, art, and myth. Some toys and sporting behaviors serve simultaneous play and ritualistic purposes. And some play stays put—it simply begins and ends as play.

As Huizinga saw it, not only does play contribute toward rite and religion, but it helps to develop man's civil institutions. Play can help to defuse a nation's anger, for example. Consider ancient Roman society. The patricians did not particularly value their captive gladiators. They let these foreign slaves enact the violence of Roman wars while, comfortable in their lightweight togas, the highborn Romans watched safely from their Colosseum seats. The ancients used gladiators in much the same way that our children today use their *Star Wars* figures, Ninja Turtles, and tiny armies. Miniaturization has actually helped society to gain some control over its violence. Not every play ritual is miniaturized, however. Our stadium spectacles—games themselves—remain enormously large-scale, while maintaining a basically nonviolent approach. For instance, our Independence Day fireworks displays, World Cup soccer matches, band competitions, Super Bowl festivities, and "March Madness" basketball tournaments all maintain a playful and ritualistic approach, while emphasizing the peaceful side to competition.

Believe it or not, play has even been built into such dead-serious institutions as the law. In early-twentieth-century Greenland, for instance, Eskimo tribal justice relied on an elaborate routine, known as a drumming contest. To the beats of a drum, a plaintiff and a defendant would take turns attacking each other with real reproaches for real grievances. Intermixed with this, however, the principals also indulged themselves in nasty songs, slanderous talk about each other's families, and witticisms meant to please the communal audience. One could get close to one's opponent, too, snorting in his face, tying him up, bumping him—and this had to be borne by the other with mocking laughter. I guess you'd have to say that some of what the Greenland natives did at these drumming contests was real and some was a game. Occasionally, these quasi-legal happenings ended quickly with a tribal vote. Other times, they extended into many drumming contests over years. In the end, however, tribal spectators would choose a winner.

When I think of the O. J. Simpson trials, I can see a connection between those Los Angeles extravaganzas and the old Greenland drumming rites. With O.J., all of America served as a spectator to a gigantic drumming contest with a "dream team" of defense lawyers, a gaggle of television attorneys, talk-show hosts, writers, opposing witnesses, gossipmongers, paparazzi, jokers, celebrities. Not only did the juries vote—not guilty in the criminal trial—but individuals all over the country "voted" about O.J. among themselves. A Santa Monica civil jury's announcement of their decision that O. J. Simpson was legally responsible for the deaths of his former wife, Nicole, and her friend Ronald Goldman interrupted the television coverage immediately following President Bill Clinton's January 1997 State of the Union address. It was that important to America!

When the O.J. "drumming contests" ended, most everyone in the United States felt some relief. There was the TV news again—real life again. But at the same time, there was an empty spot. Where was the fun over hashing and rehashing O.J.'s character? Where were the jokes? Where were all those commentators? The

Simpson trials provided a massive North American catharsis. Despite the underlying tragedies of a double murder, a hero's fall from grace, a policeman's shame, an urban community's racial divisions, and two children's losses and confusions about their parents, the O.J. trials provided a long-lasting opportunity for grownups to play.

Historically speaking, play appears to build while simultaneously offering us traces of what has been torn away. I see no problem in looking at play as a living thing. After all, bodies build at the same time as they wear down. Some mental processes erode while others are developing. The world grows as it falls to pieces. These processes occur all at once. Play comes to us from the disintegration of civilizations. But play also serves to civilize us. Play changes because it is alive. And this very aliveness enlivens us.

WHILE historians have been intrigued with the continuities between people's games and their institutions, folklorists, psychologists, and anthropologists tend to study the discontinuities. Differences in regions, genders, cultural groups, and stages of development produce differences in the way that certain games are played. Differences also account for some games' eventual extinction. But differences can also be informally measured in my consulting room, and these seem to be most noticeable at about ten-year intervals.

When I began practicing psychiatry in the mid-1960s, for instance, almost the whole idea of playing was to help children talk about their feelings. Kids weren't very talky about such things in those days, even while they were having fun. All of the child-oriented professionals I knew kept formal games in their offices. Card games, checkers, Candyland, Sorry!—each of these was a means of trying to get children to open up. I avoided chess and Monopoly because they generally took too much time and required too much concentration. The better idea was to try something mindless—war was a most useful card game for this purpose—so that the child could chat about life while relaxing at play.

We used to take little walks outside in the fresh air so that we could speak more freely.

We all had little dollhouses and doll families back in the sixties, and we kept puppets on hand, which a few children would actually pick up and use. During my training at the University of Michigan, I asked my teacher and friend Selma Fraiberg, the author of *The Magic Years,* how she and her child patients used the twenty or so gorgeous marionettes that graced Selma's walls. "We don't use them," she said. "We look at them." Kids fingered and stared at a number of playthings back then. But they often did not play past that.

We used more gloppy things in therapy then—clay and water especially. We were inevitably trying to get inhibited children to express their impulses. But most children declined the opportunity. The few who accepted became so overexcited about their new-found chance to make a mess that they had to be contained through the directions of the therapist.

Because of the anti–Vietnam War movement of the late sixties and early seventies, many parents began banning war toys at home. Children of both genders became extremely interested in enacting war at my office, partly because it was now verboten, but also because aggression is a perennial theme in play. Girls searched through the "boys' shelves" for toys to use. Boys hardly ever looked into the "girls' shelves."

In the midseventies to mideighties children tended to drop some of their compulsiveness in play and to give up their preferences for the more formal, structured games. My board games moved from my consultation-room shelves to a space high up in the receptionist's area. My deck of cards was used, but far less often. The clay and water were barely in demand and gradually disappeared. I bought some expensive dolls that girls often dressed and undressed, sometimes trying out a new hairstyle or a fancy ribbon. And I bought some toy soldiers, tanks, and guns that boys insisted on shooting, inviting me into contests to see who could propel a matchstick farther. There were road races between cars and wars between rival armies. The trends toward informality and overt expressions of aggression picked up greatly.

Somehow by the mideighties into the early nineties, the "boy" and "girl" toys that I had bought over the years became totally separated by the various child visitors who came to see me. And the boys' side of my toy cabinet was used three or four times to any one use of the girls' side. Children played with more imagination and with less compulsiveness and warlike competition than previously. They talked more. And they could contain themselves better. We hardly ever shot matches through my army guns (even though they all still worked), and we used my animal puppets far more frequently to pretend. Some small dinosaurs that I had purchased in the mideighties became the most popular toys in the office. A nineteenth-century Bavarian child's tea set, one that, when I bought it, I might have envisioned to be as untouchable as Selma's marionettes, was pressed into use—and, amazingly, has gone to this day unbroken.

In the late nineties, I have watched a few interesting developing trends—again, small-scale ones—in my office. Kids of both genders do not seem as sex- or as age-bound in their choices of play. Not only do girls choose cars, dinos, and miniature armies as frequently as before, but boys sometimes choose puppets, the fold-up dollhouse, the drawing materials. Recently I even took imaginary tea with a boy, at his request. And it was helpful. Perhaps the women's movement has made inroads in the nineties. Perhaps, too, the busyness of parents at their work has led children to make some independent choices in play. Tots only two years old know how to pretend. Sometimes they draw me scribbles and then tell me tales about them. Again, earlier day care and preschool arrangements are probably enabling toddlers to use the more sophisticated tools of play.

One late-nineties trend in my psychiatric consulting room continues to surprise me. Over the years I have gradually accumulated enough little animals, rocks, fossils, Indian artifacts, and other assorted stuff to overflow onto my office tables and desk. The adults in psychotherapy have started to pick these things up and to fiddle with them while they talk. Much as the compulsive and rule-bound little kids of the sixties fingered their toys in order to talk, my nineties adult patients find their own voices better with a wand in hand, a stylized Japanese animal at the fingertips, a lady acrobat spinning around on her double tracks. Adults are spontaneously moving my toys about, a little uncomfortably at first, but more naturally as they go on. Perhaps they are beginning to realize what a great nonmedicinal tranquilizer play can be.

And little by little, adults are going even further. Similar to a lass with a Hello Kitty collection that she insists I must see, one adult or another comes to my consulting room with poetry, a journal, some drawings, even doodles, to show me. On napkins or on restaurant paper place-mats that have carefully been folded into pants pockets and purses, adults now bring me clues to the deeper meanings of their lives. Adult play is picking up interest and therapeutic usefulness. Through our play, we might, as Johan Huizinga suggested, build civilizations while, in turn, as Phillipe Ariès told us, giving our children things to play about.

A few formal studies show us how play patterns merge, differentiate, and sometimes knock one or the other out. These projects tend to demonstrate the obvious differences in play over time and over the world. These differences were clearly pointed out by Brian Sutton-Smith, for instance, when he first began his career in New Zealand. He compared contemporary Maori children's play with pakeha (European-derived) children's play and also compared the play of both groups to descriptions made in 1925 by Eldson Best of New Zealand children's play. Sutton-Smith found that when Maori children indulged in similar activities to the pakeha—for instance, acrobatics, swimming, mock fights, racing, vine swinging, sailing flax canoes—these native activities tended to survive. But when the Maoris indulged in activities that were unique to their own group—for example, various tribal-specific hand games, string games, knucklebones, humming tops—these games tended to disappear or to fuse into the games of the dominant European society.

Knucklebones, for instance, was played in 1925 in a traditional Maori way; and at that same time, pakeha children played the game their own way. Twenty-five years later when Sutton-Smith conducted his study, knucklebones was being played by both populations of youngsters in one new version, representing a cultural fusion of the two older methods of playing.

After he moved to the United States, Brian Sutton-Smith, with Benjamin G. Rosenberg, looked at what kind of changes American children's play had undergone over sixty years. His theme, cultural differences in play, had remained intact while his home base shifted halfway around the world. By comparing observations his group made in 1960 to three earlier American folkloric studies, done in 1898, 1900, and 1926, Sutton-Smith determined that twentieth-century American child's play was in flux. Young people were increasingly turning away from what were considered girls' games—games of singing, dialogue, team guessing and acting, nonphysical competition, and kissing. The games that had been popular in the 1890s and continued to be popular in the mid–twentieth century—imitative, chasing, and central-person games—were those games that had traditionally belonged to boys. This must have been the same defeminization of games that I had begun seeing in my office in the mid to late seventies.

By the mid–twentieth century, according to Sutton-Smith and his group, the trends in child's play were making formal games almost anachronistic. Interestingly to me, the trends in my office were running about ten, fifteen years later than the playground trends that Sutton-Smith was observing. In more informal settings, children of both sexes were showing their preference for quick moments of pretend, of chasing and teasing, of pickup contests at small-scale sports. No longer did prearranged, rule-bound competitions amuse children as much. As far as Sutton-Smith and his group were concerned, this change reflected a general change in our culture, not just a change among the young. Whereas society at the turn of the twentieth century was hierarchically arranged and quite formalistic, society after the Second World War was far

less so. The formalities of games were becoming increasingly mean-
ingless to the newer generation. And by analogy, one could postu-
late that adult play was becoming less formal, as well. These
differences—at least among children—were measurable.

I have noticed that today's children are turning back slightly to
more formalized board games and more structured playground
activities. Even a three-year-old boy I recently heard about nags his
grandma to come and play Chutes and Ladders or Candyland with
him. Pendulums move back and forth in recreational activities, as
in anything else. Some of the challenges of the new century may be
impelling the younger generation toward tighter, stricter, more
defined ways of playing.

UNDER ALL those contrails and satellite signals binding together
our planetary skies, play still represents what is unique and special
to smaller societies. In looking at relatively isolated groups, the differences stand out. These dissimilarities remain prominent as long
as the underlying cultures continue to represent certain ideals and
certain ways of life. Since I am not an anthropologist myself, I put
myself in the hands of a great one, a Chicago gatherer of worldwide
observations on play, named Helen Schwartzman, to see what these
diversities would be. In her 1978 book, *Transformations,* Schwartzman
pointed me to a number of smaller anthropological studies that
have shown what makes certain modes of play special to certain
societies. Despite a general tendency to meld with other cultures,
groups who manage to remain geographically or philosophically
separate still show significant distinctions in their play.

A number of smaller societies, for instance, have not been competitive in the way that we Americans are, and their play has
reflected this noncompetitive ideal. In 1957 in Melanesia, for example, the anthropologist Kenelm Burridge watched Tangu children
playing a game called *taketak* in which the entire object was to establish a state of equilibrium between the two teams. There were no
winners here—that was not at all the goal. In 1963 within another
noncompetitive society, the Tarong tribe of the Philippines, the

anthropological duo William and Corinne Nydegger found games being played among children in which the participants purposely took turns winning. Taking turns was the underlying goal, not being a victor. Kenneth Read reported in 1959 on a form of football being played among Gahuki-Gama adults of New Guinea. In this sport, the game often went on for days because it had to be played out until the scores on both sides were equal. Again, the object was anything but winning. Yet the game was pleasurable for all.

Our culture in America is diverse, yet it is almost uniformly competitive. Still, pockets of play in our own culture represent noncompetitive ideals similar to those of the Tangu, the Tarong, and the Gahuki-Gama. Thousands of American participants enter marathons today, for instance, not for the win—which is almost always assured to a few world-class racers who travel much of the year to such places as Central Park, the Embarcadero, Boston Common. Most marathoners run just for the chance to take part. We Americans see a long, drawn-out race as an opportunity to get in shape, to make mental preparations, to override pain. Marathoning represents a subculture of self-improvement and self-mastery. This kind of no-win contest is becoming increasingly popular, despite its relative neglect of that all-American goal in play, to "win it all."

In Israeli society, many of us know of an internal culture, called the kibbutz, or collective farm, that competes with outside groups but barely competes within itself. This, like American marathons, has led to a unique outlook among kibbutzniks on aggressive play. In the 1950s, for instance, the psychologist Sara Smilansky studied grade-school players from kibbutzim. These children did not particularly like competitive games. Their society had shaped their play, and their ongoing play was helping to retain the spirit of the society.

Along these same lines, in 1970, Rifka Eifermann, a social psychologist doing large-scale research studies on children in Israel, compared the play of youngsters in two types of rural cultures, the kibbutz and the moshav. In the moshav, as in other Western enclaves, the family serves as the center of child-rearing and economics. The children of the two groups preferred very different kinds of games. Kibbutz children vastly favored those games that called for mass cooperation toward the achievement of a common goal. Moshav children played like anybody else in Israel.

Here, then, was a competitive country in which one segment was found to prefer play that reemphasized smaller community values, no matter how different those values were from those of the prevailing national culture. Within the realm of play, children did not appear to rebel against the adult values of their society. In fact, they preferred those activities that best reflected the aims of their elders.

Like competition, another frequently observed theme in play, pretend, is not seen in every culture. In one of her earliest field studies in New Guinea, for instance, Margaret Mead observed that Manus children engaged solely in active motoric games. In her view, the Manus youngsters did not imagine while they played. Mead had, in effect, thrown a small stick into the spokes of early-twentieth-century staging theories that claimed that children would inevitably go through a phase of pretend.

Speaking of imaginative play, a few studies of American and Israeli underprivileged youngsters, conducted at midcentury, implied that less privileged nursery-age children would tend to play less imaginatively than their more fortunate peers. Later studies, especially the large one I have already mentioned by Rifka Eifermann in Israel, argue for a different explanation. Eifermann found that less privileged Israeli children began their imaginative play later in life, at seven or eight years old rather than at four or five. But they pretended nonetheless.

Although it would be difficult to claim that imaginative play is universal to every single subgroup in society, it certainly appears to be a common phenomenon, especially when we allow for its spontaneous origins at different stages of childhood. In general, I would say that we need more and better research to understand exactly how the world creates its fantasy. Obviously, we cannot apply our own expectations about certain groups to the research process itself. Nor can we make value judgments about the worth of pretend over other kinds of play. Most likely there are differences in how, what, and when certain subcultures pretend, just as there are differences in how and when certain groups compete. Our differences make us interesting, just as our samenesses fascinate those who prefer to look at the world this way.

IT'S ENJOYABLE—playful, I would say—to think about world play. Helen Schwartzman noted that anthropologists themselves may be playing as they carefully transcribe the texts, contexts, and procedures of play in cultures far different from their own. What the anthropologists have found is that play and ritual often meld into a single activity.

In a monograph published to accompany a 1997 exhibit of African tribal dolls at the University of California, Los Angeles Fowler Museum of Cultural History, for instance, Elizabeth Cameron described how West African adults have tended to use their dolls simultaneously for both play and ritual. West African children traditionally employ interesting-looking, homemade dolls solely for fun and imagination. But when these dolls are used by adults, they are utilized to protect pregnancies, to ask for fertility, to plead for the health of twins, to watch over families or individuals, and to form unions with other souls who are beyond seeing. The adults using such dolls for magic also play with them. West African women tend to favor dolls, while men favor puppets (play objects that almost always require an audience, or a temporary split of the puppet master into player and audience). We see in this West African tribal use of toys that both play and ritual can exist in the very same cultures, families, and individuals . . . and at the very same time. This still occurs as the new millennium is upon us.

We might consider a comparison of the uses of Yoruba tribal dolls and puppets to our own uses of American dolls, action figures, and stuffed animals. In West Africa, boys play with puppets, girls play with dolls. In America, boys play with action figures, girls play with dolls. All of the action figures that American boys play with represent older human figures with whom the young boys wish to identify. But American girls' dolls fall into two categories—babies for the girls to "mother" and girls or teenage dolls with whom the girls wish to identify. (I saw a strange twist on this at the Dallas airport. On sale was a doll that is made to look just like the child to whom it is given. Who identifies with whom in such a case?) West African dolls function as babies or figures for identification, just as American dolls do. But they also branch out further. For adults, these dolls fit into more spiritual or wished-for categories, such as powerful protectors or make-believe lovers.

I would say that in the world of Western adults, stuffed animals, which are a form of nonhuman doll and are used by both girls and boys, fulfill some of these same magical functions. Stuffed animals frequently act as transitional objects, toys that serve both as partial parents and partial babies. In America today, a fully grown teenager might take a few Beanie Babies to college—their spiritual potential might protect the arriving freshman (as parents do) in the same sense that an African tribal doll, carried on a grown woman's back, might feel protective to her. In Western cultures, dolls or stuffed animals promise loving care forever—the kind of care that mothers and fathers provide. In Africa, a doll might, instead, stand for a loving reunion with a dead or imaginary person, perhaps a lover or a soul mate. The African doll, in other words, carries greater power.

But the American stuffed animal often carries plenty of power itself. One recent summer morning, a forty-two-year-old, highly placed business executive whom I'll call Blair told me about an abandoned stuffed animal that she had found a few years ago in a cabin that she sometimes rents to travelers. Wherever she goes now (and she goes to a great many places), Blair travels with "Weasel." "Weasel can be washed in a washer," she said, smiling, "and he serves as a customized pillow in airplanes. When I'm away from home, he joins me on my bed. On planes, children—even adults—talk to him, he's so cute. And he talks back. We all smile about Weasel.

"I plan someday to write a children's book about Weasel—about the view of the world that he's seen on his travels. And"—Blair grinned devilishly—"what he's seen in bed with me! Weasel is both a child and an adult for me. I call him my shaman. He protects me. And then, since I don't have any kids yet, he's my little one. My boyfriend likes to talk about him, too. In fact, last night—that's why I was thinking about it—Mike phoned me from Chicago to say that he'd been telling a number of people at an important business dinner about Weasel. Mike loves the idea of my children's book. And he loves Weasel almost as much as I do." In other words, Blair, well into middle adulthood, had gone almost but not quite as far as the women of West African tribes go with their dolls. Although many a Western psychologist might consider Blair's behavior "age inappropriate," I see it as creative and playful. In personifying and ritualizing her stuffed-animal playmate, Blair partly transferred her own powers of control onto "him." But at the same time, she developed a more flexible way of looking at the world.

Among the Yoruba tribe of Nigeria, adults improvise while conducting their rites. A large amount of mimicry, pretend, singing, and dancing goes on. They make their rituals into a form of playing, or *ere,* as they call it. We, too, improvise our adult American play, not just at home or in solitude, but in our Second City or *Saturday Night Live* type of nightclub and television acts, theater productions, jazz groups, cooking classes, choirs. In some American religious observances, improvisations fill the air (as in gospel singing or at a revivalist tent meeting). With improvisation, play is able to change rapidly. In improvisational American and West African rites, no gradual movement from play-to-rite or rite-to-play has to occur. Both go on simultaneously.

WHEN ONE considers the world's powerful industrialized cultures and its dominant nations, one still catches a few glimpses of the striking similarities, yet sizable differences, in the ways that people play. I recently inquired about the similarities and differences in the play in contemporary Japanese and American societies, asking my questions of a forty-five-year-old man who is extremely well imbued in both cultures. He is a native Japanese, whom I will name Yoshi Shimura, and he serves as the Western Hemisphere director of a well-known Asian photography company. He lives in San Francisco with his wife and two young boys.

Unlike the majority of native Japanese, Yoshi has practiced Christianity all his life. He attended a Christian coed preschool in Tokyo when he was four years old. The children there danced together and sang hymns well before the boys and girls, similar to American youngsters, segregated themselves by gender during his elementary school years. What was started as preschool play—singing—has become an adult play theme of Yoshi's life. A few years ago, when his center of business operations was in Washington, D.C., he and two other Japanese businessmen performed such wonderful Portuguese and Brazilian music in nightclubs that his trio made a big splash in a widely circulated American magazine.

When I asked Yoshi about the things that he did as a child strictly for fun, he realized that he played—and now plays—a great deal more than he has ever given himself credit for. "There was an American TV series we watched when we were boys, *The Man From U.N.C.L.E.* We would pretend that, over and over, together. Both sides tried to hit each other. Those who were hit were 'out.' "

I realized in thinking about Yoshi's play that the motifs in young children's play in both Japan and America were basically alike. Whether you sang in one language or the other, whether you played "good samurai, bad samurai" or cowboys and Indians, you were expressing the same ideas and underlying feelings.

There was a technical similarity, as well. American postwar culture had won over the imagination of Japanese schoolchildren. "All of the popular games and TV shows in Japan when I was a kid came from America," Yoshi told me. "In those days, we had fewer things. We imported our culture." But Yoshi was careful to inform me that Japanese culture had come back into its own. "Now we export it—Ninjas, Power Rangers, Virtual Pets, all sorts of computer games. Today many world play fads originate back home in Japan. But back then [in the midfifties], everything was American."

Baseball is one sport that has been a beloved preoccupation of the Japanese people long before the Americans took over the Japanese governmental administration after World War II. In Japanese childhood, however, the emphasis inevitably settles on teamwork. In American childhood, youngsters dream of being Mark McGwire or Sammy Sosa. At times, bickering breaks out among American teammates, something rarely seen on Japanese teams. American individualism makes the game somewhat different.

As he grew up in Japan, Yoshi Shimura told me, teenage pursuits such as baseball, skiing, and judo often felt to him more "like a discipline than like play." Judo, for instance, "wasn't play for me—it was a sports activity, a skill. I took it seriously in high school, but eventually I found I didn't have the hours for it. I had to study hard in high school. That's how I spent most of my time." Yoshi quit the Boy Scouts in junior high. He quit judo in high school. He eventually quit baseball. Studying became the essential thing to do.

In high school, however, Yoshi discovered that his true love was "hanging out." Like the most avid of American adolescent hanger-outers, Yoshi loved to talk, listen to music, bide his time. He still loves it today. "For relaxation," he said, "we went to a math teacher's house and listened to Western records of jazz—piano jazz. I loved the white American man with the glasses. Now I can't remember his name. When I was about sixteen, I started going to the coffeehouses, places where you talk and listen to music. You'd stay there an hour, two hours, and just talk. Some coffeehouses play Bach. Others play folk music. I started loving the sounds of Portugal. In college, I bought a guitar and started playing and singing those songs."

Yoshi Shimura attended a small Midwestern American college. "I put on a radio disc-jockey show there," he related. "It was fun. I ran the broadcast for two years and I liked that. I got more and more involved with all sorts of music. When I was at college, I did a lot of drinking. I hung out with my host family's son and we spent time just talking, listening to music, having beers, sitting around. The Japanese love to hang out. Their homes are small, so they leave and go out to karaoke bars, coffeehouses, places where they can relax and enjoy themselves. There's more space in a place like that—more of a community feeling—than at home. Many times, you stay out till two, three, in the morning. Next day, you're shot!"

A standard cultural practice that those of us who have visited Japan or who have watched Japanese films observe is that people who work together go out eating and drinking together. It appears that tensions that build up at work are released during the evenings away from the workplace. Sometimes alcohol helps. Yoshi Shimura feels that alcohol helps the Japanese to play. Daytime society in Japan is constrained and tight. In the Japanese daytime, you frequently sense that someone is watching your behavior. So at night, you might try to let go a little. Yoshi told me that he can't sing fado or samba when he's sober. "In front of people, in order to do things like that, I have to get my brain to feel a little wicked."

Perhaps that's the price one pays for having such a disciplined, "good" society, emphasizing teamwork. "Individuals don't come forward that much in Japan the way they do in the United States," Yoshi went on, alluding to our individualism in America and the relative lack of this quality in Japan. And it accounts for some differences in adult styles of play, not just in childhood baseball. "Almost everyone in my country loves photography. So they invest in improved equipment and go around shooting pictures. And they may show their friends a recent album of their work. But we don't really display things. We don't hang it on walls the way people do in America."

Yoshi wished that his society would learn some lessons from the Americans about how to relax. "You people take it easy. You 'hang loose.' You do many more things for pleasure. You can change your sport, your hobby. We don't. Once you start doing something in Japan, you're supposed to stick with it. You Americans relax more with the opposite sex," Yoshi went on. He was impressed with the amount of mixed-gender play he had observed in the United States. "Japanese couples play together while they are courting," he said. "Otherwise, couples mostly play together on their vacations. But we also take more separate vacations than you do in America.

That's commonly done in Japan. In Japan, when you play alone, that's for enjoyment, that's play. In Japan, it's better to be by yourself in order to relax and to feel pleasure.

"We Japanese drive ourselves hard. I play golf and I feel it's no fun unless I score in the nineties. If my Saturday golf game is off, I feel negative and the feeling lingers through Saturday night. It's terrible. If I'm below a hundred in a game, I'm very relaxed and nice with my sons. It's like being in a spacious place—when I'm relaxed. Tokyo is so jammed, so crowded. You feel free from the crowds in golf. But we don't relax enough in Japan. Not even in golf. Even with golf we have to score a certain kind of score. When I get that kind of score, I can let go. Play represents a kind of relaxation to me. Your muscles loosen, therefore you can smile. If we Japanese could do that in more situations, we'd have a more rounded country. We are rather one-sided, as it is."

Did Yoshi Shimura have any other thoughts on the similarities and differences between our cultures in play? I wondered. Yoshi wanted to reiterate his feeling that the Japanese needed to unbend a little. "I took my wife and boys skiing at Lake Tahoe starting last Wednesday. My older son had to miss school on Wednesday and Thursday, and so we had to get a permit for his absence. When the teacher learned of it, she said, 'Great! Have a good time.' That would *never* happen in Japan. If they knew that a vacation would happen, the story would leak to the principal's office. Our whole society doesn't allow such looseness, such relaxation."

The Japanese style has a more positive side, however, and Yoshi put this difference in terms of automobiles. "I have an American Jeep and a Japanese car. I paid about twenty-five thousand dollars for my American four-wheel drive and about thirteen thousand for the car. The Jeep has a lot of power, and the gadgets are okay. But it's not precise, not perfect. We don't let that happen in Japan." On the other hand, Yoshi believed that Americans exhibit exactitude in other forms. "Your plays, your musicals, your productions, your comic monologues, are so precise. I think that you are precise in your playfulness. You are so good at that! Take your *Beach Blanket*

Babylon, for instance. One song ends, and the next second, something else happens. I am so impressed with American timing. The sequences are so impressive. And I love how you improvise."

So there are noticeable differences in how the major industrial cultures play. But there are more important similarities. While play influences culture, culture also influences play. For a long time American society strongly influenced how the Japanese amused themselves. But the Japanese have always had their own ways of having fun. All of these ways carry common themes. We humans are not that different from one another.

Throughout history, some games have lived in various guises without much change—for instance, the track-and-field events of the ancient Olympic Games. But some play trends and play extinctions have also occurred through time and across cultures. One thing is sure: in other cultures and at other times, adults have played more than they do now. Perhaps that alone should inspire us to keep play in mind, to keep it on our lists of upcoming attractions, to make time for it, and to do it.

8

Underplay, Overplay, and Cure Through Play

Dana Ahern is an unmarried, thirty-five-year-old violinist, and a very good one at that. She started playing when she was six years old, and she liked, maybe loved, to practice. Why did she pick up the violin in the first place? Her Manhattan public school gave her a small fiddle in exchange for putting a little time into their elementary school orchestra. And who gave her the lessons? At first, a nice lady from the school—and soon afterward, a nice lady from the local conservatory of music. After that, a string of increasingly adept and professional teachers. You see, any musician would have recognized that Dana was gifted. She could perfectly carry a tune, she could perfectly beat out a rhythm with a triangle or drum, she could perfectly name the letter for any note that they played on a piano, and she could perfectly sing for them any A, B-flat, or F-sharp that they named. In other words, as early as when she first started school, Dana Ahern was a musical natural. For her, playing the violin was the ideal kind of play.

The child's parents and grandparents were interesting and talented, as well. Her mother, Tung Mai, who was from Singapore, was spending a couple of years studying in America when she met an aspiring young New York actor named Bill Ahern. Within just a few minutes Bill swept Tung Mai and himself into the maelstrom of love and misery that was to last them fifteen years through their wedding and the births and early childhoods of Pablo, Dana, Hermes, and Hermione. Bill arranged for Mai's parents, both well-known Chinese potters, to enter the United States. Soon, he joined an off-Broadway repertory company. Within a couple of years, he was hired for a Broadway play. The Tung grandparents settled into a big Greenwich Village house that Bill and Mai bought for the whole family. Grandma devoted herself full-time to caring for the four little Aherns while Grandpa threw his pots in an attic studio and began achieving international success with his contemporary variations on ancient pottery themes.

On the surface, everything looked rosy. But Bill was beginning to drink. Mai's interest in her marriage and her kids declined, and she went back to college for undergraduate and graduate degrees in art history. Dana lost herself in her violin practice. Nobody noticed much. They were all too busy. Grandpa's work was increasingly being purchased for museum collections. Bill was playing the lead in a new, critically acclaimed play. Their lifestyle—a private-college education for Mai, lessons of various sorts for the kids, a big house, car and driver—was costly. But the Aherns were smart and beautiful, and their extended family exceptional.

By this time, a disaster was brewing beneath the surface. Bill, who had experimented with heroin back in the East Village during his teens, developed new and destructive drug habits, using heroin, cocaine, amphetamines, and tranquilizers. At first, he said, they were just "party drugs," used by any number of actors in and around New York. Later, he had fits of temper against directors, fellow cast members, his young wife. With the children, however, Bill remained a model of politeness.

For Dana, these elementary school years were suspenseful. She tried to play sports with her father whenever he asked her to go outdoors with him. She took up jogging. Her violin helped her to cleanse her mind. When Bill wasn't around, her fiddle also filled in for him. She watched her father a number of times in each of his plays. And then, just like that, her idol toppled literally all the way to the bottom of the world.

One day just after Dana turned thirteen, her father was suddenly gone. He had taken a job with a theatrical road show, Mai said. He would send money soon and come home. Dana retreated further into her violin. She waited for her father's return. But Bill did not appear. He spent a couple of years acting in Sydney, Australia, and then, for a while, in Tasmania. The family received a clipping or two, but no cash. Mai filed for divorce. Bill ended up in New Zealand. He began spending his nights in city parks. Grandma and Grandpa Tung stayed in New York and continued to baby-sit and support their young family. By this time, the elder Tungs were in their eighties. Mai took a part-time job with a small but prestigious art museum. She dated. But she settled on no new man. Bill Ahern had taken too much out of her.

When Dana turned fifteen, she was taken on scholarship into a famous East Coast music school for gifted teens. To help support herself, she moonlighted with orchestras in and around New York. One of the suburban conductors she played for, a married, middle-aged man with five children of his own, seduced the sixteen-year-old Dana and kept her occupied with rather uninspired sex but ardent admiration. He repeatedly promised to marry the high school girl while artfully keeping his and her families in the dark. Dana could not understand why she kept up this affair. But in retrospect she realized that the conductor was around her father's age and that he, in place of her absent dad, was teaching her about art, music, and life.

Because Dana wanted a broader education than she could get at a conservatory, and because she wished to escape her by now altogether boring relationship with the conductor, she applied to a university that, along with its well-known music department, prided itself on fine academics. In her first semester there, she had a fling with a visiting violist who was teaching chamber music. But again, this did not disrupt Dana's life or play. She protected her four, five hours of daily practice. They were hers alone. Grandpa Tung, who had had a great year, bought her a wonderful old Guarnerius violin. A little bit of jogging and a lot of practicing suited Dana just fine.

Then Dana's violin teacher, a well-known concert violinist— let's call him Charles Morris—got the idea that just about ruined the young girl's promising career. He would send her to Vienna for three months to study with a colleague whose mastery of bowing, he assured her, could make all the difference in her development as a soloist. Vladimir Wasserstein's bowing was indeed superb. And his instructions were exemplary. But he did something to Dana's practice in those three months that completely robbed it of its sense of safety, security, of existing in a world apart.

As Dana Ahern stood playing in his Vienna studio, surrounded by its big windows, artworks, and sparkling sunlight, Herr Wasserstein approached her from behind, placing one hand on each breast. Dana nearly dropped her Guarnerius. A shy person, she shivered intensely.

The professor backed off. "Sorry you're cold, my dear," he said. But his retreat was only temporary. He encouraged her to play sitting down the way a chamber music performer does. He then took advantage of this position and, as she played, stood in front of her and tried to insert his exposed penis between her lips.

One wonders at this young girl's reticence. She could make herself say nothing. Dana stopped that particular encounter by clamping her mouth down, but she could not stop her teacher from making further attempts at sexual intimacy. And they always came in the midst of Dana's play, causing a break in that intense focus that had accompanied all of her practice before. The professor's lust invaded that special place in the mind that we call a playground. And Dana Ahern suffered mightily for it.

Dana returned to her American university, totally unable to practice. She told Professor Morris what had happened, and he expressed difficulty believing this. Old Wasserstein? Why, he and

Helga had been married for forty-odd years. He had coached Barbara Parsons and Mimi Bischoff, and they had never complained. "Just ignore the whole thing," Morris told Dana. "It'll fade."

But Vladimir Wasserstein's play invasions did not fade from the young woman's mind. What diminished was her enjoyment of her musical ventures. She had practiced so much in her younger years that she had developed virtuoso skills and a virtuoso name for herself. Upon graduation, she was immediately hired to sit far up in the first violin section of a fine symphony orchestra. But Dana could not, would not, practice any longer. She would only sight-read. In a way, it was a new kind of game—a pathological one that substituted for her previously healthy ones. Sight-reading was still fun for Dana. No matter how difficult a piece of symphony music was, Dana now insisted on getting it only by sight. She would not repeat a passage to perfect it. Her violin was only good for playing this tricky, new, on-the-spot, and onstage game.

To retrace Dana's story, then, her first disappointment in life was her gradual loss of her father to drugs, alcohol, and absences. To put this out of mind, Dana escaped into play—into early virtuosity and self-disciplined practice. It paid off. She became a child prodigy. The seemingly invulnerable child then suffered the total disappearance of her father. Her immediate tastes in males began to veer toward older teachers, people in authority, married persons . . . people who functioned as substitute fathers. Each of these men turned out to be a disappointment—an ardently-in-love, small-town conductor, a young and careless chamber music coach, a perverted Viennese bow master, an unbelieving professor of violin. Dana decided to take a long, perhaps permanent vacation from men.

But this is not why the story of Dana Ahern is a story about stoppage in the ability to play. Because Herr Wasserstein attacked young Dana as she played for him, he invaded the developing woman's innocent playground and thereby destroyed her ability to use her violin for pure pleasure. Dana's promising solo career vanished.

At times, a play problem goes even further than Dana's. If one of us mentally links our play completely to a parent, for instance, then we might give up on play when, as adults, we no longer depend upon our mothers or fathers. The example of a major league baseball "bonus baby" for the New York Mets, Ryan Jaroncyk, comes to mind. After performing in the minor leagues for a year and a half, the young shortstop, who had been given outright an $850,000 bonus for joining the Mets organization, quit the game entirely. When his absence became apparent, he told the inquiring press that the entire idea of a career in baseball had been his father's. Ryan still loved his dad, but he could see no further use in pursuing Papa's outline for his life.

When Ryan married his high school sweetheart and left home to be on his own, he decided never again to play baseball. Football, yes. But baseball, no. The month that he quit the Mets organization, he and his new wife drove to Ryan's parents' house to pick up his baseball memorabilia—Little League trophies, high school awards, old mitts, bats, etc. They put the stuff into a box, drove it to a park in Escondido, and shucked the whole works into a Dumpster.

Play stoppages are not usually as dramatic as Dana Ahern's or Ryan Jaroncyk's. Most of them take place silently and subtly. "I'll wait for my vacation," we mentally promise ourselves. "I'll retire early and then live it up!" By the time that we reach maturity, large numbers of us don't know any longer how to play. Some of us are too compulsive to be able to. We line things up and then put them all back up on shelves—perfectly arranged, of course. Compulsive sorts spend unnecessary time at work and come home so late there is little to no time for play. Too much of life is serious. Too much needs to be thought out in advance.

One woman I know—let's call her Yvette—is innately playful, yet her underlying personality is so compulsively controlling that any play she does has to go her own way. She is afraid to allow someone else to establish the rules. A new boyfriend wants to try, say, a local Chinese restaurant.

"Oh, I'm in such a mood for Italian," she says. "How about Mario's?"

Another new boyfriend wants to spend the afternoon walking the beach.

"I was just at the beach," she answers. "It would be great to spend the afternoon drinking wine in the Napa Valley."

Over the time that I've known her, Yvette has made and broken countless relationships through her need to direct the action. Her ideas are excellent, but they are strictly her own. If it's cold enough for a Sunday of newspapers and brunch, Yvette might bring along a few logs and insist on lighting a fire. She is the soul of concern and consideration. Yet every play move that Yvette makes spells sabotage to the bigger game of courtship. When I point out an option—say, to relax and allow her potential playmates to share in the game's planning—Yvette understands quickly and says she will try. But despite a host of psychiatric interpretations and the appropriate medications for her biologically determined compulsiveness, Yvette sees each new situation as a unique opportunity to take over control. After all, her ideas are so good, she feels, that she instinctively knows better than others how to have fun. The men who like Yvette are all passive players. But inevitably, they are forced to bow out of her games. Time and again Yvette finds herself playing alone—or worse yet, at home taking a nap.

As in both Dana's and Yvette's examples, our overarching fantasies in life often take over our day-to-day play, or lack of play. These overarching fantasies have to do with fears, anxieties, and wishes. In Dana's mind, violin play was an unconscious escape from a family at war; in Yvette's imagination, play was a clever way to put and keep her hands on the wheel.

Sometimes a situation occurs that, at least for a while, kills a person's ability to relax and enjoy. Sometimes it's mourning—grief for a lost person, grief for a lost attribute of the self (scarring after a burn, for instance)—and sometimes it's a terrible surprise. Two great athletes serve as examples here. Each of them suffered both grief and shock. Both gave up on their play.

Michael Jordan gave up basketball in 1993, shortly after his father, James Jordan, was murdered in North Carolina during a robbery. A natural athlete, Michael decided that he would switch to baseball. He went to work as a right fielder for the Birmingham Barons, a minor league team. By July 5, 1994, Jordan's batting average had slumped embarrassingly to below .200; yet he still expressed problems about returning to basketball. "I don't like to close doors," he told some reporters who wouldn't quit asking, "but if you want me to say it, okay, never! I will never play basketball again, except recreationally."

Most of us know what eventually happened to Michael Jordan. In the midst of the 1995 NBA season, he suddenly rejoined the Chicago Bulls and went on to lead them into the NBA play-offs. In later years, he led his team to one championship after another. His basketball play was great. His play stoppage was exactly the kind of slump that both mourning (for his father) and shock (at the senseless murder) would cause. It is important to note, however, that even at his worst moment in the summer of 1994, Michael was careful not to vow to give up basketball altogether. He reserved the option of playing "recreationally." He loved his sport too much to promise an end to the whole affair.

Monica Seles's play stoppage did not resolve quite as triumphantly as Michael Jordan's in his return to the Chicago Bulls. Tennis changes quickly, and a young star one year can be replaced within just a couple years' time by a new and most often younger one. On April 30, 1993, in Hamburg, Germany, Monica Seles was stabbed in the back by a German fan who had been rooting for Steffi Graf. That year, Monica was the number one woman professional tennis player in the world. The stabbing was so sudden, shocking, and completely unexpected that, in one day, the champion went from the height of physical and mental strength to muscular and mental collapse. She had to leave her game for two years, during which time she needed considerable physical rehabilitation and psychotherapy.

When she returned, Monica experienced a quick victory at the du Maurier Ltd. Open, Canada's most prestigious tennis tournament. We were overjoyed. Another triumphant sports story. But Monica's number one position could not truly be regained. During her absence from the game, she had gained weight and lost strength, and a new rival had emerged—Martina Hingis, the phenomenal Swiss teenager. Suddenly, Monica Seles was off to one side. Although her career still earned her enormous amounts of money, and although she was a finalist in the 1998 French Open tournament only a month after her father's death, her play stoppage had cost her one of the most precious commodities any of us has—time. And it had probably cost her considerable physical and mental security, as well.

IN PSYCHIATRIC practice, I find that a number of adult personality traits and disorders interfere with play. Ambivalence, for instance, tends to defeat having fun. Play is too committed a behavior to allow for "yes-no" paralyses—game decisions must be made instantly and incisively. After all, they are just play decisions. Perfectionism defeats merrymaking, as well, because play is meant strictly for enjoyment. If a person strives to be faultless, he or she would have to play for a longer time than most games—and life itself— would allow.

Other pathological traits that spell trouble for play are schizoid and paranoid tendencies. Being a loner eliminates most games, with the exception of solitaire. Yes, one can play alone on a computer. But after a while, even such a humanoid little creature as Nintendo's Mario gets under one's skin. One starts feeling as if a second person were in the room. A suspicious person, too, has trouble playing. Paranoid people respond best to dead earnestness. Their problems lie in interpreting the double meanings and the giggles of play. Are the soft laughs they hear meant against *them?*

Any number of personality problems have the potential to interfere with adult play. Some "borderline" people are too stormy, too self-focused, too unable to see the bigger picture, for worthwhile diversions to occur. And certainly, narcissism with its wholehearted centering on the self does not allow enough attention to outside factors to create much amusement. People who are dependent on others have their own problems expressing their needs and, thus, may not reap much benefit from fun-making.

Depression also strongly interferes with play. When treating conditions marked by depressed moods, we psychiatrists look for a symptom called anhedonia, the inability to experience pleasure in actions that should produce it. What better way for a clinician to inquire about anhedonia than to ask about play? And further, what better way to find out whether our depressed or grieving patients are improving than to assess whether they are beginning to amuse themselves?

Play is a good barometer with which to measure mental health. Watching mutual play is also an excellent way to assess child-parent relationships. Play would be an even better barometer if we all indulged in it when we are okay. If we all frolicked and gamboled freely, nonplayers could be spotted quickly for their abnormality. But as I have already noted, too many of us "normals" give up on play. One would have to say, in summary, that any number of personality problems and more acute mental problems can interfere with play. A good way to appreciate a patient's improvement would be to watch play reenter that person's life. But in general, we can't conclude that underplayers are unhealthy. Far too many normal people don't play to allow for any such conclusion.

SOME PEOPLE overplay, and sometimes their excessive play costs them dearly. Although overplaying is less common than underplaying, it is more obvious. The results are often dramatic. For example, one woman who suffered from bipolar disorder (manic and depressed episodes) planned elaborate vacations in Europe and gambled in Las Vegas whenever the excited phase of her illness broke through. Lynn's play worked out just fine when she and her husband had the time and the money for it. But her manic condition did not present itself only at such moments. A busy professional, Lynn was impelled to hide a $5,000 gaming debt from her husband. Then she had to earn it all back by herself and sequester these earnings from him, without cheating on her taxes. It took Lynn two years to make up for one night of overplay.

Psychological trauma, being overwhelmed emotionally by an unusual, threatening event or series of events, is an important cause of a kind of overplay that I call post-traumatic play. I initially discovered it in a group of twenty-six kidnapped schoolchildren, ages five to fourteen, who were taken from their bus in Chowchilla, California, on July 15, 1976, and were held about twenty-seven hours until they escaped. I saw the same sort of play in a comparison group of youngsters who had been separately and individually traumatized. I found that, while post-traumatic play occurred more frequently in children, it could also be observed once in a while in adults. Traumatized people, in their attempts to master the terrible events, play again and again on a theme related to their disaster. Unfortunately, because trauma is so overwhelming, it cannot be fully mastered through any kind of playful behavior. Thus, traumatized people are impelled to repeat themselves. Their play is sometimes dangerous (as was depicted so well in the postwar French film *Jeux Interdits* [*Forbidden Games*]). It is also contagious. And it doesn't stop.

Adult examples of post-traumatic play are rare because many of us stop playing as we reach maturity. Among avid adult players, however, post-traumatic play does turn up. One man in his early twenties, for example, a talented college baseball player, learned that his brother had committed suicide by shooting himself. The outfielder rushed home from spring training camp for the funeral. His brother's casket was open, and instinctively the athlete cradled his dead brother's head in his hands. The baseball star then felt what continued to horrify him for the next several years—the back of his brother's head was missing.

Two years later when I met this man, he told me he had taken up painting. His baseball career had derailed. I asked him to bring in his art portfolio. All of his drawings and paintings were of half heads. This young fellow had been unable to stop playing out his horror. Until he understood the connection between what he was picturing on canvas and what he had felt with his hands at his brother's funeral, his artistic endeavors would inexorably be repetitive and monotonous.

Let us consider a more famous and more literary example of this kind of overplay. A year and a half after her sixth child, Anne, was born, Maria Branwell Brontë died following a long and painfully wasting illness—most likely due to postpartum complications. Three years afterward, the widower, the Reverend Patrick Brontë, sent away his four oldest girls—Maria, Elizabeth, Charlotte, and Emily—to a cold, harsh evangelical boarding school in Lancashire, the neighboring county to Yorkshire, where they lived. All four girls almost immediately became ill. The two oldest, and probably the younger ones, as well, contracted tuberculosis. In late February, Patrick Brontë brought Maria home. She died on May 5, 1825. Three weeks later, he came to school to pick up Elizabeth. She died on June 15. Charlotte and Emily had both been sent back home by the time that Elizabeth died. The Brontës blamed the school's meager, ill-tasting food, harsh manner, and unhealthy living conditions for their family tragedy. The whole experience was hideously traumatic.

The next June, after the young survivors had endured the proper year of mourning, their brother, Branwell, received a gift from his father—twelve painted wooden soldiers. With these miniature men, Branwell, Emily, Charlotte, and eventually Anne invented a fictional land that they called Angria. They thought up a high-ranking nobleman, eventually named the Duke of Zamorna. They also developed the characters of several young male adventurers, their followers, their lovers, and their sequential wives. In one of their yearlong pretend "plays," the Brontë kids imagined that the children of Angria had to live in a boarding school where, if they were naughty, they were tortured and sometimes killed in a horribly grim dungeon. Here, fiction (the dungeon) imitated fact (the boarding school). Pretending about the Duke of Zamorna (who carried attributes of the Brontë children) and his thin, almost dead, and orphaned female admirers (who held other aspects of the Brontës) did not relieve the four gifted youngsters. But rather than stop playing, they continued to indulge. Eventually Emily and Anne tired of Branwell's tyranny over their game, and while Charlotte was away for a year and a half at another boarding school, they invented a new kingdom called Gondal. When Charlotte returned from school once more at age seventeen, she and Branwell returned as a dyad to their game. In this new version of their post-traumatic pretend, they no longer required the old toy soldiers, but instead they created poems, small artworks, and serialized tales that they occasionally shared with their siblings.

What makes the Brontë sisters' and brother's work "post-traumatic" is its single theme, its ongoing nature, its repeated emphasis on incarceration (one heroine nearly starved to death while she remained locked and neglected in a tower), its numerous deaths (especially of young people), and its magical resurrections of some of those who had already died. You could see both inexorable repetition of their losses side by side with their bravura attempts to make up for the damage. The tragedy of death and the terror of confinement in an awful place away from home was overplayed because the Brontës could find no realistic solution to their over-whelming childhood experiences. Emily and Anne played Gondal until they died. Branwell played Angria until his debaucheries quenched any motivations to go on. Charlotte quit playing well into her adulthood, when she was twenty-nine.

Interestingly, even though the Brontë women's play was an ongoing part of their mature lives, their published novels did not suffer from its influence. It was as if the play itself protected their public writings from their more personal experiences. Only in Charlotte's *Jane Eyre* did a tyrannical boarding school show up, along with the tubercular death of a fine little girl named Helen Burns. The Brontë women's post-traumatic play, however, was excellent soil in which to grow the techniques for three great first novels—Charlotte's *The Professor* (published after her death), Anne's *Agnes Grey,* and Emily's *Wuthering Heights.*

Throughout their lives, the Brontës strove to keep their odd overplay a secret. But in all those years that they played, they created a sizable number of miniature manuscripts and drawings. After the death of one Brontë, the survivors were supposed to destroy all of that person's play-related materials. But because Charlotte (who died of TB when she was thirty-eight) was the last surviving sibling, there was no one to destroy what was left of her play. Along with Charlotte's property, some of Emily's and Anne's play-related drawings and writings were also found. These tiny scraps sold for a pittance—after all, they weren't parts of the Brontës' acknowledged masterpieces. The Duke of Zamorna, and his young, lovelorn, and ill-fated mistresses and wives, spread themselves all over the world, finding their way into the collections of many a Brontë fan.

Post-traumatic play spreads into society and creates dreams, fears, and more play in its wake. Stephen King, the horror writer, is an adult post-traumatic player (at four years of age he witnessed a friend being hit by a train). His imaginative efforts have remained both chilling and contagious. Over the years, there have been hundreds of thousands, perhaps millions, of King-based nightmares. Alfred Hitchcock, another person traumatized as a child (at the age of five, through his father's arrangements, he was thrown into a jail cell . . . "This is what happens to naughty boys," a constable told him), played out a repetitive "wrong man" theme throughout his life as a director. In his films, not only would an innocent person be pursued by the forces of the law, but protagonists would be confined (as in a jail cell) in the most hideous of ways. Who wouldn't have had a nightmare or two over the inescapable attacks of *The Birds* or that claustrophobic and bloody shower scene in *Psycho*? Janet Leigh noted in her autobiography that for the rest of her life after starring in *Psycho,* she was unable to take a shower.

Antisocial people habitually toy with the emotions and the weaknesses of others. Their entire lives may be devoted to "play." Even though many of us think of spying or burglary as kinds of capers, for instance, a line is crossed when a supposed game is employed against the interests of another. Even though we thoroughly enjoyed jewel thieves portrayed by Clint Eastwood and Cary Grant (in *Absolute Power* and *To Catch a Thief*), what looks gamey often crosses a line from play into crime. People with antisocial personalities may conduct their lives as capers. But for others, they create anything but fun. One man I once knew prided himself on his fabulous home library made up entirely of stolen books. I couldn't force myself to browse through his collection. One man I met on a criminal psychiatric ward made a good part of his living selling his own blood. He had suffered from infectious hepatitis years before, yet when medical technicians inevitably asked him about it, he lied. At that time, there were no tests for viruses in sera. Despite my report of his name to a few blood banks, he was probably enough of a games player (he used any number of aliases) to evade detection and to infect any number of people.

Antisocial individuals sometimes make a game of their relationships to others. Those caught in their traps, as in the French novel *Les Liaisons Dangereuses,* suffer mightily for it.

Gambling is another form of dangerous overplay. Gaming costs billions of dollars of national product and even more in human lives. Before 1976, Nevada was the only state to allow casinos. But in 1976, with the opening of Atlantic City, New Jersey, to this kind of gambling, a number of other states recognized that they could raise revenue by legalizing lotteries and other betting enterprises. At about the same time, several Indian tribes set up casinos on their lands. Eventually about half of the states legalized casino gambling and/or slot and video gaming machines at racetracks and in bars. One antigambling organization estimated that in 1995, Americans wagered $550 billion on legal gambling, a 3,200 percent increase in just two decades.

In the past twenty years, gambling addictions have become more and more apparent. In 1980, the American Psychiatric Association officially recognized compulsive gambling as a disorder of impulse control. But as far as I can tell, defining gambling as a "disorder" did little to limit it or to fund its treatment. If anything, the problems have continued to mushroom.

The computer represents a form of recreation that, like gambling, can easily lead to overplay. Not only does the computer allow people to play engrossing games, but it allows them to develop pen-pal relationships, to communicate with fellow collectors and hobbyists, and to develop their own statistics and styles. As progressive as this invention has been in expanding our play choices, however, it also serves to narrow them down and to overinvolve some people to the point of disorder—already informally named cyber-addiction among the lay public. Several on-line files are devoted to the subject.

Not only do computer users complain that they or someone else in their family spends too much time at it, but they also complain of obsessive, damaging relationships over the Net. Termed cyberromance, this behavior represents a cross between addictive overplay and fantasy. One correspondent in such a romance endows the other with all sorts of desired traits that the person may not have. In psychiatry, this displacement of longing (or of hate) onto a therapist's persona is called transference. In cyberspace, the displacement is experienced as "love."

With computers, an adult overplayer may move virtual reality toward actuality. Consider, for example, the following heavily edited excerpts of cybertalk from one bulletin board that was active in the spring of 1994. From this communication, we can tell just how friendly and playful the medium is. But we can also perceive the dangers:

DEBBIE B: I am in the process of a divorce and about two months ago met someone on-line that seemed too good to be true. Unfortunately, he was. I would have left my husband eventually anyway, but I hurried things along for him. My on-line lover was talking about me moving to where he lives and spending the rest of my life with him. Suddenly he got scared, or that's what he says. I miss the fantasy we had; I'm afraid that's all it was.

EL SPLENDIDO: Things like that hurt, Debbie. Words on a screen don't make up a living human being.

OXFORD 777: Think of the millions of fizzled off-line relationships out there. Surely some fizzled on-line relationships don't mean the medium is wrong!

FLORA H 13: Déjà vu, déjà vu. Going through divorce, met wonderful man. Sold my home and business, planned to move east with him. He met another woman on-line. Then he was "gone with the wind."

VERA J 31 2: Why are people willing to "talk" about something electronically that they may not otherwise be willing to talk about (so soon in a relationship, anyway) if it were the usual meet-at-a-party kind of thing?

M STANDISH 3: Well, for one thing, you get to edit what you say before you say it. Also, there's the familiar "not in person" motif. Then, too, a person can end electronic communication swiftly, just by double-clicking the mouse button or hanging up the modem. I'd say, all in all, it's less personal. I had a relationship once with a girl I met over the modem. Starting it was a cinch. But it faded after a couple of months.

STOCKTON: It's just getting harder and harder to be intimate these days.

FOR ABOUT half a century, play has been known as a way to cure psychological ills. Our knowledge about this remedial quality came first from children. Children have been observed for years to use their play to make themselves feel better. Aside from all of their other uses of play, children have traditionally employed play to relieve their anxieties and unhappy moods. If you watch kids, you can see them do it.

Psychological cures in play come about largely through three mechanisms—abreaction, context, and correction. By abreacting, or enacting play stories with feeling, children release much of the powerful emotion that has built around their internal conflicts or their experiences with outside events. By playing in various contexts, young people come to see their problems in a new and broader perspective. The problem isn't really so big. Their own lives and the world's life is bigger than this one particular experience. By playing out new endings, or corrections, children find that there are other possibilities for next time—and, in fact, that no "next time" may ever happen.

Do we adults also use abreaction, contexts, and corrections spontaneously in our play? Of course we do. Why, if not for abreactive release, does a man go into the backyard and chop out weeds after having an argument with his teenage daughter? Why does a woman in a downsizing industry take her dog out for a two-mile run when their routine used to be half a mile? Why does a schoolteacher get drunk and sing songs in a pub toward the close of an especially tough semester? All of these activities are abreactive, and as such, they offer us spontaneous cures.

In my office, a middle-aged businesswoman picks up a magic wand on a side table and threatens to break it. She enjoys the power of her threat but never fulfills it. A depressed college student flies miniature planes about my room—planes that he himself purchased for the office toy collection. He laughs with satisfaction at a certain line of flight, a certain crash landing. The poor fellow has just been through a harrowing year trying to work his way back into a top-ranked university following a psychiatric hospitalization. No wonder he needs to buzz about my consulting room.

Abreaction, in and of itself, does not solve the majority of emotional problems. Even though the abreactive experience is powerful, the relief it brings is often too evanescent, too light, to handle something big. In my view, abreaction must be combined with broadened contexts and a repertoire of corrections before play can cure us.

Therapeutic comments bring in new contexts, either from outside the play ("You must feel shattered yourself—like that magic wand") or from within the play ("I wonder how that little Concorde is going to extract itself from this mess!"). These fresh perspectives prod us to begin reworking our habitual expectations and conflicts. We must be able to see our problems with new and broadened outlooks in order to improve. This is what children do naturally when they play cowboy, princess, rabbit and witch, lions and hunters. They insert themselves into new contexts, ones that in reality they have never experienced. In doing so they broaden the way they see their problems. A conflict doesn't look so big when compared with what Superman or Wonderwoman can do.

A delightful elderly woman who has recently recovered from a serious depression brings me a gift—some tiny magnets and some minuscule metal acrobats that can be stacked through magnetism into extraordinary shapes. "Adults will like to play with this," she says, and they do. Does fumbling with tiny human figures as we talk create some relief for us? Well, it certainly provides a new context. Marvelous things in life can be wee indeed. Sometimes they eclipse our bigger irritations.

Transference sometimes enters into remedial play. With transference, the therapist is endowed with powers, ills, malignant ideas, and loves that were originally those perceived in our parents, siblings, friends, and lovers. Among children, these attitudes may turn up in pretend play or in various competitive games. For instance, a twelve-year-old girl drew a portrait of me, complete with fangs, and labeled it "Dr. Terror!" After a serious talk about the picture, and some anguish, we were able to laugh about it. And we laughed about it many times again. Would adult patients eventually feel new ways regarding their psychiatrists, and regarding the individuals whom these professionals represent, if they played a little more in therapy? I would guess yes, but the answer is certainly not yet in.

Here is an adult example of what I mean about broader play perspectives, or contexts, as an aid in achieving emotional relief. Michael McGuire, the gifted surgeon whom we met earlier when he ran his marathon, originally came to my office to overcome a paralyzing fear of flying. This fear related to Michael's earliest days when his father beat him and threw him against walls. In one of his first sessions, I asked Michael, a playful sort, to diagram the tenement balcony from which his father had threatened to pitch him. In a diagram that looked like the ones that John Madden makes on TV for football, Michael drew an enclosure for a porch and an X and 0 for himself and his father. Suddenly, he extended his map to include his living room, as well, and placed an O in there. "I remember now," he said. "My mother was in a corner looking out of the window! She saw what was happening. Her mouth was wide open. She was protesting, maybe screaming. It's the first time I've thought of that in a long time. Maybe ever." Michael looked surprised and moved by his memory. He went on directly, almost unable to stop. "My mother has Alzheimer's disease now and is in a nursing home in Portland. I haven't seen her in a long time. I think I'll fly up there this weekend."

Michael harbored an intense fear of flying; yet he went off in a plane to Portland (and flew successfully thereafter) because he had played out and integrated the worst moment of his life. In making a football diagram of it, he fully realized that he had always had an ally, his mother. A new context was being built to surround and partially protect him from his trauma.

In addition to abreaction and contexts, corrections should come into therapeutic play before a treatment is complete. Michael McGuire needed to make some corrections to his habitual approaches to life. And so he stayed on in treatment for a while longer.

Then one day, he came into my office with a button missing from his jacket. He otherwise looked nice—that day he was to have his final interviews for membership in a city men's club.

"Do you have your button with you?" I asked. "I'll sew it back on." To fix any number of things, I keep inside my desk a few hotel sewing kits, a couple of kinds of glue, a good scissors, some toothpicks (for gluing and for wood struts), and some colored marking pens. I have learned again and again from my patients that it helps to provide corrections for bad situations. If someone breaks a toy, I try to repair it right there and then. It helps a patient to realize that objects can be fixed.

"Here it is." Michael stuck a hand into a pocket and offered me his button. We talked as I sewed. In a sense, this scene served as a kind of pretend for Michael and me. I was playing good mother, fairy godmother, healer. He was playing innocent—the child once again. This time, nobody was beating him. Instead, something broken was being repaired.

After that day, Michael no longer felt the need to see me. We had symbolically concluded treatment right there and then with his button. And he was right . . . it was ended.

Play treatments often resolve when new corrections are applied to old problems. Played-out corrections sometimes deal with uncorrectable actualities. But they still work. The idea of playing out a new ending goes back to the way that we all thought when we were kids. Superman is felled by kryptonite; but he stands back up and recovers, especially after a lead shield is placed over the deadly stuff. The coyote who chases the roadrunner is flattened by a huge truck, but he jumps up to chase that pesky old bird once again. One child who actually witnessed a murder played out with me how she and her grandmother might have prevented Grandma's killing. Why did this do any good? Grandma was dead, after all. Well, it helped because a correction within the girl's play allowed her to feel that other corrections would be found for any future horrible events or imaginings.

In my consulting room, I frequently encourage adults to play a perspective-enlarging and corrective game that one might call scenario building. How would we mature individuals handle certain situations? Many of us enjoy the drama of a verbal dialogue, and we frequently work things out by ourselves in this fashion. Here's how one such dialogue might go in the office:

"C'mon. I'll be your boss and you ask me for a raise," I say to a woman who says she'd like to ask her real boss for a raise. "I'm going to be tough on you!"

"Okay." She meekly asks me for a raise. We discuss how she asks. She is too passive and too self-effacing, as she so often is.

I, the boss, now respond negatively, but with a playfully silly voice. Is there anything else that she could try? I say in my own voice.

She comes up with something else, something new for her. I

respond differently now. My voice is still silly, but I mollify her by promising her the raise in three months.

She quickly seeks to find another new alternative. She wants a raise *now,* not later. This time, because her coping style is so much better, I gratify her by giving her an immediate, though unfortunately entirely imaginary, pay hike.

We try the whole thing again. Now she has two, perhaps three, possible ways of handling future encounters with her boss. And hopefully she has a new technique or two for handling her husband, children, friends, and coworkers, as well. All the while, we've been enjoying ourselves. She giggles over my ridiculous imitations of a boss. She is becoming more flexible through this kind of play, and she is keeping in mind some of the more important points that might help her win her raise. Most of all, through this kind of play she is becoming empowered. Flexibility, controlled drama, and humor build mental fortitude. And they sometimes resolve old conflicts.

Although lawyers do not put on silly voices as they do this, they prepare their expert witnesses for cross-examination by running through, in advance, as many potential stumbling blocks as they can identify. Because courtroom attorneys are often such terrific actors, I find this kind of trial preparation particularly enjoyable. I always feel better as an expert psychiatric witness if we've toyed in advance with a few possible scenarios.

Husbands and wives, business partners, parents and children, close friends, can run through prospective dialogues in several different ways, can critique them, and—in a playful fashion—can be honest with one another about their habitual behaviors. If a person likes this type of mini-drama or improv, the person, alone, may play out a conflict without ever speaking a word aloud. The point of an imaginary scenario is to run it two, three ways, including every stumbling block that can possibly be anticipated. In this playful fashion, we can prepare ourselves for various here-and-now situations. And it's a way to face our character flaws and possibly, hopefully, correct them.

• • •

SOMETIMES A play problem corrects itself almost as if by an act of God. Something happens that carries so much possibility for abreaction, new contexts, and correction that the problem simply resolves itself. I will end my chapter on this note because it is just where I started—with the story of the violinist Dana Ahern.

Dana wanted to play solo concerts, but she could not make herself practice. Through her psychotherapy, she was beginning to run through her orchestral music a little, but she wasn't putting in sufficient practice time for a concert career. She went two summers in a row to the psychologist Burton Kaplan's practice camp, a two-week playing program especially designed for musicians who are having motivational problems. Here, good musicians, all of whom suffer from some play blockage or the other, meet with their fellow musicians and with Dr. Kaplan, who reads them poetry, encourages them to get together and do chamber music, and works with them piece by piece, bit by bit, to reestablish positive attitudes about play. This camp is built on a cognitive/behavioral approach that centers on overcoming fears of failure and erasing perfectionism.

Both times upon coming home from practice camp, Dana was able to play her violin a couple of hours a day for a few months. And her rehearsing paid off. She performed a few solo concerts. The conductor of her orchestra, a good chamber pianist, asked Dana to join him and his brother in a chamber music trio that they were starting. Having both men to practice with, plus having a camp director who, over two summers, hadn't made any sexual advances to her, helped Dana. New, healthy contexts for play were being superimposed on the old, unhealthy ones. But the truly corrective moment to Dana's play problem came as a great surprise to both of us. And it occurred in about a moment's time.

Dana returned to my consulting room after a long absence because, of all things, Bill Ahern was coming to town. Her father had saved enough money to travel from New Zealand and would be visiting her and staying at her house for a week. What was she to do? She had no idea what kind of shape Bill was in. She hadn't spoken to him in years.

We ran through a couple of play scenarios, but Dana opted for reality. "I want to bring him to your office so that you can see him. I want you to tell him about the damage he did to me."

"No," I told Dana. "Although I'll see him with you, I don't think we should get into the damage part. Let's play it by ear. You haven't seen him for more than twenty years. Let's find out if you two might be friends."

"Well, I want you to see him early when he first gets to town."

In retrospect I do not think that either Dana or I could have anticipated with a play scenario exactly what eventually did take place. Into my office came a neat, well-groomed, nondefensive, sober-looking, and clever man who, for the last few years, had been making a living doing bit parts in Australian and New Zealand films. Bill Ahern was completely off alcohol and drugs, he said, and was extremely contrite about his past. He told us that he could remember few things about Dana from about age eight on. From the time that his drug use in New York had gained momentum, his life was one big blur.

But he remembered Dana with fondness before she was eight and told her a few stories that reflected this warmth. He was extremely proud of Dana now. "Despite everything I did to turn you off on your life," he said, "you made it and you've become a wonderful person." Bill Ahern wanted nothing from his daughter except to know her. And he offered her no criticisms, except toward himself.

Dana smiled. Yes, they could have a relationship now. And she relaxed in a way that demonstrated how starved she had been for a father, her father, the person who had always been her favorite.

Well, Bill went off within a few days to New York to stay with some old friends, to visit with Dana's sister and brothers, and to see Grandma and Grandpa Tung in Greenwich Village. Grandpa was turning one hundred years old that year and was still producing his fabulous ceramic pieces. His homeland was celebrating his centennial with a series of concerts and museum shows, including a violin recital by Dana Ahern. And guess what? Dana began practicing steadily. All that play energy that she had lost years ago reappeared with a simple apology from her father and a proposal to reopen their prized relationship.

I do not see Dana in my office anymore. But I do see her once in a while onstage. She looks wonderful and sounds great. As for Bill Ahern, was he playing a game, a "people game," with us during his one-week jaunt in California? After all, a week of contrition, of reacquaintance, and most of all, of charm wouldn't have been too much for an adept actor to pull off. As far as Dana was concerned, it didn't matter. She had a father again, gamey or no. And she had her violin playing.

9

Play as Work, Play as Life

From my garden, I turn away from the Presidio Wall and walk up a steep sidewalk. Panting a bit, I climb Presidio Hill, which rises for three city blocks above my house. I attain the top a little past Clay Street, then cruise down a couple of blocks farther to the intersection of California and Presidio to a wonderful little neighborhood restaurant called Ella's. Ella's co-owner is a chef named Danny Wilser. Danny is a bachelor, lives out by Ocean Beach, and is a specialist in forties and fifties American home cooking. If you want super-duper comfort food—pea soup with ham, homemade bread, chicken fried steaks, stew, potpie, chocolate cake—Danny is your man. You can always find something unusual on Danny's menus, too—fiddlehead ferns in the salad, if they are in season, or a mango sauce, if he's in the mood.

It's been plain to me in the time that I've known Danny that he thrives on being a chef. But what I didn't know before I walked up the hill to interview him was that Danny is really a baker at heart. I should have realized earlier that his broad chest and huge forearms argue for a life of kneading dough. "Pies, cakes, fruit crisps," he says, "I enjoy them all. But I love bread the best because it's alive!"

From the beginning of his life, young Danny hung out around food. "I used to have fun helping my mother in the kitchen," he remembered about his boyhood in the South Bay (what is now Silicon Valley). "It was funny. My brother and sister were picky eaters, but it was rare for me not to like something. My dad is pretty much a meat-and-potatoes man; that's how we all ate. But my father worked at Stanford with an Indian woman who once invited our family over for dinner. I was six years old and I can remember that meal to this day. It was so good, yet so different. It was fascinating."

Danny Wilser smiled his big, beautifully innocent smile. "Actually I aggravated my mom in the kitchen more than anything else. I was always underfoot and asking too many questions. I guess I got thrown out of the kitchen a lot. But I always loved the kitchen because I loved to eat. Mom occasionally baked bread at home. I relished it 'cause it was the only time that we were allowed to eat white bread. Whole wheat and rye were better for us, Mom thought. But if she baked it herself, white bread was okay. Now, every day, I bake white bread for my restaurant."

I asked Danny if he and his siblings ever played "restaurant," the way my two kids used to do for hours on end. "No," Danny said, "playing restaurant wasn't my thing. When I was a child, we never went out to eat. So I wouldn't have known *how* to play restaurant!"

So here had been a young boy, a boy who preferred staying at home with his family, whose best place in the whole house was the kitchen, whose curiosity, interest, and spirits rose when he was around food. And then the serendipity came up in Danny's early adolescence that charted the course of the rest of his life. He turned thirteen and wanted to get a job.

The family who lived across the street and down a couple of houses—"the South Bay was pretty rural, and so you met your neighbors back then"—owned a bakery. They asked Danny if he'd like to help out. He did, along with their two younger children. Danny began with menial tasks. "Actually," he said, "John, the owner, snuck me into the bakery as a family member, sort of, because I was too young to work." Danny's first regular assignment was to wash pots; but if it was late and not busy, "John would show me things. Then we would talk, too."

We have already seen that during the teenage years, many people begin to make a switch—imposed on them by society—from play to work. But Danny Wilser did not have to make this switch. Going to work at John's bakery was the same as going to play. Certainly, Danny had to wash pots, wipe off the kneading surfaces, clean up at night when they closed. And John paid him for it. But Danny didn't think of all this activity as aimed toward baking someday. His life choices were happening beyond his conscious knowledge. His love for his home kitchen and his pleasure in helping John were leading him there.

"I would say I was pretty attached to John," Danny told me. "He was the opposite of my father—real easygoing and patient. I can remember making major errors. Once, I was mixing a whole batch of chocolate cake batter and put salt in it instead of sugar. And John just said, 'We'll have to make this again.' Sometimes there'd be a couple of us cleaning up and having dough fights—we thought we'd cleaned up!—and I found out years later that John knew all about it." So, for the adolescent Danny Wilser, work equaled satisfying relationships. Work was fun.

"My father *had* to eat on time," he went on, less comfortable at the thought of Dad. "Eating on time was the most important thing to him. We made a real evening meal each day—a vegetable, starch, meat—*never* lamb, though. And we *never* heated up frozen-package foods. I mean TV dinners were a sin. You'd *never* do that. And there was no convenience food involved. You *never* ate boxed mashed potatoes, for instance."

Despite having a formidable and possibly demanding father at home, Danny liked to improvise, even with his dad's mandatory, on-schedule dinners. But by the time that Danny turned seventeen, his father's meals were no longer an issue. The Wilsers divorced, and Danny's mother started working swing shifts. "I still baked at John's place," Danny recalled, "and John would let me make fillings for the pies and bake some bread myself. We'd make the fillings early in the morning before we made the piecrusts, and then we'd mix the whole thing with our arms. And I'd go to high school purple up to my elbows from blackberries. I'd get kidded terribly for stuff like that."

Danny graduated and automatically figured he'd go on to college. "But I didn't really want to, it turned out. I got a job in a restaurant washing dishes forty hours a week. It was," he said, laughing "right next to the freeway—a truck stop, a greasy spoon. It was a 'You come up to the counter and order and we'll call you' kind of place. After six months or so, they trained me to cook. I worked there for two years. Then I tried about a year of junior college and was bored out of my mind. So I got a job at a real restaurant on the Klamath River in Oregon. I started working with fish for the first time in my life—I hadn't eaten it before. I tried lamb, too. I'd taste everything. But I also did hard physical labor. I think my big arms came from lifting hundred-pound sacks of potatoes at places like that. That and kneading were, and still are, my only physical exercise."

In his early twenties, Danny Wilser wandered to New York, southern California, Nevada. "That was one of the good things about cooking," he said. "You could always get a job. And then a kind of amazing thing happened—my mom married John. I can't remember when he and his wife broke up—sometime in my late teens maybe—but there it was. Mom and John were married.

"So I came back to the Bay Area." Danny consistently worked in restaurant kitchens, but occasionally thought he should be doing something truly "serious." Restaurants felt too playful. "It's not that I've ever been criticized about being playful with food, but I thought I should prepare for a *real* job, like being a doctor or a lawyer or something." He smiled a little slyly, knowing what I do for a living. He did not realize how much enjoyment—play, if you will—someone else might reap from medicine or law.

"Well, eventually I realized that food would be what I'd be

doing for the rest of my life." But Danny noted that his cooking has not rigidified. Even though he had coowned Ella's for six years at the time I interviewed him, he still found himself seeking new adventures along the way. His hours were "kind of crazy," for instance. He visited the produce market at three in the morning— "looking, tasting, talking to people, looking, tasting." And then he made his breads late into the evening. "I kind of sleep when I get the chance." But Danny never dreaded coming to his kitchen-away-from-home. "There are days when something worrisome is looming—or when I'm so tired that I need sleep. But I like what I do. I'm learning Spanish at the restaurant. There are only two English-speaking people right now in our kitchen, so we're both enjoying getting good at our Spanish. I've learned to say stuff you can't translate directly. And also, their whole food thing is completely different. I catch jokes in Spanish now, and I can tell a joke myself, and now I'm making my shopping and prep lists in Spanish. In fact, have you noticed? I've started to cook under Spanish influence."

Because he is a true player, Danny Wilser does not "age." He was forty years old when I interviewed him, and he was still finding his work a source of continuous change. "I always thought my job would be to cook," he told me, "but I see now that my job is to teach others to cook. We have a crew working here twenty-four hours a day, seven days a week. I never have the opportunity to work alone. And that's too bad. I like being alone in a kitchen. But I love the produce market. And I love to pound bread." He smiled that beatific smile once again. "Besides, whatever anyone is doing in the way of cooking—if I'm around—I always have to have my nose in it."

WORK AS play, play as work. Is this possible in situations other than Danny Wilser's? We already know from a number of adult examples that it is. Tiger Woods loves golf enough to inspire thousands of children to want to be just like him and thousands of adults to follow him along the fairways. And Dana Ahern loves her Guanerius, especially now that she has overcome her practice block. In eulogizing the great Italian film actor Marcello Mastroianni, at his funeral in Rome, Italian deputy prime minister Walter Veltroni quoted the actor as having said, "Movies were the most beautiful set of toy trains that I ever found." The skeptic might say that Mastroianni died without ever growing up. But I would hold, instead, that he grew past a number of us.

The ninety-two-year-old cartoonist Al Hirschfeld told the *New York Times* in an interview, "People just enjoy different things. I'm not a great nature lover, and I'm terrible at sight-seeing. But when I'd come back from Paris, I would sit for hours in the window of Howard Johnson's at the corner of Broadway and Forty-sixth Street making little sketches, watching people go by. I find that stimulating."

But must a person be a professional at play to achieve the goals of play—enjoyment and release—at work? No, not at all. When in 1997 a couple of Danish biologists, Peter Funch and Reinhardt Mobjerg Kristensen, discovered a possible new animal phylum that fed parasitically on lobsters' lips, Frederick Harrison, an American invertebrate biologist at Western Carolina University, was quoted by the *New York Times* as saying, "This is going to be neat. People are going to talk, it will be controversial, and that's so much fun." Science can be extraordinarily enjoyable for those who love it. And a lobster's lips can be good for a "lotta laughs."

I know some people who work at relatively routine jobs for large companies and nonetheless play at them. Once in a while an elevator operator, for example, makes it a practice to know by name the various people who work in the building. The game of making personal greetings to regulars makes a workday speed along. A professional dog walker who cruises by my house a couple of times each day with eight or nine dogs in tow—a changing pack of canines according to who's in, who's out of, town—knows his charges well by name and habit. "Hey, Rosa, stop being so lazy. I know you can keep up with us. Hey, Caesar, don't get up so far ahead. *I'm* the boss today." I watch him push a few small dogs by their rumps up and over the wall. And I spot him urging a few older or lazy ones over the top any way he can. He's obviously having fun . . . and they are, too.

People who make a personal game of what they do seem more successful at what they do. And they appear happier. Then, too, they demonstrate heightened and pleasurable concentration—a mental state long associated with play. The University of Chicago psychologist Mihaly (Mike) Csikszentmihalyi calls this kind of superconcentration "flow."

Early in his career, Mike Csikszentmihalyi conducted interviews and distributed questionnaires to people who spent their time doing precisely what they preferred to do, often making financial or social sacrifices to do so. He questioned artists, athletes, musicians, chess masters, surgeons. What became clear was that a number of these individuals achieved a sense of deep happiness, or "optimal experience," by setting up smallish, doable challenges and then staying intensely focused on these. In a sense, they achieved the same sort of "flow" that children routinely achieve in play.

The University of Chicago group developed an interesting technique, called the Experience Sampling Method, for studying flow. They asked over a hundred men and women to wear a pager for a week and to write down what they were feeling and thinking whenever a transmitter, set to go off at random intervals, paged them. In this experiment, there would be somewhere between thirty-five and fifty written records of selected moments during each person's week. The Chicago psychologists defined their subjects as being "in flow" if, at the moment they were beeped, they rated their immediate level of challenge and usage of skills as above their mean level for the week. When beeped at work and while actually working (not gossiping, doing personal business, or daydreaming, which took about one-quarter of people's work time), a little more than half of these people's responses indicated that they were in flow.

When the Chicago investigators asked their subjects whether their sense of challenge was, at that moment, above the mean, this was similar to asking, "Do you have a personally determined goal in mind, a game plan, something nonessential that you're trying to carry out?" In a sense, people were being asked, "Are you playing?" For instance, we know that while he was at work, our chef Danny Wilser set up small goals—little game plans. He wanted to get his "nose into food," taste things, seek adventure, teach cooking, learn Spanish. The University of Chicago research subjects played at their work in the same kinds of ways. One of them, for instance, wished to change his rate of speed of inserting a certain car part into an assembly-line-made automobile. First he determined that his average speed was forty-three seconds per part. Then he silently and secretly challenged himself to work faster until he reached his ultimate best of twenty-eight seconds. Another man, who installed fittings into railroad cars, wanted to understand every other man's job at the plant. His self-sought knowledge became invaluable to factory managers. This kind of doable side-task creates above-average concentration. But it also serves as an entirely internal sort of game.

Another essential of flow—using skills more complex and at a higher level than ordinary skills—is met whenever a person plays. Whenever, say, Danny Wilser challenged himself to joke in Spanish, his Spanish skills improved. If Danny asked himself to cook something new, his skills as a chef rose. Rather than considering flow studies strictly as research into consciousness, one can view them also as studies of play.

However, we must consider an interesting paradox in regard to the Chicago beeper study. When the subjects were paged at their leisure, only 18 percent of their responses qualified as flow. At work, on the other hand, 54 percent of the responses were graded as flow. If flow is truly an experience of deep pleasure, why would the vast majority of individuals still say on their research questionnaires that they would rather be at leisure than at work?

To solve this paradox, we need to understand what most people like to do at their leisure. "Leisure," as we have already determined, is in no way the same as "play." Leisure is "time off." Play is "time on." I believe that no one can be "on" all of the time, even half of the time, much as creative and active people might hope. We cannot expect huge amounts of flow, or play, to occur at our leisure, just as we cannot expect ourselves to flow, or play, all of the time that we work. Just as we need a certain amount of rapid eye movement (REM) active or dream sleep, along with deep sleep and some light sleep, we also need various states of consciousness during our waking hours. One of these conditions is rest, or "couch potato" time. In many instances, after the more active mental activities of work, we must slow down and let our tired minds go on idle. When else, but at leisure, can we kill, bide, and while away the time? We look forward eagerly to this sort of mini-vacation.

But when our kids come over and say, "Mommy, you wanna look at this new toy?" or "Daddy, what's a 'tango'?" we might just happen to have a few spare minutes for play. And for the concentration, or flow, that goes along with it. Okay, so Dr. Csikszentmihalyi's beeper system will probably not pick up our heightened mental activity at these moments. And our considerable pleasure. But the benefits will flow nonetheless.

WE ADULTS show an amazingly varied number of play preferences. Some of the cleverer ones among us use play to alter our selling approaches or work environments. Jordan Furniture of Boston, for instance, is owned by two brothers, Elliott and Barry Tatelman, who have brought their love for play into retailing. They built a specialized and original kind of movie theater right into their store. The idea, imported from Japan, was that their theater would show an action documentary, while the seats, perfectly computer-synchronized with the film, would move every which way to accompany the movements on the screen. People would bank to one side if a turn was shown. They'd jiggle and shake in their seats if the camera did the same. When it first opened, Jordan Furniture's theater was so special, in fact, that families in and around Boston planned their Saturday or Sunday excursions around a visit to Jordan's. And while playing there, why not pick up that new mattress set they've advertised—or an end table for the family room?

If a business owner is going to do something like the Jordan Furniture project, the owner has to remain flexible, however. Over time, other shopping malls, theaters, and museums will install similar recreational devices. Over time, too, such devices, like ever so many toys, lose their luster. I have heard that, for a newer store that Jordan Furniture has more recently designed, instead of putting in another theater, they installed the first branch of a well-loved local roast-beef restaurant. If you enjoyed roast beef, you might just stop in. And while there, why not look at a bunk bed for José?

Playful store windows draw crowds of shoppers. Everybody enjoys something that promises play. Years ago, I especially liked the windows at Sloan's (a furniture store that unfortunately is no more). They were set up to look like storyboards. After Christmas, for instance, Sloan's featured a well-furnished living and dining room that—from the way that everything was arranged—looked as if a New Year's Eve party had taken place there the night before. A little spilled confetti, a newspaper dated January 1, a cupful of coffee near the paper, two or three popped balloons, an empty champagne bottle and a couple of used glasses—just a few things—conveyed the whole picture. I stood in front of such windows for long minutes during my lunch hours. And I bought a lamp and a small table while I was at it.

Retailers' windows with kinetic objects in them, even live objects in them—such as Gump's early-1990s "adopt-an-animal" Christmas windows—traditionally beg for customers to enter the store. The beckoning to play is an offer that is hard to refuse. Long after we grown-ups think that we have forgotten how to play, we can be invited back into the action. Play inducements, if attractive enough, are universal.

Since the early seventies, John Cleese, the English actor who helped to start Monty Python's Flying Circus and who costarred in the films *A Fish Called Wanda* and *Fierce Creatures,* has co-owned a business-consultation company called Video Arts. Video Arts makes industrial training films about corporate skills and strategies, emphasizing playful frames of mind and good humor. John Cleese, so amusing on film, has taken an equally fun-loving approach to the serious goals of the commercial world.

Whenever a person struggles with an important business problem, Mr. Cleese has found, that person "needs to create a little distance from the problem." This distance is established by momentarily changing the "mood or emphasis." As an example of this kind of abrupt change, Cleese spoke of Alfred Hitchcock's behavior with his coscreenwriters. When the writing committee came up against a block and their attitudes became tense, the director would break into their conversation and tell a story that had nothing at all to do with the struggle in which they were all engaged. At first, Hitchcock's writers were annoyed with their boss's tendency to go totally off-point. Later, they realized that the master of suspense was behaving this way on purpose. "Relax," Hitch said one day when the group's irritation was obvious. "It will come." And, indeed, after a break for a story, the ideas did come.

Play does not tackle a problem head-on. In fact, more innovative solutions to work problems are often to be found in play fashion—by avoiding staring straight ahead and, instead, trying out ideas that come from somewhere off to the side. John Cleese recalled that a number of the Monty Python sketches were inspired by "random trawls through a dictionary." He also thought that every person responsible for creative contributions needs an "oasis of quiet"—a specific period each day with the door closed and no phone calls. If you pose a subject to your mind during this time and then toy with all sorts of ideas around it, even apparently unusable ones, chances are you will "get a reward from your unconscious." Finally, Cleese believes that people's egos often interfere with the excellence of their work. Interestingly, a number of researchers on play have found that ego also interferes with play. So if you play at your work, your ego is less likely to get in the way.

Because work and play are not the direct opposites that people have traditionally thought, toys and pleasurable gadgets can be used to advantage in business and professional settings. Sometimes one sees such toys in an office in a motion picture scene. Also, one sometimes sees toys in a real-life consulting or waiting room. National retailers, such as the Nature Company or the Sharper Image, have been selling a number of toys for offices. In fact, one

Christmastime a spokesperson for the Sharper Image company noted that four business categories called for the use of toys.

First, you can use toys to dispel work stress. This has traditionally been a well-accepted use for play, the kind of thing that Alfred Hitchcock was attempting by telling one of his off-point stories. Sharper Image suggested clay, putty, or foam balls for when a person's office pressures mount up. But you might also consider pretty things, such as shakable snow globes, movable toys like the friction car and the mouse on roller skates on my desk, and tiny personal information managers (PIMs) like the ones that U.S. Robotics has manufactured. Virtually any kind of pleasantly tactile and attractive object can temporarily relieve your mind of work-related anxiety.

The second purpose of office toys is to inspire creativity. The Sharper Image company suggested that people use puzzles or novel writing instruments to push these imaginative buttons. Any toy or gadget that diverts your mind from the immediate task at hand will allow creative ideas to strike from somewhere to the side. It doesn't take hours, just a few minutes. One rearrangement of the rock collection on the desk, one setup of a magnetic tower of acrobats, and a good idea often comes. Not always. But often.

Two other potential corporate uses the Sharper Image spokesperson suggested for toys and gadgets are for breaking the ice at business meetings and for gift-giving to coworkers. Both of these, however, may not always be appropriate. People who do not know each other well, especially adults, often feel awkward in forced-play situations. Even when everyone is given the tiny miniature cars or the sets of balls-and-jacks that were suggested by the gadget company, many a normal adult entering such a meeting might feel imposed upon. Do you remember the children on the playgrounds whom the play researchers the Opies watched being play-managed by adults? They didn't play at all nicely.

Two play therapists offered me a good illustrative story in this regard. At a national psychology meeting, they had set up a seminar on "group play therapy" that was open to any interested mental health professional. The two psychologists spent the evening before their seminar arranging the assigned conference room with a tableful of attractive toys that they had brought from home. They wanted all of the seminar participants to spontaneously begin playing as a group, a living example of their topic. The next day when the seminar participants, all of them professionals, arrived, these people sat stiffly in their chairs, facing the toys, their hands folded in their laps. In other words, the more that you arrange for people to play, the less likely they are to play.

As for giving little gifts at the office, this, too, can easily take on a forced or manipulative quality. Unless the gift celebrates a special birthday, Christmas, or a job well done, presents—even of toys—are better left for the worlds of family and friends.

WHEN THE great San Francisco quarterback Joe Montana decided to quit football in 1995 at age thirty-eight, he told the twenty thousand people who had come to a street party in his honor that he had decided to leave football when "it felt like a job."

When work feels as if it no longer allows for play, it is time to think about making some kind of modification. The remarkable, but eccentric, pianist Glenn Gould stopped concertizing and turned entirely to making piano recordings and radio commentaries, for instance, when he concluded that live audiences, before which he had only one shot to play near perfection, were robbing him of his musical pleasures. Gould once said that if, during a performance, he was displeased with how it was going, he fervently wished to be able to stop playing, turn to the audience, and say, "Take two." And so the pianist readjusted. In making recordings, he could have as many takes as he wanted.

People who are truly enjoying their play, even when this is combined with work, are not at all eager to stop. For example, in a note published as a newspaper advertisement after the 1995 National Basketball Association finals, Shaquille O'Neal, who played at the time for the losing Orlando Magic team, wrote to Hakeem Olajuwon, the winning Houston Rockets star: "Hakeem—The Series may be a done deal, but it ain't over between you and me. Sure you're pretty good with your team behind you, but I want you one-on-one."

I don't think that these two great basketball stars ever did play that highly touted one-on-one game. Or if they did, it was lost to me, even though I was watching for it. In a sense it was a fiction, as was the legal secretary Maida's attitude about her work, as expressed in Robert Traver's novel *Anatomy of a Murder*. When her boss, the small-town attorney Parnell, assigns Maida away from her everyday duties to do a little private-detective work, she says, "To think, just to think that I've been pounding a typewriter all these years when—when there's work like this to be done. Work my eye, absorbing play." Yes, a person can make a change toward learning to play again. Or toward playing in a new and different fashion. But it takes some self-observation. And it takes some planning.

Robert Fagen made the point that play is a regulator of nonhuman animals' developmental rates—in other words, that playing controls the speed of maturation. In late maturity, the corollary may be true: play may be able to slow down maturation into senescence. I know a married couple from Columbus, Ohio, Jinny and Dick Sherman, who both ski competitively. When I first met her, Jinny was well into her seventies and was ranked second for women over seventy in the United States. Her husband, Dick, was number seven among American men skiers over eighty. Both of the Shermans looked and acted remarkably young. Both of them met their fellow skiers at get-togethers and competitions throughout the darker, colder months of the year. Interestingly, Dick led an intellectual life all through his working career—he was a professor at Ohio State University. Yet his pleasure in retirement was to play actively and physically.

I WASN'T looking for a second player at food to illustrate how mature adults can play at their work and at their leisure; but that's exactly what did occur when I learned what had become of one of America's greatest athletes. Nate Thurmond, or "Nate the Great," was the hero of the Golden State Warriors for years and was selected in 1997 as one of the fifty best players in National Basketball Association history. Yet Nate had two themes going for him throughout his life of play—basketball and down-home cooking. Late one afternoon, I interviewed Nate in the minimalist office atop his San Francisco restaurant. We talked at a small, squarish table for a little more than two hours. Although he did not smile much, spending time with Nate Thurmond was pleasant and sometimes downright funny.

Nate grew up in Akron, Ohio, home of the American rubber industry. His dad worked as a laborer for Firestone Tire and Rubber Company, and, Nate said, "My father decided for me and my older brother that we wouldn't ever have to work there unless we messed up in college." His parents consistently saved for their boys' college educations. And neither Thurmond lad "messed up."

Their mother was a full-time beautician, and Nate and Ben's maternal grandmother ran the house. Both of Mrs. Thurmond's parents lived with the two growing boys and the boys' mother and father. "Grandma made sure everything was okay at home," Nate remembered. "She always knew what we were doing. We didn't have that free rein that people shouldn't have at a certain age. I love my grandma."

I wondered, since Nate spoke of this special person in the present tense, whether his grandmother was still alive. "No, she died at eighty-four." Nate immediately switched to the past tense to talk about this formative life force behind his own. He was flexible. "She was very religious, my grandmother. Very straight. Typical. She loved her grandboys. Grandma was from Alabama. She taught us manners—how to say 'mister' and 'missus.' She'd drop little wisdoms of life as she cooked. Eventually it soaked through you. I loved it in the kitchen with Grandma."

When Nate was four years old, his father, at six feet three inches, had to convince people that his exceptionally tall boy "shouldn't be in school yet." But Nate sees his height as coming from the tall line of women on his mother's side. "Mom is eighty-five years old and she's five feet eleven. Grandma hit five feet nine, and that was taller than her husband."

Though Nate, even at a young age, hung around his grandma

and the kitchen, he also loved sports. "In my early elementary school years," he recalled, "I played playground softball. I was a pitcher. My coordination just wasn't there, and I had trouble fielding. Also, I couldn't be 'on' every few days, like pitchers are, and still make myself improve. I needed more practice." Nate's mother tried hard to encourage him—"You're growing ahead of your coordination," she told him a number of times. "In a matter of years, you'll catch up." But Nate Thurmond did not feel he absolutely *had* to catch up. He loved his sports, but he also loved to cook.

"Grandma wouldn't let anybody into the kitchen without an apron on," Nate recalled. "So I'd put one on. Man, was she a rib cooker!" Her Thanksgiving feasts were memorable. "We'd have turkey, dressing, ham, fresh collard greens, macaroni and cheese, candied sweet potatoes, fresh rolls, mashed potatoes, and sweet potato pie. As a boy, I wasn't skilled enough to do the Thanksgiving cooking, but I started learning other things from my grandmother. I guess I started cooking on my own at about the same time that I started basketball—when I was about eleven years old."

Nate went to a public school that spanned kindergarten through eighth grade. Spicer Grade School had something that a number of elementary schools do not have—a basketball program. Nate joined the program in the sixth grade. After that, basketball was his only sport, his only athletic endeavor. It was perfect, he felt, for him. He was a "beanpole" as a child with "no meat" on him. His back hurt him from his earliest childhood on—"my right leg is a half inch shorter than my left. But I got that corrected. They built up one of my shoes and nobody knew." His coordination, though never his strong point, was far better suited to basketball than baseball. And best of all, "it was fun." Nate considered his height to be only his second advantage in basketball ("People eventually catch up to you in height"). His primary advantage was that he liked the game so much. Basketball may have included some drudgery, and some pain due to that always-overburdened back of his. But his enjoyment overrode everything else.

At the time in life—eleven and twelve years old—when those

children who are going to develop prodigious capacities for play often do so, Nate Thurmond became a prodigious cook. Unlike Rich Davis—a psychiatrist I know and admire who found his true play form, barbecue, as an adult and went on to invent KC Masterpiece barbecue sauce after serving first as the dean of a medical school—Nate was becoming a homebred chef while still a child. Although he lived in the industrial North, he cooked in the mode of the small-town South from whence his grandmother came. "I was great at frying chicken," he said. "And I was good at baking a cake from scratch. We didn't know nothin' about cakes from boxes in our house. I could make a fun dinner of fried corn off the cob in the pan, or okra, tomatoes, onions. And even then, I had a terrific recipe for sweet potato pie."

So two play trends were developing simultaneously in this young boy from a hardworking and loving family. Neither of these trends had anything but an "I *like* it" goal. He was not looking for any scholarships to college, nor was he looking à la *Hoop Dreams* toward a National Basketball Association career. He was looking for enjoyment at two pastimes at which he knew he was getting "great."

But then something emerged that changed the nature of Nate's play—intense competition. The competition assumed the guise of just one boy, Elijah Chatman, who played basketball at Akron's Henry Grade School. "He was the same age as me," said Nate, "and he was better than me. He wasn't taller—we were about the same size—but he was more coordinated. He played a lot of basketball at the Akron Community Center. He lived at that gym. We met in the seventh and eighth grades when we started playing against each other. And I learned from him that you have to play against older guys to get better."

By eighth grade, Nate was playing basketball hard and continuously. "I *really* played in the summers—I did six hours a day. I'd do three hours by myself in the mornings—I'd do speed and footwork drills, lateral movements, and other things essential to basketball players. I was having success and I wanted to be better. I was the best on our elementary school team, but Elijah was better. I matured late. Elijah matured early. We'd play outside in the park all afternoon in the summers. And we'd play together one-on-one. At first, I couldn't beat him. He lived across the street from Grace Park, where he always practiced—that's one way that he got such an early jump on me. Sometimes we played on Saturday mornings at the Community Center. But it's softer on your knees to play in a dirt place. So we played a lot of one-on-one in the park. And I took a lot of beatings there from Elijah."

Why did a boy like Nate stick with basketball? Obviously he had strong backing for basketball at home. But there were minuses, too. He worried a great deal about his coordination and worked on it for hours during his summertimes. His back hurt at times. He also became self-conscious about playing in front of his parents: "I didn't want my parents to come see me—I thought I'd be too nervous. And then I let the thing go on too long. The first time in high school that my parents came to see me play, I was just horrible."

But the pros far outweighed the cons as far as Nate's favorite game was concerned. And the rewards were becoming complex and multiple. "The competition was great," he told me. "I liked to play. I liked the adulation. My pictures were in the newspapers. People in our small city knew who the two of us were—Elijah and me. And it wasn't because I was going to jail! By the time I was in my junior and senior years in high school, I realized that I would go to college on a basketball scholarship. At sixteen, I was six feet seven inches tall and weighed a hundred sixty-five pounds. And about half of the time now, I was beating Elijah at one-on-one. He was six feet seven, too. A handful of colleges, all in the Midwest, came after me. And Elijah and I decided to go on scholarship to Bowling Green State University [Ohio]. We could room together. And my parents could keep their college money in the bank."

Nate was still cooking all through his basketball days at Akron's Central High. "Guys would come by the house to see me," he remembered, "and they'd find me in an apron [at six feet seven] in the kitchen with Grandma. She had all kinds of things to say to me while we were cooking or baking alone. Like, 'Don't unzip your pants for anything but going to the bathroom' or 'Don't smoke any funny cigarettes.' Grandma and Mom started telling me all kinds of those sayings early on. I had no idea what a 'funny cigarette' was until I saw one much later. Then I realized. It *was* a funny-looking cigarette."

In his freshman and sophomore years at Bowling Green State, Nate grew four more inches. Suddenly he was six feet eleven inches tall and capable of beating his old friend and nemesis, Elijah, just about every time that they played. "It all started coming together for me in my college sophomore year," Nate said. "My coordination, my strength—they caught up to my height. That's what my mother and grandmother had told me about growing ahead of my coordination. They were right. You can be eight feet tall, but if your coordination is off, you can't play basketball." True. And if you can't stand the heat of having "the guys" see you in the kitchen with an apron on and at the command of your grandmother, you can't cook either.

We know the rest of Nate's sports story. In college, he realized that he might have a chance of making the pros. As a pro he thought he might become a star. Even as a star, "I never would have guessed I'd be in the top fifty players ever to play in America." Playing as a professional carried one important difference for Nate Thurmond: "I knew if I didn't perform, it would affect my livelihood." In Nate's case, as in Dr. Rich Davis's "play" with his KC Masterpiece barbecue sauce, once there were big monetary stakes, play moved closer to work. Nate had to practice basketball even when he didn't want to. "So I saw it as a job," he said. "But I can't think of a better job than working in the NBA. It was the best fun job that you could ever have!"

Nate retired when he was thirty-six years old, during the 1977–78 season. Afterward, he did some television commentary, and since 1981 he has worked for the Golden State Warriors as a goodwill ambassador. But as for basketball itself, Nate told me he can't even play a short game of one-on-one in his neighborhood. "My knees are shot," he said.

Having a second game to play certainly helps, however. "During my basketball career, I started a restaurant up on Fillmore Street called The Beginning," he said. "The name was a reference to my grandmother because she is 'the beginning' of our family tree as I know it." Again, Nate broke into the present tense at the thought of his major source of inspiration. "There was a need in San Francisco for a sit-down, black restaurant that would be presented in a way in which all races could be comfortable. Also at around the time that I started the restaurant, I used to go to a little restaurant up the block where the lady who ran it was a lot like my grandmother. Her name was Ollie Butler, and she came to work for me as my first chef. It was too bad, but Grandma was never here in San Francisco to try out the food. Grandma didn't fly."

Nate found it difficult to keep The Beginning at the same time that he played basketball. "When you cook soul food," he said, "you have to have a lot of things cooked in advance—things like chitlins, macaroni and cheese, short ribs, gumbo—and if it's a slow, rainy night, it's hard to make it. So after nine years of having the restaurant, I sold it."

At The Beginning, Nate had been unable to barbecue because "you'd smoke out the residents who lived above the restaurant. But I had been noticing all of those Domino's trucks delivering pizza all over town. So I thought after we closed down in 1979—and I was talking to friends about it, too—'Why wouldn't barbecued ribs and chicken be a good option to pizza?' And if it was a good option, people would call in."

In 1982, Big Nate's, a restaurant, carryout, and delivery barbecue, opened in the Civic Center area of San Francisco. No apartments were above it—just the small business office where we sat. "This place does much better than The Beginning," said Nate. "A lot of Big Nate's is work, plain and simple. Ordering, bill paying, all of that is work. And sometimes I have conflicts about a Warriors game or something—but that's life. But a lot of it is fun, too." He smiled. "I have a manager here who can get me out of 'situations.' I'm blessed with good employees, and it's a nice feeling of camaraderie. I get to meet a lot of people here. And somebody sometimes says something to me like, 'Hey, Nate, I like your ribs.' That's fun, too.

"We bottle our own sauce now." He proudly stood up from our table to show me six label mock-ups on his wall for "Big Nate's Hall of Fame Bar-B-Que Sauce." When he stood up, a huge, towering frame emerged—still thin—on long, stiltlike legs. The labels had a yellow background with brown writing, a black picture of Nate's face, and such words as *mild* and *original* designating the varieties. The first recipe, the one used in setting up the restaurant and known as Nate's "original," is "the same recipe as Mom's."

A few days after I interviewed Nate Thurmond, I ran into him at—of all places—Ella's. Nate was there for lunch with his wife, Marci, a lovely-looking, tall, blond woman of about Nate's age, who works downtown as a legal secretary. The couple have no children, and as Nate had told me back at his office, they were both getting to an age when they occasionally talked of retirement. Nate said a few words to me at Danny Wilser's restaurant about how much he had enjoyed our interview and how much he and Marci liked Danny's food. It reminded me that Thanksgiving was coming up soon and that Nate had told me that five couples, friends of theirs, were coming over for the holiday meal. In addition to all of Nate's Southern specialties, which he'd be cooking himself, they'd also be having, Nate said, "Marci's peas and carrots, apple pie, and fresh cranberry sauce—food which I knew *nothing* about as a kid!"

Ab and I tried Big Nate's ribs the night that I interviewed Nate. My brother Bob joined us, and we ate ourselves stuffed, without a calorie in mind. It was great fun, and we promised ourselves to have more of Nate's ribs the next time we were all off our diets.

As to Nate's retirement from both basketball and food, his last words to me at Big Nate's stuck in my memory: "If my sauce is like Rich Davis's KC Masterpiece, then I really *will* retire."

WE MUST look at our commitments to play as lifelong promises to ourselves. Conscious promises. Important ones. When I considered the two male food lovers whose stories summarized my thoughts on adult play, along with the three gardeners—two women and one man—whose tales inspired me to begin writing this book, I found that all five held these commitments in common. As they passed through critical developmental moments of their lives, each was able to hang on to his or her recreational interests, while finding suitable new variations on these interests. They went through their transitions from one period of life to another without changing their dedication to play. And they went through transitions in their playing abilities without changing this commitment.

In the same regard, I remember reading a professional paper, written in 1948 by William Menninger, one of the leading American psychoanalysts of his day and the son of Charles Frederick (C. F.) Menninger, the founder of the Menninger Clinic and its subsequent family psychiatric dynasty. In his article, William spoke of his father's life in the two-plus decades that followed his retirement. After age seventy-five, C.F. no longer had the spryness and stamina to play in his garden, so he found a new way to serve the same interests—inside his house with rock polishers and cutting tools. After a decade of mineralogy, the eighty-five-year-old man went on to investigate and collect various mollusks and their shells. In C. F. Menninger's later life, his activities centered on natural-science themes. No matter what end-of-life barriers arose, play continued to impel him into new solutions and enjoyments. He passed from midlife into old age seamlessly and without gloom.

A single story line ran through these later-life interests of C. F. Menninger. And a single story line runs through the tales of the three gardeners and the two cooks who start and finish this book. Their play did not change that much, even though their specific subjects of interest might have altered considerably. In a sense, these adult players maintained a fantasy that kept their lives unique and ran like a ribbon of continuity through whatever they did.

For Danny Wilser, for instance, the idea of connecting with a gentler, more flexible father than the one whom he had known as a young boy pushed him into new and more complex cooking projects. For Nate Thurmond, his strong connection to the remarkable women in his life induced him to go his own way—regardless of any pressures to go in other directions. The images of mothers and grandmothers became constant, undying icons that Nate could keep before his eyes—propelling him toward a belief in himself and a belief in his own "beginnings."

Governing fantasies are seen in all sorts of interesting lives, most likely in all lives. By dedicating a good part of our energies to play, we can express these fantasies more fully, without creating the kinds of harm to others that would easily follow were our spirits less devoted to the sense of fun. Because play is ordinarily one step removed from the sexual and aggressive drives, it remains more innocent and more creative than the more direct expressions of these impulses.

All of us need to pause at times and to assess our lives. What are we doing too much? What is missing? What's good? What's bad? What's the problem? And what can be done about it?

Today, these assessments often revolve around sex, friendships, communication skills, family troubles, work. But we rarely, if ever, give much pause to the idea of play. Preachers don't preach about it. Psychotherapists don't often mention it or ask about it. They rarely, if ever, watch it. After all, Freud himself overlooked it. Family physicians act as if they have never heard the word. Play presents far too upbeat a story to attract much media attention, so we see little of it in our newspapers or on our TV sets.

Yet a trickle of researchers continue to study play. Most of them are almost paralytically underfunded because the drug companies, toy companies, institutes of health and medicine, private foundations, even groups funding special programs for children, have tended to shy away from the subject. Anything ordinarily associated with childhood is thought to be small and frivolous. As a result, we have not yet perceived the ultimate importance of play. But these few researchers go on, despite the difficulties. And every year or so, something new and interesting emerges.

A good way for any of us—researchers or not—to appreciate the benefits of adult play is to informally watch other people's play.

When we observe play—situation by situation, individual by individual—we find certain adults who seem particularly creative and happy. How do they play? Is it obvious? Or does their play take place entirely on the inside? If their play is largely solitary, how do these individuals accomplish it? If we know an adult player well, sometimes he or she will tell us.

One such person loved to farm. She behaved as if corn were the only thing that was worth growing. She meticulously watched each and every type of corn that she grew and began formulating genetic principles from them. Another such person loved to imagine things. He couldn't imagine a species of life, bacteria such as *E. coli* for instance, cloning itself endlessly without once in a while—just once in a while—having sex. He set out to prove it. Perhaps genes might be manipulated—that is, *if* bacteria did have sex. A third such person sat in an old Ann Arbor student hangout, the Pretzel Bell, watching his beer. Most of the bubbles went up straight, but a few veered off in wild pathways. Why? He stared and stared. Maybe bubbles could signal the intrusions of space particles by veering off in new directions. Would that same principle work in a specialized chamber? He began to look into it. These three solitary players, Barbara McClintock, Joshua Lederberg, and Donald Glaser, each eventually won a Nobel Prize in science. But at first, they were "just playing."

There are as many ways to play as there are people. Because of our unique personalities, we all have unique contributions to make to the world of play. And to the world at large. Once a person becomes aware of these possibilities, the person will not have to wait long for a good play idea to come. Once an idea comes along, another will arrive even sooner.

This leads me to the best single way to appreciate the benefits of adult play—to play oneself. A person's play can be solitary or mutual, imaginative or strictly preset, athletic or stationary. Play benefits the individual and the individual's surroundings. One can feel it.

Play feeds on play. All play researchers seem to agree that once a person knows how to play, it becomes easier to play under other circumstances and at other times of life. Anyone can begin taking a more playful approach. And today is a good day to start.

I AM AT my garden fence, looking over at the Presidio Wall and mentally drifting. It is early June, and most of the bearded iris that I put in last fall bloomed while I was away from home in May. But one iris is still coming up, and I'm so eager to see what it does that I look for it every morning. No, it's not out yet! I pause and look again at the shiny black buds. Will the flowers be black? I doubt it, but I'll have to wait till tomorrow to find out.

My poppies are blooming intensely. It seems as if every small poppy plant I set into the ground last March is offering me a new surprise in color, texture, ruffles, edging. I am particularly enjoying, too, some sunrise-to-sunset-colored snapdragons that I put into one spot together. I tell myself to do that combination again— and in more places.

An acquaintance stops by my fence to tell me that my minuscule next-door neighbors, Frankie and Robin, are coming back home next week from Hong Kong. They will be spending the summer in San Francisco. I know that they love the way my snapdragons' "mouths" pop open when they press their "cheeks" toward the vertical. And I know that they like the idea that white sweet alyssum is called "fairy carpet." What else could I do in the garden that would be fun for them? Show them the faces of my pansies? Tell them the names that people call columbines—"little doves," "granny's bonnets"? Get them to figure out why? Should I quickly put some woolly lamb's ear into the ground so that they can feel the fuzz? Or some bachelor's buttons so they can weave a chain? Here's a new lily as dark and as red as blood. I can't tell them *that*. But here are some jet-black pansies. Frankie and Robin will enjoy searching for them, I'll bet, especially if we make a game of it.

I drift away for a second or two. There comes the idea—in from somewhere off to the side, the direction playful ideas always seem to come from. Last fall I harvested the seeds from my giant stock.

I'll give my two little neighbors my envelopes of seed and let them plant it in some pots that I've got behind the house. Stock grows fast from seed and smells wonderful. Frankie and Robin will be able to grow some flowers from scratch before they have to get back onto that plane to Hong Kong.

Looking at the Wall reminds me of a scene early in April 1997, when Ab and I came home late from work. It was after dark. We were pulling into our garage when a neighbor, Jed Tully, who was walking his two dogs, Homer and Lily, and whose cat, Mikey, was following close behind, motioned for us to stay outside for a minute. Jed carried a pair of binoculars and asked if we'd seen the Hale-Bopp comet yet. Yes, we had, but only with our naked eyes and a hundred-year-old pair of opera glasses. We'd mislaid our binoculars and needed to search for them.

Well, Jed is a player and he'd come along with the proper equipment. We stared at Hale-Bopp with Jed's high-powered lenses, and the three of us marveled at its amazingly spiraled tail. Was it a double spiral? We were pretty sure that it was. Another person approached us—a woman we didn't know. She joined us in peering at the comet. Then two more neighbors joined in. A couple of new dogs came along, too. Pretty soon, Jed had attracted a little knot of adults to the Wall—all of us playing with the miracle of Hale-Bopp, with the miracle of binoculars, with the miracle of a national recreational area so close at hand, with the miracle of a nonfoggy night in an ordinarily foggy town.

It was a memorable evening at the Presidio Wall. Almost a rite. And I will always think of Hale-Bopp with great pleasure, not just because of its spectacular appearance in the night sky but because of Jed Tully, his binoculars, his dogs, his cat, and our neighbors. Jed and Hale-Bopp created a moment of adult play, a moment for remembrance, a moment of high enjoyment. At such moments we are at our best.

Notes

Preface

12 "In his 1930": *Civilization and Its Discontents* is published in *The Standard Edition of the Complete Psychological Works of Sigmund Freud* (hereafter, *Standard Edition*), vol. 21, trans. and ed. J. Strachey (London: Hogarth Press, 1961), 59–145.

12 "In his writings": "Beyond the Pleasure Principle" (1920) is in *Standard Edition*, vol. 18 (1955), 7–64.

13 " 'We cannot improve' ": E. Erikson, *Childhood and Society* (New York: W. W. Norton, 1950), 264.

13 "In fact, in 1972": Erikson's lectures at Harvard, the Godkin lectures, are published as *Toys and Reasons: Stages in the Ritualization of Experience* (New York: W. W. Norton, 1977).

1: Why Play? And How Do We Know We're Playing?

21 "In his classic 1938 book": J. Huizinga discussed the word *fun* on page 3 of *Homo Ludens*, trans. F. F. C. Hull (London: Routledge & Kegan Paul, 1949).

21 "Mihaly Csikszentmihalyi": Csikszentmihalyi wrote about play and possibility in "Leisure and Socialization," *Social Forces* 60 (1981): 332–40.

21 "Early in my studies": I first discovered post-traumatic play from the

behaviors of the Chowchilla kidnapping group. Later, I found post-traumatic play in my own patients and, at about the same time, in a rural comparison group to the Chowchilla children whom I interviewed five years after the kidnapping. These references are (1) L. Terr, "Children of Chowchilla: A Study of Psychic Trauma," *Psychoanalytic Study of the Child* 34 (1979): 547–623; (2) L. Terr, " 'Forbidden Games': Post-Traumatic Child's Play," *Journal of the American Academy of Child Psychiatry* 20 (1981): 741–60; (3) L. Terr, "Life Attitudes, Dreams, and Psychic Trauma in a Group of 'Normal' Children," *Journal of the American Academy of Child Psychiatry* 22 (1983): 221–30; and (4) L. Terr, "Chowchilla Revisited: The Effects of Psychic Trauma Four Years After a Schoolbus Kidnapping," *American Journal of Psychiatry* 140 (1983): 1543–50.

21 "Post-traumatic play has a ripple effect": This subject can be found in a published lecture I gave, "Childhood Trauma in Society: The Pebble and the Pool," in ed. J. Hammer III, *The 1990 Distinguished Visiting Professorship Lectures* (Memphis: University of Tennessee, Memphis, Health Science Center), 75–91. A discussion of ripple effects also appears in my book *Too Scared to Cry* (New York: Harper & Row, 1990; paper ed., New York: Basic Books, 1992).

22 "A generation ago": D. W. Winnicott's ideas about teaching patients to play are in his *Playing and Reality* (New York: Basic Books, 1971), 63. Winnicott wrote, "If the therapist cannot play, then he is not suitable for the work. If the patient cannot play, then something needs to be done to enable the patient to become able to play, after which psychotherapy may begin."

22 "Though teas are": Some of my happiest memories of North American teas come from the Empress Hotel, Victoria, BC; the Windsor Court, New Orleans; a teahouse on the Beehive Trail, Banff National Park, Canada; and the Pierpont Morgan Library, New York City.

25 "We even sleep less": J. Schor, *The Overworked American: The Unexpected Decline of Leisure* (New York: Basic Books, 1993).

26 "The practice of relegating play": This discussion of the Greek words for education and play comes from two sources, Huizinga's *Homo Ludens* and from a learned Greek friend.

26 "But I wondered": My favorite biography of Mozart is M. Davenport, *Mozart* (New York: Charles Scribner's Sons, 1932).

27 "In his syndicated": The Brazelton correspondence was published in his "Families Today" newspaper column on November 13, 1995 (*San Francisco Chronicle*, E8).

27 "And we recognize": I found the Jung quote in chapter 1 (p. 82) of his *Psychological Types*, trans. H. Godwin Baynes (Great Britain: T. & A. Constable, 1923; New York: Pantheon, 1953). The Frost poem, "Two Tramps in Mud-Time," is quoted in Erikson's *Toys and Reasons* (New York: W. W. Norton, 1977). It can be found in *The Poetry of Robert Frost,* ed. E. C. Lathem (New York: Holt, Rinehart and Winston, 1969).

28 "Huizinga called": The "play-ground" concept comes from *Homo Ludens.* Gregory Bateson's ideas about the "framed event" come from Bateson's *Steps to an Ecology of the Mind* (New York: Ballantine, 1972). His classic professional paper on the communications involved in play is "The Message 'This Is Play,' " in ed. B. Schaffner, *Group Processes: Transactions of the Second Conference* (New York: Josiah Macy Foundation, 1956), 145–246.

29 " 'The closer she came' ": The quote about Steffi Graf is from R. Finn, "Graf's Year Is Difficult Till End, but Successful," *New York Times,* November 20, 1995, B7.

29 "David Mamet's film": *House of Games,* 1987, marked Mamet's film-directing debut. It starred his then-wife, Lindsay Crouse, and his stage-acting friend Joe Mantegna.

30 "The playwright S. N. Behrman": Behrman's quote was recorded in G. Clarke, "Broadway Legends: George Gershwin: The Celebrated Composer's Manhattan," *Architectural Digest* 52 (11) (November 1995): 192.

30 "After the tower": The psychiatrist Stuart Brown described his "psychological autopsy" of Charles Whitman in his article "Animals at Play," *National Geographic* 186 (6) (December 1994): 2–35.

31 "According to Prof. Robert Fagen": Fagen's classic work on nonhuman play is *Animal Play Behavior* (New York: Oxford University Press, 1981).

33 "Consider the case": On January 22, 1998, in federal court in Sacramento, California, Theodore Kaczinski pleaded guilty to several crimes, including murder, in exchange for a sentence of life imprisonment without possibility of parole and the forgoing of his right to appeal. W. Glaberson, "Kaczinski Avoids a Death Sentence with Guilty Plea," *New York Times,* January 23, 1998, A1.

34 "The second day": The Eickelman account comes from Richard Péres-Pena, "Memories of His Brilliance, and Shyness, but Little Else," *New York Times,* April 5, 1996, A11.

38 "Then Kelly's husband": The Rockefeller Foundation's Villa Serbelloni is one of the great places in the world for combining work and play. I spent one-month scholar-in-residence terms there in October 1981 and in March 1988.

40 "As Robert Fagen": The Fagen quote is from Stuart Brown's article "Through the Lens of Play," *ReVision* 17 (4) (Spring 1995): 4–12.

2: Revisiting the Lowest Rungs of the Play Ladder

43 "The important concept of developmental staging": G. Stanley Hall, *Adolescence,* vol. 1 (New York: D. Appleton, 1904).

44 "By categorizing the phases": The psychoanalytic concept of phases is to be found throughout the writings of Sigmund Freud, beginning with his

1905 paper on Little Hans, "The Analysis of a Phobia in a Five-Year-Old Boy," in *Standard Edition,* vol. 10, trans. and ed. J. Strachey (London: Hogarth Press, 1955), 3–149.

44 "Let's briefly think": In opting for readability and clarity, I left out a number of psychoanalytic contributions concerning the development of play. For those readers particularly interested in the analytic approach to play, I would suggest an overview, edited by Albert J. Solnit, Donald J. Cohen, and Peter B. Neubauer, entitled *The Many Meanings of Play: A Psychoanalytic Perspective* (New Haven: Yale University Press, 1993). I would also suggest L. Peller, "Models of Children's Play," in eds. R. E. Herron and B. Sutton-Smith, *Child's Play* (New York: John Wiley & Sons, 1971), 110–25; E. H. Erikson, "Configurations in Play," *Psychoanalytic Quarterly* 6 (2) (1937): 139–214; "Sex Differences in the Play Configurations of American Pre-Adolescents," in eds. R. E. Herron and B. Sutton-Smith, *Child's Play,* 126–44, and *Play and Development* (New York: W. W. Norton, 1972); P. Greenacre, "Play in Relation to Creative Imagination," in *Psychoanalytic Study of the Child* 12 (1959): 47–72; M. Klein, "The Development of a Child," *International Journal of Psychoanalysis* 4 (1923): 419–74; and "Personification in the Play of Children," *International Journal of Psychoanalysis* 10 (1929): 193–204.

46 "In the mid-1960s": Anna Freud's developmental lines are proposed in *Normality and Pathology in Childhood* (New York: International Universities Press, 1965). Anna Freud's thoughts on the need for an early shift to work about when a kindergartener enters school come from "The Dynamic Psychology of Education" (1976), in *The Writings of Anna Freud,* vol. 8 (New York: International Universities Press, 1981), 307–14.

46 "Jean Piaget painstakingly studied": J. Piaget, *Play, Dreams, and Imitation in Childhood* (1945) (London: Hienemann, 1951; New York: W. W. Norton, 1962). His early theories on childhood thought are to be found in *The Language and Thought of the Child* (New York: Harcourt Brace, 1926). A good summary of Piaget's theories is in J. H. Flavell, *The Developmental Psychology of Jean Piaget* (New York: Van Nostrand Reinhold, 1963).

49 "Whenever they slip in space": The infantile instincts are described well in various medical textbooks of neonatal neurology. For a good list of instincts, see either J. J. Volpe, *Neurology of the Newborn,* 3rd ed. (Philadelphia: W. B. Saunders, 1995), 95–124, or G. M. Fenichel, *Neonatal Neurology* (New York: Churchill Livingstone, 1990), 4–14.

50 "We grown-ups indulge vicariously": The films I cite are *Downhill Racer* (1969, directed by Michael Ritchie), *Wind* (1992, directed by Carroll Ballard), *Deliverance* (1972, directed by John Boorman), *River Wild* (1994, directed by Curtis Hanson), *Endless Summer* (1966, directed by Bruce Brown), *Endless Summer II* (1994, directed by Bruce Brown), *Cliffhanger* (1993, directed by Renny Harlin).

54 "Perhaps Kareem should have patented": For an interesting article on the possibility of trademarking or patenting specific play techniques, read C. Marine, "All the Copyrighted Moves," *San Francisco Examiner,* June 23, 1996, D1.

54 "Mimicry is frequently used": Michael Lewis's book on infant communication is M. Lewis and L. Michalson, *Children's Emotions and Moods: Developmental Theory and Measurement* (New York: Plenum, 1983). See especially chapter 7, "How Emotions Are Managed, Labeled, and Interpreted," pp. 193–230. In another book, edited by Michael Lewis and his colleague Leonard A. Rosenblum, *The Effect of the Infant on Its Caregiver* (New York: John Wiley, 1974), R. Q. Bell wrote an interesting chapter on infantile influences over parental behavior: "Contributions of Human Infants to Caregiving and Social Interaction," pp. 1–19. Bell suggested that there are two social exchange systems between parent and infant, one to give care, and a second to play together. Daniel Stern, M.D., an infant psychiatrist and researcher, proposed that the baby's caretaker provides a communication system with the baby that allows for mutually sportive behaviors. This system includes a usual time and place for play, a play gaze, play face, special play vocalizations, peekaboo face presentations (zooming in and out), and making play bubbles. See D. Stern, *The First Relationship: Infant and Mother* (Cambridge, Mass.: Harvard University Press, 1977).

56 "Animals with more advanced": Some of these observations on young animals come from Robert Fagen, *Animal Play Behavior* (New York: Oxford University Press, 1981). Fagen also specifies that play develops earlier in those species that grow up more quickly. See R. Fagen, "Animal Play, Games of Angels, Biology, and Brian," in ed. A. D. Pellegrini, *The Future of Play Theory: A Multidisciplinary Inquiry into the Contributions of Brian Sutton-Smith* (Albany: State University of New York Press, 1995), 23–44.

56 "Once they have the capacity": R. G. Patton and L. I. Gardner described infantile inabilities to grow and thrive in their pioneering monograph, *Growth Failure and Maternal Deprivation* (Springfield, Ill.: Thomas, 1963). Réné Spitz wrote two classic papers on infantile cognitive and emotional shutdowns: "Hospitalism: An Inquiry into the Genesis of Psychiatric Conditions in Early Childhood," *Psychoanalytic Study of the Child* 1 (1945): 53–74; and R. Spitz and K. M. Wolf, "Anaclitic Depression: An Inquiry into the Genesis of Psychiatric Conditions of Early Childhood," *Psychoanalytic Study of the Child* 2 (1946): 313–42.

58 "Peekaboo is based on symbolism": Jean Piaget was the first person to recognize that in the eyes of young babies, material objects are impermanent. He presented and explained his experiments on children's development of object permanence in his *Construction of Reality in the Child* (1937) (New York: Basic Books, 1954). The American psychologist Jerome Bruner saw peekaboo as the first important game with rules. For his take on this infantile game, see J. S. Bruner and V. Sherwood, "Peekaboo and the Learning of Rule Struc-

tures," in eds. J. S. Bruner, A. Jolly, and K. Sylva, *Play—Its Role in Development and Evolution* (New York: Basic Books, 1976), 277–85.

59 "Attachment and loss are primary themes": The most important work in this field was written by John Bowlby, *Attachment and Loss* (New York: Basic Books, 1969). Its three volumes are vol. 1, *Attachment;* vol. 2, *Separation: Anxiety and Anger;* vol. 3, *Loss: Sadness and Depression.* They originated in Bowlby's work for the World Health Organization on the mental status of homeless children after World War II. Bowlby then went on to consider what happens when young children temporarily lose their mothers, or when they have to be admitted to a hospital.

59 "The mid-twentieth-century English": Winnicott's theories about "transitional phenomena" being at the root of creative mind play were expressed in D. W. Winnicott, *Playing and Reality* (New York: Basic Books, 1971).

60 "Erikson believed that": Autocosmic, microspheric, and macrospheric play were explained in E. Erikson, *Childhood and Society* (New York: W. W. Norton, 1950).

62 "In 1997, the Nobel Prize": Articles summarizing Dario Fo's accomplishments leading to the Nobel Prize in literature, and also summarizing the criticisms against Fo's work, are M. Gussow, "The Not-So-Accidental Recognition of an Anarchist," *New York Times,* October 15, 1997, E2; T. Kushner, "Fo's Last Laugh," *The Nation* 265 (14) (November 3, 1997): 4; and C. Hitchens, "Lotta Continua," *The Nation* 265 (15) (November 10, 1997): 8.

62 "But language play can": The story of E. Mason Cooley's epigrams was told to me in August 1997 by Carl F. Hovde, professor emeritus of American literature at Columbia University. A bit of Dr. Cooley's language play can also be found under "Apothegms" in ed. L. Peterson, *The Norton Reader* (New York: W. W. Norton, 1996), 805–15.

64 "For some people": William Steig's *CDB* (1968) and *CDC* (1984) are published in New York by Aladdin and by Farrar, Straus, Giroux, respectively. St. Elizabeth's Hospital, Washington, D.C., censored patients' mail throughout the 1940s and 1950s when Ezra Pound was there. Pound's postcards to friends were read at that time and decoded by a psychiatric friend of mine. Occasionally, one may also find a crossword puzzle that uses these letter codes. See, for instance, those of Matt Gaffney, the *New York Times.*

65 "When it's great": *All About Eve* (1950, directed by Joseph L. Mankiewicz). Mankiewicz's superbly witty screenplay was based on Mary Orr's story "The Wisdom of Eve."

3: Biological Reasons We Pick Certain Playgrounds and Ways of Playing

68 "Even though we are raised": A group of developmental psychologists at Harvard, led by Jerome Kagan, physiologically and psychologically studied

behaviorally inhibited (shy) toddlers versus uninhibited ones as they grew older. The shyness trait appeared to last at least through age five and a half. See J. S. Reznick, J. Kagan, N. Snidman, M. Gersten, K. Baak, and A. Rosenberg, "Inhibited and Uninhibited Children: A Follow-up Study," *Child Development* 57 (1986): 660–80.

68 "Agassi, the 1994 winner": The physical differences between Sampras and Agassi and the ways each tennis player was marketed were amusingly discussed in G. Vecsey, "Next Year Switch Wardrobes," *New York Times,* September 11, 1995, C2. The lengths of their walks to the court were highly visible from the TV coverage of the event.

69 "One clue as to how": The two professional articles on the novelty-seeking gene are R. P. Ebstein, R. H. Belmaker, M. Katz, L. Nemanov, E. R. Bennett, D. Blaine, Y. Osher, B. Priel, R. Umansky, and O. Novick, "Dopamine D4 Receptor (D4DR) Exon III Polymorphism Associated with the Human Personality Trait of Novelty Seeking," *Nature Genetics* 12 (1) (1996): 78–80; and J. Benjamin, D. H. Hamer, D. L. Murphy, B. D. Greenberg, C. Patterson, and L. Li, "Population and Familial Association Between the D4 Dopamine Receptor Gene and Measures of Novelty Seeking," *Nature Genetics* 12 (1) (1996): 81–84. The findings were reported to the general public by N. Angier, "Variant Gene Tied to a Love of New Thrills," *New York Times,* January 2, 1996, A1.

69 "Years before the American": Robert Cloninger is a prolific psychiatric writer on temperament, personality, and brain chemistry. For one paper that described his thesis on temperament, read C. R. Cloninger, "The Genetics and Psychobiology of the Seven-Factor Model of Personality," in ed. K. R. Silk, *The Biology of Personality Disorder* (Washington, D.C.: American Psychiatric Association, 1998), 63–91.

73 "Two scientists, for instance": J. D. Lazell Jr. and N. C. Spitzer, "Apparent Play in an American Alligator," *Copiea* (1977): 188.

73 "And an evolutionary": G. M. Burghart commented on his pet sea turtles in "Precosity, Play, and the Ectotherm-Endotherm Transition: Profound Reorganization or Superficial Adaptations?" in ed. E. M. Blass, *Handbook of Behavioral Neurobiology,* vol. 9 (New York: Plenum, 1988), 107–48.

73 "young mice apparently do": R. Fagen, "Animal Play, Games of Angels, Biology, and Brian," in ed. A. D. Pellegrini, *The Future of Play Theory: A Multidisciplinary Inquiry into the Contributions of Brian Sutton-Smith* (Albany: State University of New York Press, 1995), 23–44.

74 "But animal curiosity": G. Burghardt, "On the Origins of Play," in ed. P. K. Smith, *Play in Animals and Humans* (Oxford, England: Basil Blackwell, 1984), 5–42.

74 "Unrelated to either sex or survival": The idea of the aesthetics of evolution was rediscovered and reworked by Michael Ghiselen from unpublished and relatively unstudied notebooks and papers of Charles Darwin as well as

from Ghiselen's new thinking and observations. These ideas can be further explored in M. T. Ghiselen, *The Economy of Nature and the Evolution of Sex* (Berkeley: University of California Press, 1974), and in M. T. Ghiselen, "On the Evolution of Play by Means of Artificial Selection," *Behavioral and Brain Sciences* 5 (1982): 165.

75 "One late-summer afternoon": It's possible to argue endlessly about what is *real* animal play. If my Cape Cod sighting of the back-and-forth scramble between the crow and the three little birds had been in May or early June, it would most likely have been a real war between a nest raider and three tiny nest guardians. Later in the summer, however, it was more likely to have been a game.

75 "hard-fought hockey game": At the 1998 Winter Olympics in Nagano, Japan, the American women's team, led by Cammi Granato, won the first gold medal ever awarded for the sport of women's hockey.

75 "Along these same lines": Video games appeal more to boys than girls. In one report, 80 percent of video-game play among children of ages nine to fifteen was done by boys (R. Kubey and R. Larson, "The Use and Experience of the New Video Media Among Children and Young Adolescents," *Communications Research* 17 [1990]: 107–30). Jeffrey H. Goldstein, a play researcher especially interested in gender differences in children's choices of toys, wrote "Sex Differences in Aggressive Play and Toy Preference," in eds. K. Bjorkqvist and P. Niemela, *Of Mice and Women: Aspects of Female Aggression* (San Diego: Academic Press, 1992), 65–76. A Japanese computer invention, Virtual Pets, has, however, appealed to girls. It is worn like a watch on the wrist by a child interested in raising, cleaning, and caring for a developing being. The toy has beeped and interrupted classes enough, however, that a number of American elementary schools have banned it from their premises. As a bow to the boys' computer-toy market, Virtual Pets were modified to include play fighting.

75 "This, in fact, is exactly": Susan Goldberg and Michael Lewis's study of infants at six and thirteen months old is "Play Behavior in the Year-Old Infant: Early Sex Differences," *Child Development* 40 (1) (1969): 21–31.

76 "Of the 225 members": An article for the general public, noting the striking gender disparity in chess, is B. Weber, "For Girls, an Early Endgame," *New York Times,* December 19, 1996, B1.

77 "Only four obviously female": Doing a count of first names would not bring more than a rough estimate. A number of first names are used for either sex, and some authors publish only under their initials.

77 "In a 1979 summary": The chess chapter, a fascinating one, is E. Hearst and M. Wierzbicki, "Battle Royal: Psychology and the Chessplayer," in ed. J. Goldstein, *Sports, Games, and Play* (Hillsdale, N.J.: Lawrence Erlbaum, 1979), 29–63. Hearst and Wierzbicki quote the psychologist L. J. Harris, on gender differences in brain functions, from "Sex Differences in Spatial Ability: Possible Environmental, Genetic, and Neurological Factors," in ed. M. Kinsbourne,

Asymetrical Functions of the Brain (Cambridge, England: Cambridge University Press, 1978), and Alfred Binet from *Mnemonic Virtuosity* (1893), trans. M. L. Simmel and S. B. Barron (Genetic Psychology Monographs, 1966). They cite Bobby Fischer from a media interview.

77 "Interestingly, studies in the 1990s": The changes in girls' math and science skills, as evidenced by a four-year gender study conducted by the Educational Testing Services (ETS), were reported by T. Henry, "Gender Gap in Math Skills Grows Slim," *USA Today,* May 7, 1997, D1.

82 "Young girls test": The 1997 *USA Today* report of the four-year ETS study findings cited in the previous note indicated that girls accomplish their strongest leap above the boys in writing and verbal skills in the middle-school years, between about fourth and eighth grades. Boys make their greatest gains over girls in math and science in the high school years. The superiority of girls over boys in verbal and writing skills has been previously well-established by a number of educational and developmental psychologists.

82 "In studies of how the genders": B. Sutton-Smith and B. G. Rosenberg, "Sixty Years of Historical Change in the Game Preferences of American Children" (1961), reprinted in eds. R. E. Herron and B. Sutton-Smith, *Child's Play* (New York: John Wiley, 1971).

83 "In a 1973 study": N. G. Blurton Jones and M. J. Konner, "Sex Differences in Behaviour of London and Bushman Children," in eds. R. P. Michael and J. H. Crook, *Comparative Ecology and Behaviour of Primates* (London: Academic Press, 1973).

83 "Cary Grant, awkward": The films I refer to are *Bringing Up Baby* (1938, directed by Howard Hawks), *Tootsie* (1982, directed by Sydney Pollack), and *National Velvet* (1944, directed by Clarence Brown).

85 "He diagnosed the young man": In 1998, Gabriel let me know that the genetics department at a nationally respected medical school did not agree with his previous diagnosis of Noonan's syndrome—because of his normal intelligence, facial appearance, and heart functioning. However, they came up with no alternative diagnosis and continued his treatment as is.

4: Play Built on Fantasies About Aggression or Sex

89 "After going through much": When one combines the research interests of the nonhuman-animal observers (ethologists) and nursery-age- and school-age-child observers (developmentalists, sociologists, anthropologists), it appears that rough-and-tumble play (R&T play) is a strong commonality and organizer for these fields to communicate and collaborate about.

90 "In one rat lab": D. F. Einon and M. J. Morgan, "A Critical Period for Social Isolation in the Rat," *Developmental Psychobiology* 10 (1977): 123–32; Graham J. Hole and Dorothy F. Einon, "Play in Rodents," in ed. P. K. Smith, *Play in Ani-*

mals and Humans (Oxford, England: Basil Blackwell, 1984), 95–118; and D. Einon and M. Potegal, "Enhanced Defense in Adult Rats Deprived of Playfighting," *Aggressive Behavior* 17 (1991): 27–46.

90 " 'Play faces,' marked by smiles": The Dutch primatologist J. A. R. A. M. Van Hoof was the first scientist to carefully study the facial expressions of animals prior to their play. His work is exemplified by "A Comparative Approach to the Phylogeny of Laughter and Smiling" (1972), reprinted in eds. J. S. Bruner, A. Jolly, and K. Sylva, *Play—Its Role in Development and Evolution* (New York: Basic Books, 1976), 130–39.

91 "A group of Kalahari San children": M. J. Konner, "Aspects of the Developmental Ethology of a Foraging People," in ed. N. Blurton Jones, *Ethological Studies of Child Behaviour* (Cambridge, England: Cambridge University Press, 1972), 285–304.

92 "Peter Smith and Kevin Connolly": Their research can be found in "Patterns of Play and Social Interaction in Pre-School Children," in ed. N. Blurton Jones, *Ethological Studies,* and in P. K. Smith and K. J. Connolly, *The Ecology of Preschool Behaviour* (Cambridge, England: Cambridge University Press, 1980). For an interesting review of the play-fighting and chasing literature, see A. P. Humphreys and P. K. Smith, "Rough-and-Tumble in Preschool and Playground," in ed. P. K. Smith, *Play in Animals and Humans,* 241–66.

92 "one Pennsylvania study": K. Conner was working in Philadelphia with Brian Sutton-Smith when she wrote "Aggression: Is It in the Eye of the Beholder?" in *Play and Culture* 2 (1989): 213–17.

93 "Certainly, however, the way": Sutton-Smith wrote an interesting and inclusive review chapter, "The Play of Girls," in eds. C. B. Kopp and M. Kirkpatrick, *On Becoming Female* (New York: Plenum, 1979), 229–57.

94 "Along these lines, the": Barrie Thorne wrote her journal entries into a footnote in *Gender Play: Girls and Boys in School* (New Brunswick, N.J.: Rutgers University Press, 1994), 193.

94 "Critical mass contributes": Thorne, *Gender Play,* 53. Settings have a great deal to do with whether gender lines can be crossed during enjoyable but nonaggressive activities. There was more cross-gender grouping, for instance, at a museum trip of elementary school children (80 percent of small groups were of mixed gender) than on a school playground—Z. Luria and E. Herzog, "Sorting Gender Out in a Children's Museum," *Gender and Society* 5 (1991): 224–32.

95 "Anthony Pellegrini of the": "Boys' Rough-and-Tumble Play and Social Competence: Contemporaneous and Longitudinal Relations," in ed. A. D. Pellegrini, *The Future of Play Theory* (Albany: State University of New York Press, 1995), 107–26.

95 "In an interestingly analogous finding": The dark side of nonhuman

play was discussed by Fagen in his *Animal Play Behavior* (New York: Oxford University Press, 1981). In the case of human play, the shadowy aspects were pointed out in a number of examples in B. Sutton-Smith, *A History of Children's Play: The New Zealand Playground, 1840–1950* (Philadelphia: University of Pennsylvania Press, 1982). This negative side to play was also summarized in a dark article by B. Sutton-Smith and D. Kelly-Byrne, "The Idealization of Play," in ed. P. K. Smith, *Play in Animals and Humans,* 305–21.

96 "Amateur karate and judo": This is a clinical observation of my own, but I have heard from a number of other mental health professionals dealing with trauma that self-defense classes can be helpful.

96 "I once heard on national": The Madras, India, nuns' karate lessons were featured on *ABC Nightly News* with Peter Jennings, May 28, 1996.

96 "Take a Steven Seagal": Perhaps I shouldn't admit to enjoying these, but sometimes after a bad day at the psychiatric office, I need to watch cat and mouse, mouse and cat. I think the best Seagal action flick is *Under Siege* (1992, directed by Andrew Davis). Chuck Norris's play chase, play fights are well exemplified in *Delta Force* (1986, directed by Menachem Golan). Bruce Willis is at his jostling best in *Die Hard* (1988, directed by John McTiernan). *From Russia with Love* (1963, British, directed by Terence Young) is noted by *Leonard Maltin's 1998 Movie and Video Guide* (New York: Plume) to have "one of the longest, most exciting fight scenes ever staged."

97 "Among the older groups": B. Thorne, *Gender Play,* 82–83.

98 "Thorne observed that": Crossing the gender lines is a central theme of chapters 5, 6, and 7 in B. Thorne, *Gender Play.*

98 "A study by the Illinois psychologist": J. Gottman, "The World of Coordinated Play: Same- and Cross-Sex Friendship in Young Children," in eds. J. M. Gottman and J. G. Parker, *Conversations of Friends: Speculations on Affective Development* (New York: Cambridge University Press, 1986), 139–91.

103 "As a matter of fact, he": D. Kaplan and D. Pedersen, "The Best Happy Ending: At Last, Dan Jansen Wins One for His Family and Himself," *Newsweek* 123 (9) (February 28, 1994): 44.

105 " 'Displacement' (moving the wish": For a good professional review of the defense mechanisms, see ed. G. Vaillant, *Ego Mechanisms of Defense: A Guide for Clinicians and Researchers* (Washington, D.C.: American Psychiatric Press, 1992). For the classic monograph on defenses, see A. Freud, *The Ego and the Mechanisms of Defense* (1937) (New York: International Universities Press, 1946).

106 "A. A. Milne's poem": "Nursery Chairs" appears in *When We Were Very Young,* reprinted in A. A. Milne, *The World of Christopher Robin* (New York: E. P. Dutton, 1958).

107 "The developmental psychologist": G. Fein, "Toys and Stories," in ed. A. D. Pellegrini, *Future of Play Theory,* 151–64.

107 "*Immature pretend* sounds funny": Ibid.

108 "Parents or teachers help": An excellent review of the importance of cuing in helping children to remember and to frame well-structured stories is R. Fivush, "Developmental Perspectives on Autobiographical Recall," in eds. G. S. Goodman and B. L. Bottoms, *Child Victims, Child Witnesses: Understanding and Improving Testimony* (New York: Guilford, 1993), 1–24. Another source on narrative beginnings, middles, and ends is J. Hudson and L. R. Shapiro, "From Knowing to Telling: Children's Scripts, Stories, and Personal Narratives," in eds. A. McCabe and C. Peterson, *Developing Narrative Structure* (Hillsdale, N.J.: Lawrence Erlbaum, 1991), 59–136.

109 "Some of the sexual games": J. Goodall, "Chimpanzees and Others at Play," *ReVision* 17 (4) (1995): 14–20.

110 "Adult sexual games and fantasy": This comment is based on a small number of clinical examples of what adults have told me in my practice. Some sex manuals suggest employing fantasy—see, for instance, A. Comfort, *The New Joy of Sex* (New York: Crown, 1991), or B. Zilbergeld, *The New Male Sexuality: The Truth About Men, Sex, and Pleasure* (New York: Bantam, 1992). Mutual, shared-out-loud fantasies are noted in Zilbergeld as helpful for some couples, but potentially dangerous for others; see especially pages 129 and 353.

5: Rules of the Game, Tools in the Game, Fools for the Game

115 "Consider the films": The motion pictures cited here are *Shoot the Piano Player* (1960, French, directed by François Truffaut), *The Right Stuff* (1983, directed by Philip Kaufman), and *Nina Takes a Lover* (1994, directed by Alan Jacobs).

115 "Even when a film is": *The Sting* (1973, directed by George Roy Hill).

115 "Near the end, when": Our responses to readings and films are explored in an interesting comparative-literature book by Evelyne Keitel, entitled *Reading Psychosis: Reader's Text in Psychoanalysis* (Oxford, England: Basil Blackwell, 1989).

116 "One of the most": I. Opie and P. Opie, *Children's Games in Street and Playground* (1969) (Oxford, England: Oxford University Press, paper ed., 1984).

116 "Once in a while": The children I knew who were harmed by the pedophilic "it" joined in a lawsuit against the church. Cases were settled prior to any trials.

118 "Here, Iona and Peter": Opie and Opie, *Children's Games in Street and Playground.*

118 "In Chaucer's *Canterbury Tales*": Geoffrey Chaucer (d. 1400), *The Canterbury Tales,* ed. and intro. A. C. Cawley (New York: E. P. Dutton, Everyman's Library, 1975).

119 "opening day of the Olympics": The ceremonies at the Olympic Winter Games, Nagano, Japan, on Friday, February 6, 1998, were an amazingly colorful blend of rite and the invitation to play.

119 "At times like this": J. Huizinga, *Homo Ludens*, trans. F. F. C. Hull (London: Routledge & Kegan Paul, 1949).

120 "In 1969, in a book": Opie and Opie, *Children's Games in Street and Playground*.

120 "Robert Louis Stevenson once": The Stevenson comment is taken from Opie and Opie, *Children's Games in Street and Playground*, 2.

120 "Consider this statement": I. Opie, *The People in the Playground* (Oxford, England: Oxford University Press, paper ed., 1994), 2.

121 "It was composed at": In June 1996, two third-grade teachers at San Francisco Day School, Ms. Hildy Burness and Ms. Kristy Price, arranged for their classes to subdivide into small gender-based groups and to compose a set of tree-house rules. My thanks to both of them, and to their inventive pupils.

123 "In his memoirs": M. Ali (with R. Durham), *The Greatest: My Own Story* (New York: Random House, 1975).

124 "George Foreman admitted": T. Hauser, *Muhammad Ali: His Life and Times* (New York: Simon & Schuster, 1991). An interesting documentary about the fight was filmed in 1974 in Zaire. More than twenty years later, it was released as *When We Were Kings* (1996, directed by Leon Gast).

124 "Yet if you're playing": The Spirlea-Williams bump is noted in S. L. Price, "Venus Envy," *Sports Illustrated* 87 (11) (September 15, 1997): 32; and R. Williams, "Father of Tennis Star Venus Williams Charges Racism During Recent U.S. Open," *Jet* 92 (19) (September 29, 1997): 49.

125 "The Tonya Harding story": Tonya's tale set off a media storm that lasted for about three months until she failed to place in the Olympic Games, Lillehammer, and was banned from American skating. Two articles written at that time are J. Adler, "Thin Ice," *Newsweek* 123 (January 24, 1994): 68–73; and S. Orlean, "Figures in a Mall," *The New Yorker* 70 (February 21, 1994): 48–63. The day prior to the opening of the 1998 Winter Olympics in Nagano, Japan, Thursday, February 5, the Fox Television Network featured a double interview by sportscaster James Brown of Tonya Harding and Nancy Kerrigan in which Tonya apologized to Nancy. The public fascination with Tonya had lasted.

127 "Tonya's agent put a spin": The agent, David Hans Schmidt, was quoted in T. Keown, "Hard Sell," *San Francisco Chronicle*, February 19, 1997, D1.

128 "They become 'trolley jollies' ": My brother-in-law, Leonard Ronis, who, for years, ran the Regional Transit System of Greater Cleveland, told me on several occasions about various bus- and streetcar-watching kids who eventually became bosses in the municipal transportation industry. Leonard himself was not a trolley jolly as a child.

130 "If the only purpose": Garry Chick and Lynn Barnett based a paper they wrote on the premise that play stimulates more play—"Children's Play and Adult Leisure," in ed. Anthony D. Pellegrini, *The Future of Play Theory* (Albany: State University of New York Press, 1995), 45–69. Chick and Barnett began their article with a 1993 quote from Sutton-Smith: "Still some things seem reasonable. Namely that my early intensive and later successful game play provided a disposition to be interested in games."

133 "In the eighteenth and early nineteenth": I base what I say about safe conversation two hundred and more years ago upon the dialogue in Jane Austen's (1775–1817) six novels: *Emma, Mansfield Park, Northanger Abbey, Persuasion, Pride and Prejudice,* and *Sense and Sensibility.* I read these novels in the London, Folio Society (1975), editions.

134 "Huizinga-style play ritual": J. Huizinga, *Homo Ludens,* trans. F. F. C. Hull (London: Routledge & Kegan Paul, 1949).

134 "The story of Charlotte Brent": "Charlotte" is the same person who appeared in my book *Too Scared to Cry* (New York: Harper & Row, 1990; paper ed., New York: Basic Books, 1992).

6: Adolescent Turning Points in Play

139 "Playing in adolescence": Much of the theorizing of the early-twentieth-century developmentalists failed to take adolescent play into account. However, midcentury observers of games and sports recorded a great deal of this kind of play.

139 "At the end of 1996": Sutton-Smith's autobiographical statement comes from "A Memory of Games and Some Games of Memory," in ed. D. J. Lee, *Life and Story: Autobiographies for a Narrative Psychology* (Westport, Conn.: Praeger, 1994), 125–42.

141 "In 1966, for instance, he": The Piaget–Sutton-Smith debate is reprinted as two articles in eds. R. E. Herron and B. Sutton-Smith, *Child's Play* (New York: John Wiley, 1971), 326–39. A third, rebuttal-style article was written later by Sutton-Smith for his and Herron's 1971 *Child's Play,* pages 340–42.

142 " 'the romance of risk' ": I borrowed this phrase from Lynn Ponton's fine book on teenage daring, *The Romance of Risk* (New York: Basic Books, 1997).

142 "Fads, such as Russian roulette": Occasionally we child and adolescent psychiatrists are alerted to such adolescent behaviors through our local professional newsletters, for instance, M. Persky, "The New Adolescent Risk Taking: Russian Roulette," *The Northern California Psychiatric Physician,* February/March 1996, 4. A psychiatrist recently found that 20 percent of teenage boys who were confined in a southeastern U.S. detention center admitted, when asked, to having played Russian roulette—Kevin M. Denny, "Russian Roulette: A Case

of Questions Not Asked?" *Journal of the American Academy of Child and Adolescent Psychiatry* 34 (1995): 1682–83. Walt Disney's *The Program* (1993) was directed by David S. Ward. Without the highway scene, it rated two stars (out of four) in *Leonard Maltin's 1998 Movie and Video Guide* (New York: Plume). For an article on copycatting relating to this film, see M. de Courcy Hinds, "Not Like the Movie: A Dare to Test Nerves Turns Deadly," *New York Times,* October 19, 1993, A1.

142 "A study by Brian Sutton-Smith's ": B. Sutton-Smith, "The Kissing Games of Adolescents in Ohio," *Midwestern Folklore* 9 (1959): 189–211.

143 "In 1991, the pop star": *Truth or Dare* (1991, directed by Alek Keshishian).

143 " 'the dark side of play' ": For the most pessimistic of the dark-side papers by Brian Sutton-Smith, see B. Sutton-Smith and D. Kelly-Byrne, "The Idealization of Play," in ed. P. K. Smith, *Play in Animals and Humans* (Oxford, England: Basil Blackwell, 1984), 305–21.

144 "the singer Karen Carpenter's death": This sudden, unexpected death on February 4, 1983, of a teenage idol was attributed to anorexia and bulimia.

145 "But it was particularly heartening": The numbers behind teenage information-seeking behaviors following the 1986 space-shuttle tragedy can be found in L. Terr, D. Bloch, B. Michel, H. Shi, J. Reinhart, and S. A. Matayer, "Children's Thinking in the Wake of *Challenger*," *American Journal of Psychiatry* 154 (1997): 744–51. If the reader is interested in the rest of the *Challenger* series, see L. Terr, D. Block, B. Michel, H. Shi, J. Reinhart, and S. A. Matayer, "Children's Memories in the Wake of *Challenger*," *American Journal of Psychiatry* 153 (1996): 618–25. A third paper, L. Terr, D. Bloch, B. Michel, H. Shi, J. Reinhart, and S. A. Matayer, "Children's Symptoms in the Wake of *Challenger*," is awaiting publication.

146 "For a few lucky adolescents": A story about a famous young person's solitary mind play was told by Lonnie Sherrod and Jerome Singer in "The Development of Make-Believe Play," in ed. J. Goldstein, *Sports, Games, and Play* (Hillsdale, N.J.: Lawrence Erlbaum, 1979), 1–28. As he was recovering from an injury, the incomparable French skier Jean-Claude Killy practiced the entire course for a future downhill race entirely in his mind. When Killy eventually competed on that course, he gave one of his greatest performances.

152 "The Australian film": *Shine,* 1996, was directed by Scott Hicks. David Helfgott is credited with consulting on the writing of the screenplay. The quotes from his quasi-internal monologue come from S. Mydans, "For the Pianist of 'Shine' a Life Depicted Is a Life Transformed," *New York Times,* January 21, 1997, B1.

154 "The story of Shirley Temple": I based the majority of what I wrote about Shirley's life on her autobiography, S. Temple Black, *Child Star* (New York: McGraw-Hill, 1988).

156 "Meglin's Dance Studio": In addition to what Shirley told her readers about Meglin's in her autobiography, we were shown Meglin's in a two-hour Arts and Entertainment cable-network program, *Biography,* centering on Shirley Temple, December 8, 1996. *Biography* also broadcast film clips of the Baby Burlesk series. For me, it felt intensely uncomfortable to watch preschoolers in such obviously sexual situations.

156 "Verging on pedophilia": *Pretty Baby* (1978, directed by Louis Malle).

156 " 'I wanted her to be artistic' ": C. J. Foster, "Mrs. Temple on Bringing Up Shirley," *Parents* (13) (October 1938): 22–23.

157 "Shirley's first spoken phrase": Temple Black, *Child Star.*

157 "Her break came": *Stand Up and Cheer* (1934, directed by Hamilton Mac-Fadden), *Little Miss Marker* (1934, directed by Alexander Hall), *Baby Take a Bow* (1934, directed by Harry Lachman).

157 "In the films made": I watched hours of Shirley Temple movies to reach the conclusions written on these pages. For example, I watched her smile and bow in her first two film appearances—on videotape, of course.

158 "Like Babe, the Australian": *Babe* (1995, Australian, directed by Chris Noonan).

158 "The leading lady": Temple Black, *Child Star.*

158 "Her on-screen dances": Shirley danced that famous staircase number with Bill (Bojangles) Robinson in *The Little Colonel* (1935, directed by David Butler). They also performed brilliantly together in *The Littlest Rebel* (1935, directed by David Butler), *Rebecca of Sunnybrook Farm* (1938, directed by Allan Dwan), and *Just Around the Corner* (1938, directed by Irving Cummings).

159 "From the ages of seven": Shirley's relationship with Darryl Zanuck and the Fox Studio is a story in itself. For further details on this problematic union, see L. Mosely, *Zanuck: The Rise and Fall of Hollywood's Last Tycoon* (Boston: Little, Brown, 1984).

159 "At a garden party at Val-Kill": This story was told on herself by Shirley in *Child Star,* 235–39.

160 "Lolita did not": V. Nabokov (1899–1977), *Lolita* (New York: Putnam, 1955).

160 "H. I. Philips wrote": The *Washington Post* quote comes from S. Temple Black, *Child Star,* 307.

161 "Films started revealing": *Heidi* (1937, directed by Raymond Griffith), *Rebecca of Sunnybrook Farm* (1938, directed by Allan Dwan), *The Little Princess* (1939, directed by Walter Lang).

162 "In the movies she made": *The Blue Bird* (1940, directed by Walter Lang) and *Young People* (1940, directed by Allan Dwan).

162 "She could not make herself": Judy Garland's studio, MGM, hired Shirley to act in one movie, *Kathleen* (1941, directed by Harold S. Bucquet).

162 "In her later teens": *Since You Went Away* (1944, directed by John Cromwell) and *I'll Be Seeing You* (1944, directed by William Dieterle).

163 "Shirley married": In her autobiography, *Child Star,* Shirley writes that during her senior year of high school, she decided to be the first in her senior class to become engaged. She implies she wanted the status and wished to leave her family. Her marriage at seventeen to John Agar lasted from August 1945 to December 1949. Their child, Susan, was born January 30, 1948. Shirley then married Charles Black on December 16, 1950. There are two children from that marriage, Charlie Jr., born April 28, 1952, and Lori, born April 9, 1954.

7: How Play Moves through History and around the World

164 "We didn't always think": My main source for the historical views on "childhood," and for Louis XIII as an example of a child of historical transition, was Phillipe Ariès, *Centuries of Childhood: A Social History of Family Life* (1960) (New York: Alfred A. Knopf, 1962).

165 "A special physician, Jean Héroard": Not only did Ariès, in *Centuries of Childhood,* use Héroard's journals to illuminate the life of Louis XIII, but the British writer Lucy Crump did so, as well, in her *Nursery Life Three-Hundred Years Ago* (London: Routledge & Kegan Paul, 1929). I used both books as sources for my telling of the tale of Louis's young life.

166 "Young Louis performed his dances": Ariès, *Centuries of Childhood.*

169 "Today's historians characterize": I picked up the dour idea from the *Columbia Encyclopedia,* fifth edition, article on Louis XIII (New York: Columbia University Press, 1993), 1616. Actually, the editors used the terms "melancholy" and "retiring" to describe the adult Louis.

169 "He was married to the infanta": This story is told with Gaellic gusto in Ariès, *Centuries of Childhood.*

171 "During the late sixteenth": The journals of Felix Platter (1536–1614) are available today as *Beloved Son Felix: The Journal of Felix Platter, a Medical Student in Montpellier in the Sixteenth Century,* trans. and intro. S. Jennett (London: F. Muller, 1961). However, my quotes are taken from Ariès, *Centuries of Childhood.*

172 "Johan Huizinga, concluded": J. Huizinga, *Homo Ludens,* trans. F. F. C. Hull (London: Routledge & Kegan Paul, 1949).

173 "known as a drumming contest": This example was originally cited by Huizinga, *Homo Ludens,* 84–86. He based what he described on the Danish anthropological literature on tribal life in Greenland.

174 "When I began practicing psychiatry": I finished residency and fellowship training at the University of Michigan in 1966. I then went to Case Western Reserve University in Cleveland, where I taught and did research full-time from 1966 to 1971 (I had a small practice at the university). I began

my full-time private practice in San Francisco in 1971 and joined the volunteer clinical faculty at the University of California, San Francisco.

176 "I have gradually accumulated": What is most amazing is what stuff I wound up *not* buying for my office. Like Tantalus, I have habitually been tempted. But thankfully, I have had to continually bear in mind the ultimate practicality of my consulting room.

177 "He compared contemporary Maori": B. Sutton-Smith, *The Games of New Zealand Children* (Berkeley: University of California Press, 1959). Reprinted in B. Sutton-Smith, *The Folkgames of Children* (Austin: University of Texas Press, 1972), 5–257. Elsdon Best's earlier study of Maori children was "Games and Pastimes of the Maori," *Dominion Museum Bulletin* 8 (1925).

178 "After he moved to the United States": B. Sutton-Smith and B. G. Rosenberg, "Sixty Years of Historical Change in the Game Preferences of American Children," *Journal of American Folklore* 74 (1961): 17–46, reprinted in Sutton-Smith, *Folkgames of Children,* 258–94. Here, the authors compared the results of the three earlier studies to their own. They used T. R. Crosswell, "Amusement of Worcester School Children," *The Pedagogical Seminary* 6 (1898): 314–71; Z. McGhee, "A Study in the Play Life of Some South Carolina Children," *The Pedagogical Seminary* 7 (1900): 459–78; and L. M. Terman, *Genetic Studies of Genius,* vol. 1 (Stanford, Calif.: Stanford University Press, 1926). For these comparisons, see B. G. Rosenberg and B. Sutton-Smith, "A Revised Conception of Masculine-Feminine Differences in Play Activities," *Journal of Genetic Psychology* 96 (1960): 165–70.

179 "In her 1978 book": H. Schwartzman, *Transformations: The Anthropology of Children's Play* (New York: Plenum, 1978).

179 "In 1957 in Melanesia": K. O. Burridge, "A Tangu Game," *Man* 57 (1957): 88–89.

179 "In 1963 within another": W. Nydegger and C. Nydegger, "Tarong: An Ilocos Barrio in the Philippines," in ed. B. Whiting, *Six Cultures: Studies of Child Rearing* (New York: John Wiley, 1963), 693–867.

180 "Kenneth Read reported in 1959": K. E. Read, "Leadership and Consensus in a New Guinea Society," *American Anthropologist* 61 (1959): 425–36.

180 "In Israeli society": S. Smilansky, *The Effects of Sociodramatic Play on Disadvantaged Preschool Children* (New York: John Wiley, 1968).

180 "Along these same lines": R. Eifermann, "Cooperation and Egalitarianism in Kibbutz Children's Games," *Human Relations* 23 (1970): 579–87; and R. Eifermann, "Social Play in Childhood," in eds. R. Herron and B. Sutton-Smith, *Child's Play* (New York: John Wiley, 1971), 270–97.

181 "Speaking of imaginative play": In addition to Smilansky, *The Effects of Sociodramatic Play,* one finds the conclusion that underprivileged children play less imaginatively in J. L. Singer and D. Singer, "Imaginative Play and Pretend-

ing in Early Childhood: Some Experimental Approaches," in ed. A. Davids, *Child Personality and Psychopathology,* vol. 3 (1976). Eifermann, "Social Play in Childhood," showed that rather than not developing at all, imaginative play begins later in underprivileged children.

182 "In a monograph": E. Cameron, "Playing with Dolls," in ed. E. Cameron, *Isn't She a Doll? Play and Ritual in African Sculpture* (Los Angeles: UCLA Fowler Museum of Cultural History, 1996), 18–41.

184 "Among the Yoruba": Ibid.

187 "Yoshi wished that his society": One of the most amazing cinematic depictions of Japanese lesson-learning along these lines is *Shall We Dance?* (1996, directed by Masayuki Suo). The ballroom dancing in this film is Western, but the way the dancing is carried out, and the characteristics of the dancers, are traditionally Japanese. For an associated article, see J. Coleman, "Japan Gripped by Ballroom Dancing," *San Francisco Chronicle,* June 11, 1996, E2.

188 "Take your *Beach Blanket Babylon*": This show, a nightclub-style San Francisco review, celebrates its silver anniversary in 1999.

8: Underplay, Overplay, and Cure through Play

193 "Dana returned to her American": In *Childhood and Society* (New York: W. W. Norton, 1950), Erik Erikson wrote of "play disruption," a situation in which play momentarily creates enough anxiety in a child that the youngster can no longer play coherently. But underplay in adults has not been well studied, partly because—after Freud and Piaget—adults have been assumed to stop playing as a matter of course.

195 "The example of a major league baseball": B. Olney, "Major League Prospect Quits a Game He Dislikes," *New York Times,* May 30, 1997, C17.

197 "Michael Jordan gave up basketball": The murder of James Jordan occurred in the summer of 1993, and Michael's decision to stop playing was announced on October 6, 1993. See D. Remnick, "Back in Play," *The New Yorker* 71 (11) (May 8, 1995): 38. Jordan's miserable baseball season with the Birmingham Barons and his quotes about basketball are in "Jordan 'Never' Again in NBA," *USA Today, International Edition,* July 5, 1994, B5. Jordan's return to basketball is chronicled in P. Taylor, "What Goes Up" and "Resurrection," *Sports Illustrated* 82 (11,12) (March 20 and March 27, 1995).

197 "On April 30, 1993": The man who attacked Monica Seles was not sentenced in Germany to a prison term. Monica's reaction was chronicled in J. Howard, "Home Alone," *Sports Illustrated* 82 (14) (April 10, 1995): 44. Her return to tennis was noted in R. Finn, "No Contest: Seles Roars Down Comeback Trail," *New York Times,* August 21, 1995, A1. That summer she commented that she had been struck down "at the peak" of her career—R. Finn, "For Seles,

Exhibition Promise," *New York Times,* July 30, 1995, Sports, 19. Two years later, after she lost at Wimbledon to unseeded Sandrine Testud of France, she was called "over the hill and strangely adrift at twenty-three" by S. Ostler in "Seles' Woes Continue in Defeat," *San Francisco Chronicle,* July 1, 1997, D1.

199 "But in general, we can't conclude": One ironic example of a virtual nonplayer who has made his living from the play of others is Hiroshi Yamauchi, president of Nintendo. His story was told by Andrew Pollack, "Nintendo Chief Is All Work, No Play," *New York Times,* August 26, 1996, C1.

199 "Some people overplay": The problems of the physically injured athlete have only recently attracted psychiatric attention. Marjorie Shuer, M.D., and her colleague Mary Dietrich, Ph.D., wrote an article, "Psychological Effects of Chronic Injury in Elite Athletes," in the *Western Journal of Medicine* 166 (1997): 104–9, in which they showed that injured athletes, even with mild or minor injuries, often denied their problem and overdid exercise to the malfunctioning areas of their body. This may lead to worsening, not bettering, of their condition.

200 "Psychological trauma, being": L. Terr, "Children of Chowchilla: A Study of Psychic Trauma," *Psychoanalytic Study of the Child* 34 (1979): 547–623; L. Terr, " 'Forbidden Games': Post-Traumatic Child's Play," *Journal of the American Academy of Child Psychiatry* 20 (1981): 741–60.

200 "observed once in a while in adults": Adult post-traumatic play was first described by L. Terr. Ibid.

200 "*Jeux Interdits*": The French film was made in 1952, directed by René Clement. It was based on a French novel by E. Boyer, *The Secret Game* (New York: Harcourt Brace, 1950).

201 "A year and a half after": My biographical information on the Brontë family comes from R. Keefe, *Charlotte Brontë's World of Death* (Austin: University of Texas Press, 1979); R. Fraser, *The Brontës: Charlotte Brontë and Her Family* (New York: Crown, 1988); and Mrs. *Gaskell's Life of Charlotte Brontë* (1857), ed. and intro. W. Gérin (London: Folio Society, 1971).

201 "The next June": My sources on the ongoing pretend of the Brontë children are F. E. Ratchford, *The Brontës' Web of Childhood* (New York: Columbia University Press, 1941); Keefe, *Charlotte Brontë's World;* and *The Juvenilia of Jane Austen and Charlotte Brontë,* ed. F. Beer (Harmondsworth, England: Penguin, 1986).

203 "After the death": The story of the secret withholding—and then the posthumous spread—of the Brontë Angria and Gondal works was told by Ratchford, *Brontës' Web,* ix–xv.

203 "His imaginative efforts": I wrote about Stephen King's post-traumatic play in a professional paper, "Terror Writing by the Formerly Terrified: The Life and Works of Stephen King," *Psychoanalytic Study of the Child* 44 (1989): 369–90. King is also prominent in my book *Too Scared to Cry* (New York: Harper

& Row, 1990; paper ed., New York: Basic Books, 1992). For King's biography, I used S. King, *Danse Macabre* (New York: Berkeley, 1983), 83–84; D. Winter, *Stephen King* (New York: Plume, 1986); and J. Underwood and C. Miller, *Bare Bones* (New York: McGraw-Hill, 1988).

203 "Alfred Hitchcock, another person": For materials about Hitchcock's life of post-traumatic play, see Donald Spoto's biography *The Dark Side of Genius: The Life of Alfred Hitchcock* (Boston: Little, Brown, 1983) and Spoto's discussion of the films in his *Art of Alfred Hitchcock: Fifty Years of His Motion Pictures* (Garden City, N.Y.: Doubleday/Dolphin, 1976). Consider, also, a psychiatric paper I wrote on creative artists, including Hitchcock—"Childhood Trauma and the Creative Product," *Psychoanalytic Study of the Child* 42 (1987): 545–72. *The Birds* and *Psycho* were directed by Alfred Hitchcock in 1963 and 1960, respectively.

203 "Janet Leigh noted": J. Leigh, *House of Destiny* (New York: Harlequin, 1996).

203 "spying or burglary": One type of store, the "spy shop," straddles on an invisible line between selling toys for those who enjoy a little fun with mysteries and those interested in out-and-out criminal activity. See R. E. Milloy, "Spying Toys for Adults or Supplies for Crimes?" *New York Times,* August 28, 1995, A6.

204 "Clint Eastwood and Cary Grant": *Absolute Power* (1997, directed by Clint Eastwood); *To Catch a Thief* (1955, directed by Alfred Hitchcock).

204 "as in the French novel": *Les Liaisons Dangereuses,* the eighteenth-century book written by Choderlos de Laclos entirely in letter form, was made into the film of the same name (1959, French, Roger Vadim). See also *Dangerous Liaisons* (1988, directed by Stephen Frears) and *Valmont* (1989, directed by Milos Forman).

204 "Gambling is another form": "Compulsive Gambling Program," in the Isaac Ray Center, Rush-Presbyterian–St. Luke's Medical Center's *Combined Annual Report,* 1996; and B. Castellani and L. Rugle, "A Comparison of Pathological Gamblers to Alcoholics and Cocaine Misusers on Impulsivity, Sensation Seeking, and Craving," *International Journal of the Addictions* 30 (1995): 275–89.

205 "cyberaddiction . . . cyberromance": D. Renshaw, "Delights and Dangers of the Internet," *Psychiatric Times,* October 1996, 64; and "The Popular Peril of Cyberaddiction: One for the Books?" *Psychiatric Times,* April 1995, 35.

205 "cybertalk from one bulletin": One of my patients, as a favor to me, pulled from the Net this back-and-forth discussion about love in cyberspace. I have changed people's "handles" and have shortened or deleted some of their statements.

206 "For about half a century": Spontaneous cures through play are described in Robert Waelder's classic Freudian paper "The Psychoanalytic Theory of Play," *Psychoanalytic Quarterly* 2 (1932): 208–24.

206 "Psychological cures in play": Melanie Klein suggested using a child's

play in a child's psychoanalysis, thus pioneering the field of play therapy. Here, she and Anna Freud differed seriously in their approach. Miss Freud was far more committed to talking with children (and originally their parents before analysis began) than she was to playing with them. See M. Klein, *The Psychoanalysis of Children* (1932) (New York: Dell, 1975); and M. Klein, *Contributions to Psychoanalysis: 1921–1945* (New York: McGraw-Hill, 1964). Klein and A. Freud differed in their theories as well as in their practices with children.

206 "By abreacting, or enacting": The New York child analyst David Levy wrote three important papers just before and at the time of World War II, comparing children who had undergone hospital procedures to soldiers evacuated from the European front because of emotional stress, and offering these children play therapy without psychiatric interpretation (pure abreaction). This treatment was later paralleled by abreactive barbituate-facilitated interviews, given to men behind the battle lines. Levy's papers were "Release Therapy in Young Children," *Psychiatry* 1 (1938): 387–90; "Release Therapy," *American Journal of Orthopsychiatry* 9 (1939): 713–36; and "Psychic Trauma of Operations in Children," *American Journal of the Diseases of Childhood* 69 (1945): 7–25.

207 "use abreaction, contexts, and corrections": I have given a number of lectures on these three principles of play treatments, but this is the first time I have put them to print. The idea of the three occurred to me as I privately supervised psychologists, psychiatrists, social workers, and counselors on play-treatment cases that appeared to be "stuck." What became gradually apparent was that at least one of these three elements had been relatively neglected.

208 "In a diagram that looked": Michael McGuire, mentioned only as a "man" appeared briefly in my book *Unchained Memories* (New York: Basic Books, 1994), 232.

210 "One child who actually witnessed": This case is more thoroughly discussed in L. Terr, "Play Therapy and Psychic Trauma," in eds. C. E. Schaefer and K. J. O'Connor, *Handbook of Play Therapy* (New York: John Wiley, 1983), 308–19.

212 "She went two summers": Dr. Kaplan ordinarily gives his musician campers an excellent handout explaining his corrective approach to fears of failure and fears of not being perfect. This pamphlet is entitled "Practicing for Artistic Success: The New Frontier."

9: Play as Work, Play as Life

220 "In eulogizing the great Italian": The Mastroianni funeral and the Veltroni quote can be found in J. Tagliabue (*New York Times*), "Thousands Mourn Marcello Mastroianni in Rome," *San Francisco Chronicle,* December 23, 1996, E5.

220 "The ninety-two-year-old cartoonist": Al Hirschfeld was interviewed

by Alex Witchel, "Anarchy Within a Smile Behind a Beard," *New York Times,* December 14, 1995, B1.

220 "When in 1997 a couple": N. Angier, "Flyspeck on a Lobster Lip Turns Biology on Its Ear," *New York Times,* December 14, 1995, A1.

221 "Early in his career": M. Csikszentmihalyi, *Beyond Boredom and Anxiety: The Experience of Play in Work and Games* (San Francisco: Jossey-Bass, 1975).

221 "The University of Chicago group": The pager system of recording "flow" and "nonflow" is described in M. Csikszentmihalyi, *Flow: The Psychology of Optimal Experience* (New York: Harper Perennial, 1991).

222 " 'Are you playing?' ": Brian Sutton-Smith has been critical of Dr. Csikszentmihalyi's theoretical merging of work with play in his flow concept. See B. Sutton-Smith and D. Kelly-Byrne, "The Idealization of Play," in ed. P. K. Smith, *Play in Animals and Humans* (Oxford, England: Basil Blackwell, 1984), 305–22; and B. Sutton-Smith, *The Ambiguity of Play* (Cambridge, Mass.: Harvard University Press, 1997).

223 "we also need various states": Corinne Hutt, an English play researcher, has studied the various daytime physiological states of young children's play. In a recorded conversation with a number of other experts on play in ed. B. Sutton-Smith, *Play and Learning* (New York: John Wiley, 1979), 180–86, she proposed that there are a number of daytime states of arousal.

223 "Jordan Furniture of Boston": I learned of Jordan Furniture's exploits in play through my cousin Hershel Alpert, whose furniture store, Alpert's, outside of Providence, Rhode Island, is also a playful place, though not as spectacularly playful as Jordan's.

224 "Since the early seventies": The Cleese interview is reported in R. Lane, "Laughter Is Good for Business," *Business News,* Summer 1996, 14–19. Cleese's most successful films, *A Fish Called Wanda* and *Fierce Creatures,* were released respectively in 1988 (directed by Charles Crichton) and in 1996 (directed by Robert Young and Fred Schepisi).

226 "a spokesperson for the Sharper Image": H. Oeltjen, "Office Toys: The Fun and Games of Business," *Women in Business,* November/December 1992.

226 "Do you remember": I. Opie and P. Opie, *Children's Games in Street and Playground* (Oxford, England: Oxford University Press, 1984).

227 "When the great San Francisco": T. Friend, "Cool to the End, Montana Says Goodbye," *New York Times,* April 10, 1995, B10.

227 "The remarkable, but eccentric, pianist Glen Gould": The Gould story was related in a pamphlet printed by Burton Kaplan, who, for years, has taught a course on the psychology of practice at the Manhattan School of Music and runs a practice camp for musicians. His pamphlet, "Practicing for Artistic Success: The New Frontier," summarizes his approach.

228 "In a sense it was a fiction": R. Traver, *Anatomy of a Murder* (New York: St. Martin's Press, 1958), 148.

228 "Robert Fagen made the point": See R. Fagen, "Play and Behavioural Flexibility," in ed. P. K. Smith, *Play in Animals and Humans* (Oxford, England: Basil Blackwell, 1984), 159–73.

228 "When I first met her, Jinny": The Shermans told me that *Sports Illustrated* has consistently published the names of the overseventy skiing champions at the end of their racing season. But the magazine does not print the names of the overeighty winners. So Jinny's, not Dick's, name and ranking have appeared.

231 "Unlike Rich Davis": I have known Rich Davis, a child and adolescent psychiatrist from Kansas City, since 1988 when he gave an outdoor barbecue party for a number of us psychiatric oral examiners when the boards were being conducted in Kansas City. In 1996, Rich let me interview him about his invention of KC Masterpiece sauce. It had been a playful enterprise, especially during the inventing phase.

231 "He was not looking for": The documentary film *Hoop Dreams* was released in 1994 (directed by Steve James).

232 "People in our small city": Elijah Chatman played basketball at Bowling Green State University but did not make it into the professional ranks. He died of a heart attack in his early thirties.

233 "In Nate's case, as in": Both Nate Thurmond and Rich Davis commented in their interviews that when large amounts of money were involved, the play qualities in their work noticeably diminished.

236 "William Menninger, one of the leading": The Menninger family, with its four generations of practicing psychiatrists, is one of the great dynasties of American medicine. When he heard about my book project, Walter Menninger sent me his father's article about his grandfather's late-life play— W. C. Menninger, "Recreation and Mental Health," *Recreation* 42 (1948): 340–56.

238 "One such person loved": Brief summaries of the contributions of the three Nobel laureates whom I mention here can be found in *The Columbia Encyclopedia*, 5th ed. (New York: Columbia University Press, 1993). (Glaser is listed under "bubble chamber.") My take on the play behind their discoveries is my own viewpoint, based on orally transmitted stories that have been around for a long time.

239 "next-door neighbors, Frankie and Robin": A number of my ideas on how to interest children in a flower garden come from Steve Albert, "A Place in the Garden for Your Children," *Gardener's Notebook,* Sloat Garden Center, June/July 1997, 1.

Bibliography

Ariès, P. *Centuries of Childhood: A Social History of Family Life* (1960). New York: Alfred A. Knopf, 1962.

Bateson, G. "The Message 'This Is Play.' " In ed. B. Schaffner, *Group Processes: Transactions of the Second Conference.* New York: Josiah Macy Foundation, 1956.

————. *Steps to an Ecology of the Mind.* New York: Ballantine, 1972.

Beer, F., ed. *The Juvenilia of Jane Austen and Charlotte Brontë.* Harmondsworth, England: Penguin, 1986.

Bell, R. Q. "Contributions of Human Infants to Caregiving and Social Interaction." In eds. M. Lewis and L. A. Rosenblum, *The Effect of the Infant on Its Caregiver.* New York: John Wiley, 1974.

Benjamin, J., D. H. Hamer, D. L. Murphy, B. D. Greenberg, C. Patterson, and L. Li. "Population and Familial Association Between the D4 Dopamine Receptor Gene and Measures of Novelty Seeking." *Nature Genetics* 12 (1) (1996): 81–84.

Best, E. "Games and Pastimes of the Maori." *Dominion Museum Bulletin* 8 (1925).

Binet, A. *Mnemonic Virtuosity* (1893). Trans. M. L. Simmel and S. B. Barron. Genetic Psychology Monographs, 1966.

Bowlby, J. *Attachment and Loss.* New York: Basic Books, 1969.

Boyer, E. *The Secret Game.* New York: Harcourt Brace, 1950.

Brontë, C. *Jane Eyre* (1847). London: Folio Society, 1965.

Brown, S. "Animals at Play." *National Geographic* 186 (6) (December 1994): 2–35.

———. "Through the Lens of Play." *ReVision* 17 (4) (Spring 1995): 4–12.

Bruner, J. S., and V. Sherwood. "Peekaboo and the Learning of Rule Structures." In J. S. Bruner, A. Jolly, and K. Sylva, eds., *Play—Its Role in Development and Evolution.* New York: Basic Books, 1976.

Burghardt, G. "On the Origins of Play." In ed. P. K. Smith, *Play in Animals and Humans.* Oxford, England: Basil Blackwell, 1984.

———. "Precosity, Play, and the Ectotherm-Endotherm Transition: Profound Reorganization or Superficial Adaptation?" In ed. E. M. Blass, *Handbook of Behavioral Neurobiology,* vol. 9. New York: Plenum, 1988.

Burridge, K. O. "A Tangu Game." *Man* 57 (1957): 88–89.

Cameron, E. "Playing with Dolls." In ed. E. Cameron, *Isn't She a Doll? Play and Ritual in African Sculpture.* Los Angeles: UCLA Fowler Museum of Cultural History, 1996.

Castellani, B., and L. Rugle. "A Comparison of Pathological Gamblers to Alcoholics and Cocaine Misusers on Impulsivity, Sensation Seeking, and Craving." *International Journal of the Addictions* 30 (1995): 275–89.

Chick, G., and L. Barnett. "Children's Play and Adult Leisure." In ed. A. D. Pellegrini, *The Future of Play Theory.* Albany: State University of New York Press, 1995.

Cloninger, C. R. "The Genetics and Psychobiology of the Seven-Factor Model of Personality." In ed. K. R. Silk, *The Biology of Personality Disorder.* Washington, D.C.: APPI, 1998.

Columbia Encyclopedia, 5th ed. New York: Columbia University Press, 1993.

"Compulsive Gambling Program." In the Isaac Ray Center, Rush-Presbyterian–St. Luke's Medical Center, *Combined Annual Report,* 1996.

Conner, K. "Aggression: Is It in the Eye of the Beholder?" In *Play and Culture* 2 (1989): 213–17.

Crosswell, T. R. "Amusement of Worcester School Children." *Pedagogical Seminary* 6 (1898): 314–71.

Crump, L. *Nursery Life Three-Hundred Years Ago.* London: Routledge & Kegan Paul, 1929.

Csikszentmihalyi, M. *Beyond Boredom and Anxiety: The Experience of Play in Work and Games.* San Francisco: Jossey-Bass, 1975.

———. "Leisure and Socialization." *Social Forces* 60 (1981): 332–40.

———. *Flow: The Psychology of Optimal Experience.* New York: HarperPerennial, 1991.

Davenport, M. *Mozart.* New York: Charles Scribner's Sons, 1932.

de Laclos, P. C. *Les Liaisons Dangereuses* (1782). Trans. R. Aldington. New York: Alfred A. Knopf, 1992.

Denny, K. M. "Russian Roulette: A Case of Questions Not Asked?" *Journal of the American Academy of Child and Adolescent Psychiatry* 34 (1995): 1682–83.

Ebstein, R. P., R. H. Belmaker, M. Katz, L. Nemanov, E. R. Bennett, D. Blaine, Y. Osher, B. Priel, R. Umansky, and O. Novick. "Dopamine D4 Receptor (D4DR) Exon III Polymorphism Associated with the Human Personality Trait of Novelty Seeking." *Nature Genetics* 12 (1) (1996): 78–80.

Eifermann, R. "Cooperation and Egalitarianism in Kibbutz Children's Games." *Human Relations* 23 (1970): 579–87.

———. "Social Play in Childhood." In eds. R. Herron and B. Sutton-Smith, *Child's Play.* New York: John Wiley, 1971.

Einon, D. F., and M. J. Morgan. "A Critical Period for Social Isolation in the Rat." *Developmental Psychobiology* 10 (1977): 123–32.

Einon, D., and M. Potegal. "Enhanced Defense in Adult Rats Deprived of Play-fighting." *Aggressive Behavior* 17 (1991): 27–46.

Erikson, E. "Configurations in Play." *Psychoanalytic Quarterly* 6 (2) (1937): 139–214.

———. *Childhood and Society.* New York: W. W. Norton, 1950.

———. "Sex Differences in the Play Configurations of American Pre-Adolescents." In eds. R. E. Herron and B. Sutton-Smith, *Child's Play.* New York: John Wiley, 1971.

———. *Play and Development.* New York: W. W. Norton, 1972.

———. *Toys and Reasons: Stages in the Ritualization of Experience.* New York: W. W. Norton, 1977.

Fagen, R. *Animal Play Behavior.* New York: Oxford University Press, 1981.

———. "Play and Behavioural Flexibility." In ed. P. K. Smith, *Play in Animals and Humans.* Oxford, England: Basil Blackwell, 1984.

———. "Animal Play, Games of Angels, Biology, and Brian." In ed. A. D. Pellegrini, *The Future of Play Theory: A Multidisciplinary Inquiry into the Contributions of Brian Sutton-Smith.* Albany: State University of New York Press, 1995.

Fein, G. "Toys and Stories." In ed. A. D. Pellegrini, *The Future of Play Theory.* Albany: State University of New York Press, 1995.

Fenichel, G. M. *Neonatal Neurology.* New York: Churchill Livingstone, 1990.

Fivush, R. "Developmental Perspectives on Autobiographical Recall." In eds. G. S. Goodman and B. L. Bottoms, *Child Victims, Child Witnesses: Understanding and Improving Testimony.* New York: Guilford, 1993.

Flavell, J. H. *The Developmental Psychology of Jean Piaget.* New York: Van Nostrand Reinhold, 1963.

Fraser, R. *The Brontës: Charlotte Brontë and Her Family.* New York: Crown, 1988.

Freud, A. *The Ego and the Mechanisms of Defense* (1937). New York: International Universities Press, 1946.

———. *Normality and Pathology in Childhood.* New York: International Universities Press, 1965.

———. "The Dynamic Psychology of Education" (1976). In *The Writings of Anna Freud,* vol. 8. New York: International Universities Press, 1981.

Freud, S. "The Analysis of a Phobia in a Five-Year-Old Boy" (1905). In trans. and ed. J. Strachey, *The Standard Edition of the Complete Psychological Works of Sigmund Freud,* vol. 10. London: Hogarth Press, 1955.

————. "Beyond the Pleasure Principle" (1920). In trans. and ed. J. Strachey, *The Standard Edition of the Complete Psychological Works of Sigmund Freud,* vol. 18. London: Hogarth Press, 1955.

————. "Civilization and Its Discontents" (1930). In trans. and ed. J. Strachey, *The Standard Edition of the Complete Psychological Works of Sigmund Freud,* vol. 21. London: Hogarth Press, 1961.

Gérin, W., ed. and intro. *Mrs. Gaskell's Life of Charlotte Brontë* (1857). London: Folio Society, 1971.

Ghiselen, M. T. *The Economy of Nature and the Evolution of Sex.* Berkeley: University of California Press, 1974.

————. "On the Evolution of Play by Means of Artificial Selection." *Behavioral and Brain Sciences* 5 (1982): 165.

Goldberg, S., and M. Lewis. "Play Behavior in the Year-Old Infant: Early Sex Differences." *Child Development* 40 (1) (1969): 21–31.

Goldstein, J. H. "Sex Differences in Aggressive Play and Toy Preference." In eds. K. Bjorkqvist and P. Niemela, *Of Mice and Women: Aspects of Female Aggression.* San Diego: Academic Press, 1992.

Goodall, J. "Chimpanzees and Others at Play." *ReVision* 17 (4) (1995): 14–20.

Gottman, J. "The World of Coordinated Play: Same- and Cross-Sex Friendship in Young Children." In eds. J. M. Gottman and J. G. Parker, *Conversations of Friends: Speculations on Affective Development.* New York: Cambridge University Press, 1986.

Greenacre, P. "Play in Relation to Creative Imagination." *Psychoanalytic Study of the Child* 12 (1959): 47–72.

Hall, G. S. *Adolescence,* vol. 1. New York: D. Appleton, 1904.

Harris, L. J. "Sex Differences in Spatial Ability: Possible Environmental, Genetic, and Neurological Factors." In ed. M. Kinsbourne, *Asymmetrical Functions of the Brain.* Cambridge, England: Cambridge University Press, 1978.

Hearst, E., and M. Wierzbicki. "Battle Royal: Psychology and the Chessplayer." In ed. J. Goldstein, *Sports, Games, and Play.* Hillsdale, N.J.: Lawrence Erlbaum, 1979.

Hole, G. J., and D. F. Einon. "Play in Rodents." In ed. P. K. Smith, *Play in Animals and Humans.* Oxford, England: Basil Blackwell, 1984.

Hudson, J., and L. R. Shapiro, "From Knowing to Telling: Children's Scripts, Stories, and Personal Narratives." In eds. A. McCabe and C. Peterson, *Developing Narrative Structure.* Hillsdale, N.J.: Lawrence Erlbaum, 1991.

Huizinga, J. *Homo Ludens.* Trans. F. F. C. Hull. London: Routledge & Kegan Paul, 1949.

Humphreys, A. P., and P. K. Smith. "Rough-and-Tumble in Preschool and Playground." In ed. P. K. Smith, *Play in Animals and Humans.* Oxford, England: Basil Blackwell, 1984.

Jones, N. G. B., and M. J. Konner. "Sex Differences in Behaviour of London and Bushman Children." In eds. R. P. Michael and J. H. Crook, *Comparative Ecology and Behaviour of Primates.* London: Academic Press, 1973.

Jung, C. *Psychological Types.* Trans. H. G. Baynes. Great Britain: T. & A. Constable, 1923; New York: Pantheon, 1953.

Kaplan, B. "Practicing for Artistic Success: The New Frontier." (Private pamphlet.)

Keefe, R. *Charlotte Brontë's World of Death.* Austin: University of Texas Press, 1979.

Keitel, E. *Reading Psychosis: Reader's Text in Psychoanalysis.* Oxford, England: Basil Blackwell, 1989.

King, S. *Danse Macabre.* New York: Berkeley, 1983.

Klein, M. "The Development of a Child." *International Journal of Psychoanalysis* 4 (1923): 419–74.

———. "Personification in the Play of Children." *International Journal of Psychoanalysis* 10 (1929): 193–204.

———. *Contributions to Psychoanalysis: 1921–1945.* New York: McGraw-Hill, 1964.

———. *The Psychoanalysis of Children* (1932). New York: Dell, 1975.

Konner, M. J. "Aspects of the Developmental Ethology of a Foraging People." In ed. N. Blurton Jones, *Ethological Studies of Child Behaviour.* Cambridge, England: Cambridge University Press, 1972.

Kubey, R., and R. Larson. "The Use and Experience of the New Video Media Among Children and Young Adolescents," *Communications Research* 17 (1990): 107–30.

Lazell, J. D., Jr., and N. C. Spitzer. "Apparent Play in an American Alligator." *Copiea* (1977): 188.

Leigh, J. *House of Destiny.* New York: Harlequin, 1996.

Levy, D. "Release Therapy in Young Children." *Psychiatry* 1 (1938): 387–90.

———. "Release Therapy." *American Journal of Orthopsychiatry* 9 (1939): 713–36.

———. "Psychic Trauma of Operations in Children." *American Journal of the Diseases of Childhood* 69 (1945): 7–25.

Lewis, M., and L. Michalson. *Children's Emotions and Moods: Developmental Theory and Measurement.* New York: Plenum, 1983.

Luria, Z., and E. Herzog. "Sorting Gender Out in a Children's Museum." *Gender and Society* 5 (1991): 224–32.

McGhee, Z. "A Study in the Play Life of Some South Carolina Children." *Pedagogical Seminary* 7 (1900): 459–78.

Menninger, W. C. "Recreation and Mental Health." *Recreation* 42 (1948): 340–56.

Nydegger, W., and C. Nydegger. "Tarong: An Ilocos Barrio in the Philippines."

In ed. B. Whiting, *Six Cultures: Studies of Child Rearing.* New York: John Wiley, 1963.

Opie, I. *The People in the Playground.* Oxford, England: Oxford University Press, paper ed., 1994.

Opie, I., and P. Opie. *Children's Games in Street and Playground* (1969). Oxford, England: Oxford University Press, paper ed., 1984.

Patton, R. G., and L. I. Gardner. *Growth Failure and Maternal Deprivation.* Springfield, Ill.: Thomas, 1963.

Pellegrini, A. D. "Boys' Rough-and-Tumble Play and Social Competence: Contemporaneous and Longitudinal Relations." In ed. A. D. Pellegrini, *The Future of Play Theory.* Albany: State University of New York Press, 1995.

Peller, L. "Models of Children's Play." In eds. R. E. Herron and B. Sutton-Smith, *Child's Play.* New York: John Wiley, 1971.

Persky, M. "The New Adolescent Risk Taking: Russian Roulette." *Northern California Psychiatric Physician,* February/March 1996, 4.

Piaget, J. *The Language and Thought of the Child.* New York: Harcourt Brace, 1926.

————. *Play, Dreams, and Imitation in Childhood* (1945). London: Hienemann, 1951; New York: W. W. Norton, 1962.

————. *The Construction of Reality in the Child* (1937). New York: Basic Books, 1954.

Piaget, J., and B. Sutton-Smith. "Debate." In eds. R. E. Herron and B. Sutton-Smith, *Child's Play.* New York: John Wiley, 1971.

Platter, F. *Beloved Son Felix: The Journal of Felix Platter, a Medical Student in Montpellier in the Sixteenth Century.* Trans. and intro. S. Jennett. London: F. Muller, 1961.

Ponton, L. *The Romance of Risk.* New York: Basic Books, 1997.

Ratchford, F. E. *The Brontës' Web of Childhood.* New York: Columbia University, 1941.

Read, K. E. "Leadership and Consensus in a New Guinea Society." *American Anthropologist* 61 (1959): 425–36.

Renshaw, D. "The Popular Peril of Cyberaddiction: One for the Books?" *Psychiatric Times,* April 1995, 35.

————. "Delights and Dangers of the Internet." *Psychiatric Times,* October 1996, 64.

Reznick, J. S., J. Kagan, N. Snidman, M. Gersten, K. Baak, and A. Rosenberg. "Inhibited and Uninhibited Children: A Follow-up Study." *Child Development* 57 (1986): 660–80.

Rosenberg, B. G., and B. Sutton-Smith. "A Revised Conception of Masculine-Feminine Differences in Play Activities." *Journal of Genetic Psychology* 96 (1960): 165–70.

Schor, J. *The Overworked American: The Unexpected Decline of Leisure.* New York: Basic Books, 1993.

Schwartzman, H. *Transformations: The Anthropology of Children's Play.* New York: Plenum, 1978.

Sherrod, L., and J. Singer. "The Development of Make-Believe Play." In ed. J. Goldstein, *Sports, Games, and Play.* Hillsdale, N.J.: Lawrence Erlbaum, 1979.

Shuer, M., and M. Dietrich. "Psychological Effects of Chronic Injury in Elite Athletes." *Western Journal of Medicine* 166 (1997): 104–9.

Singer, J. L., and D. Singer. "Imaginative Play and Pretending in Early Childhood: Some Experimental Approaches." In ed. A. Davids, *Child Personality and Psychopathology,* vol. 3. 1976.

Smilansky, S. *The Effects of Sociodramatic Play on Disadvantaged Preschool Children.* New York: John Wiley, 1968.

Smith, P. K., and K. J. Connolly. "Patterns of Play and Social Interaction in Pre-School Children." In ed. N. Blurton Jones, *Ethological Studies of Child Behaviour.* Cambridge, England: Cambridge University Press, 1972.

————. *The Ecology of Preschool Behaviour.* Cambridge, England: Cambridge University Press, 1980.

Solnit, A. J., D. J. Cohen, and P. B. Neubauer, eds. *The Many Meanings of Play: A Psychoanalytic Perspective.* New Haven, Conn.: Yale University Press, 1993.

Spitz, R. "Hospitalism: An Inquiry into the Genesis of Psychiatric Conditions in Early Childhood." *Psychoanalytic Study of the Child* 1 (1945): 53–74.

Spitz, R., and K. M. Wolf. "Anaclitic Depression: An Inquiry into the Genesis of Psychiatric Conditions in Early Childhood." *Psychoanalytic Study of the Child* 2 (1946): 313–42.

Spoto, D. *The Art of Alfred Hitchcock: Fifty Years of His Motion Pictures.* Garden City, N.Y.: Doubleday/Dolphin, 1976.

————. *The Dark Side of Genius: The Life of Alfred Hitchcock.* Boston: Little, Brown, 1983.

Stern, D. *The First Relationship: Infant and Mother.* Cambridge, Mass.: Harvard University Press, 1977.

Sutton-Smith, B. *The Games of New Zealand Children.* Berkeley: University of California Press, 1959. Reprinted in *The Folkgames of Children* (Austin: University of Texas Press, 1972).

————. "The Kissing Games of Adolescents in Ohio." *Midwestern Folklore* 9 (1959): 189–211.

————. "The Play of Girls." In eds. C. B. Kopp and M. Kirkpatrick, *On Becoming Female.* New York: Plenum, 1979.

————. *A History of Children's Play: The New Zealand Playground, 1840–1950.* Philadelphia: University of Pennsylvania Press, 1982.

————. "A Memory of Games and Some Games of Memory." In ed. D. J. Lee, *Life and Story: Autobiographies for a Narrative Psychology.* Westport, Conn.: Praeger, 1994.

————. *The Ambiguity of Play.* Cambridge, Mass.: Harvard University Press, 1997.

————, ed. *Play and Learning.* New York: John Wiley, 1979.

Sutton-Smith, B., and D. Kelly-Byrne. "The Idealization of Play." In ed. P. K. Smith, *Play in Animals and Humans.* Oxford, England: Basil Blackwell, 1984.

Sutton-Smith, B., and B. G. Rosenberg. "Sixty Years of Historical Change in the Game Preferences of American Children" (1961). Reprinted in eds. R. E. Herron and B. Sutton-Smith, *Child's Play.* New York: John Wiley, 1971.

Temple Black, S. *Child Star.* New York: McGraw-Hill, 1988.

Terman, L. M. *Genetic Studies of Genius,* vol. 1. Stanford, Calif.: Stanford University Press, 1926.

Terr, L. "Children of Chowchilla: A Study of Psychic Trauma." *Psychoanalytic Study of the Child* 34 (1979): 547–623.

———. " 'Forbidden Games': Post-Traumatic Child's Play." *Journal of the American Academy of Child Psychiatry* 20 (1981): 741–60.

———. "Chowchilla Revisited: The Effects of Psychic Trauma Four Years After a Schoolbus Kidnapping." *American Journal of Psychiatry* 140 (1983): 1543–50.

———. "Life Attitudes, Dreams, and Psychic Trauma in a Group of 'Normal' Children." *Journal of the American Academy of Child Psychiatry* 22 (1983): 221–30.

———. "Play Therapy and Psychic Trauma." In eds. C. E. Schaefer and K. J. O'Connor, *Handbook of Play Therapy.* New York: John Wiley, 1983.

———. "Childhood Trauma and the Creative Product." *Psychoanalytic Study of the Child* 42 (1987): 545–72.

———. "Terror Writing by the Formerly Terrified: The Life and Works of Stephen King." *Psychoanalytic Study of the Child* 44 (1989): 369–90.

———. "Childhood Trauma in Society: The Pebble and the Pool." In ed. J. Hammer III, *The 1990 Distinguished Visiting Professorship Lectures.* Memphis: University of Tennessee, Memphis, Health Science Center.

———. *Too Scared to Cry.* New York: Harper & Row, 1990; paper ed., New York: Basic Books, 1992.

———. *Unchained Memories.* New York: Basic Books, 1994; paper ed., 1995.

Terr, L., D. Bloch, B. Michel, H. Shi, J. Reinhart, and S. A. Matayer. "Children's Memories in the Wake of *Challenger.*" *American Journal of Psychiatry* 153 (1996): 618–25.

———. "Children's Thinking in the Wake of *Challenger.*" *American Journal of Psychiatry* 154 (1997): 744–51.

———. "Children's Symptoms in the Wake of *Challenger.*" Submitted.

Thorne, B. *Gender Play: Girls and Boys in School.* New Brunswick, N.J.: Rutgers University Press, 1994.

Underwood, J., and C. Miller. *Bare Bones.* New York: McGraw-Hill, 1988.

Vaillant, G., ed. *Ego Mechanisms of Defense: A Guide for Clinicians and Researchers.* Washington, D.C.: American Psychiatric Press, 1992.

Van Hoof, J. A. R. A. M. "A Comparative Approach to the Phylogeny of Laughter and Smiling" (1972). Reprinted in eds. J. S. Bruner, A. Jolly, and K. Sylva, *Play—Its Role in Development and Evolution.* New York: Basic Books, 1976.

Volpe, J. J. *Neurology of the Newborn,* 3rd ed. Philadelphia: W. B. Saunders, 1995.

Waelder, R. "The Psychoanalytic Theory of Play." *Psychoanalytic Quarterly* 2 (1932): 208–24.

Winnicott, D. W. *Playing and Reality.* New York: Basic Books, 1971.

Winter, D. *Stephen King.* New York: Plume, 1986.

Index

About the Author

Lenore Terr, M.D., is a clinical professor of psychiatry at the medical school of the University of California, San Francisco. She is the author of *Too Scared to Cry* (1990) and *Unchained Memories* (1994) as well as a distinguished body of work in academic journals. She won the American Psychiatric Association's Blanche F. Ittleson Award for her research on the kidnapped children of Chowchilla and other childhood trauma victims. A graduate of Case Western Reserve University and the University of Michigan Medical School, Dr. Terr now lives in San Francisco with her husband.